GODLESS AMERICANA
RACE AND RELIGIOUS REBELS

SIKIVU HUTCHINSON

Publisher's Cataloging-in-Publication
(Provided by Quality Books, Inc.)

Published 2013 by Infidel Books

Hutchinson, Sikivu.
Godless Americana : race and religious rebels / by
Sikivu Hutchinson.
p. cm.
Includes bibliographical references and index.

ISBN 978-0-61-558610-6
ISBN-10: 0615586104

1. African Americans—Religious life. 2. Civil rights—United States.
3. Religious fundamentalists—United States. I. Title.
E185.615.H88 2012 323.1196'073
QBI12-600185

GODLESS AMERICANA: RACE AND RELIGIOUS REBELS

SIKIVU HUTCHINSON

INFIDEL BOOKS
Los Angeles, CA

Table of Contents

Acknowledgments vii

Introduction: Prison House of Textbook History ix

American Terror 1

God's Body, Science's Brain 25

Straight to Hell: Christian Fascism and Americana 53

White Picket Fences, White Innocence 71

Prayer Warriors and Freethinkers 99

Seeing Things 151

Ungrateful Dead 165

Endnotes 181

Selected Bibliography 211

Index 219

Acknowledgments

In the two years since the publication of my book, *Moral Combat: Black Atheists, Gender Politics, and the Values Wars*, there has been growing interest in non-believers of color. Nonetheless, there are still few book length analyses on the sociopolitical views, lived experiences, and belief systems of contemporary non-believers of color. Until *Moral Combat*, there were no books that placed the emergence of non-believers of color within the broader context of deepening class, race, and gender disparities in the United States. *Godless Americana* continues that discussion. This essay collection is the culmination of cross-disciplinary research, conversation, community organizing, and classroom teaching. The issues it addresses are in response to a global climate in which the forces of bigotry, discrimination, and intolerance have rolled back human rights in the name of God and public morality. The central question the book poses is how Humanism can become culturally relevant in an era in which socioeconomic and educational conditions for communities of color are increasingly dire.

Given these circumstances, I am grateful to all of the interview respondents who provided candid feedback on the intersection of atheism, humanism, feminism, and racial politics. My deep appreciation to my parents, Earl Ofari Hutchinson and Yvonne Divans Hutchinson, my husband Stephen Kelley, and friend Kamela Heyward-Rotimi for their support as well as patient, thoughtful critiques of early drafts of this book. Tom Melchiorre also provided invaluable assistance with editing and fine tuning. Over the past several years, I've always been able to rely on the support, friendship, and crystal clear insights of Kamela, Diane Arellano, Heather Aubry, and Sumitra Mukerji for unconditional affirmation. Thanks are also due to Naima Washington and Donald Wright for their encouragement, as well as their commitment to social justice radical humanism. Finally, I am indebted to my students in the

Women's Leadership Project, especially Eclasia Wesley, Imani Moses, Lizeth Soria, Janeth Silva, Miani Giron, and Ronmely Andrade. These strong young women continue to teach, challenge, and inspire me. They are the next generation of feminist humanist visionaries who will set the stage and lead the way.

Introduction
Prison House of Textbook History

In 1781, Afro-Latinos and Indians founded the city of Los Angeles. Their settlement followed the design of the original inhabitants, the Gabrielino Indians. In this so-called city without a history, legend has it that undocumented Anglos were the real "o.g." (original) illegals. A few years before the founding of Los Angeles, a "new" revolution in what it meant to be human unfolded on the opposite shore in the British colonies. My students know the "romance" of the American Revolution but not the secret of Los Angeles. In the prison house of textbook history, they know each other mostly as enslaved "niggers" and "wetback" interlopers. Growing up, elbow-to-elbow in the same deeply religious neighborhoods, many are taught to believe that black and Latino culture can be distilled down to media stereotypes. The dominant culture programs them to read each other through the narrative of get-rich-or-die-tryin' hip hop and ghetto dysfunction, or big Catholic families and job stealing "illegals". As kindergartners they were taught to cite the pledge of allegiance as sacred chapter and verse, hand solemnly over heart, in homage to royal theft. Founding myths of heroic white men bootstrapping to liberty are intimately bound to their imagination of the classroom, to its rhythm of shrill discipline and stench of ground chalk; to a regime of time in which white supremacy and narratives of progress are the currency of American faith.

Over the past several years, the Right has spun the fantasy of colorblind, post-racial, post-feminist American exceptionalism. This Orwellian narrative anchors the most blistering conservative assault on secularism, civil rights, and public education in the post-Vietnam War era. It is no accident that this assault has occurred in an era in which whites have over twenty times the wealth of African Americans.[1] For many communities of color, victimized by a rabidly Religious Right, neo-liberal agenda, the American dream has never been more of a nightmare than it is now. *Godless Americana* is a radical humanist analysis of this climate. It provides a vision of secular social justice that challenges Eurocentric traditions of race, gender, and class-neutral secularism. For a small but growing number of non-believers of color, humanism and secularism are inextricably linked to the broader struggle against white supremacy, patriarchy, heterosexism, capitalism, economic injustice, and global imperialism. *Godless Americana* critiques these titanic rifts and the role white Christian nationalism plays in the demonization of urban communities of color.

Historically, Americana has symbolized mom, Apple pie, and the idyllic innocence of little white kids with fishing poles grinning from Norman Rockwell paintings. The dark underbelly of Americana is the lawless urban racial Other—the fount of all that threatens American progress. During the 2012 presidential campaign, this apocalyptic theme was sounded again and again by Religious Right GOP presidential candidates like Newt Gingrich and Rick Santorum. Dubbing President Obama the "food stamp president", Gingrich was an especially effective demagogue for capitalist class entitlement. Railing against child labor laws, Gingrich commented that:

> Really poor children, in really poor neighborhoods have no habits of working and have nobody around them who works so they have no habit of showing up on Monday…They have no habit of staying all day, they have no habit of I do this and you give me cash unless it is illegal.[2]

When I mentioned Gingrich's diatribe during a training session with a group of African American and Latino teachers, it was clear to them that the "really poor children" Gingrich was talking about weren't Appalachian white children or Honey Boo Boo from the hit reality show of the same name. Gingrich's "really poor neighborhoods" (rife with illegal activity) were not the mythic trailer parks and Bruce Springsteen blue collar salt-of-the-earth suburbs where the majority of the nation's white welfare presumably recipients live. These were not the neighborhoods that produced the really poor children Gingrich exhorted to work as unpaid janitors in under-resourced, overcrowded "inner city" schools.

As a symbol of moral failure and ghetto pathology, American public education has always been red meat for the far right. But what is more insidious is that both the Obama administration and the Right have joined forces in ravaging public education. The Obama administration's 2009 Race to the Top policy has opened the floodgates to privatized schools, dumbed-down curricula, and a permanent regime of high stakes testing that undermines teacher creativity and guts teachers' unions.[3] Nationwide, public schools have been targeted for charter conversion by foundations, corporations,[4] and hedge fund managers on the hunt for desperate inner city school districts. The neo-liberal magic bullet for "reforming" K-12 education is carving schools up for the highest corporate bidder. Special needs students, English language learners, and other "problem" demographics are then shoved out the back door.

As the gutting of American public education proceeds, aided and abetted by both liberals and conservatives, radical and progressive education activists continue to reshape the dialogue about the so-called achievement gap in public schools. Culturally relevant or culturally responsive pedagogy that builds on the lived experiences, cultural knowledge, language, and world views of children of color has become a standard, if still controversial, approach to redressing race and class disparities in education. Culturally relevant pedagogy rejects myths of meritocracy, colorblindness, and exceptionalism. At its most radical, cultural relevance critiques institutional structures of racist power and control that render children of color invisible within mainstream curriculum and instruction. It is based on the view that challenging traditional Western notions of what it means to be moral, to be a citizen, and to be human is implicit within the politics of education and that "teaching to transgress" is a social obligation.

In all my years of post-Jim Crow public education no one ever handed me a book written by a black woman and said that what she wrote is universal truth. I was never told that so-called civilizations rose and fell on the power of her words, or that entire belief systems sprung from her ideas. I was never taught that the world's greatest intellectuals worked plantations, were herded onto reservations, or traveled every day from barrios and "ghettoes" to keep white people's children. Intellectuals and philosophers—serious thinkers—were white men, with no need for a living wage job. They did not ride public buses or clean houses or go to schools where stop-and-frisk was a routine practice. They did not have to worry, like my students do, about being assigned to special education classes because they were chronic discipline "problems" or didn't speak "proper" English. They were never told that they would be more likely to get pregnant and drop-out of school than go on to a four-year college. These vaunted intellectuals and philosophers were certainly not seventeen year-old East L.A. girls like Paula Crisostomo, a Mexican-American Filipina activist who helped spearhead the Chicano student walkouts of 1968. The East L.A. walkouts were the largest high school student protests in this nation's history. Thousands of students boycotted their classes in protest over lack of college access, tracking policies, discrimination against speaking Spanish in the classroom, and racist curricula. In 2012, Crisostomo came and spoke to a group of my students at Washington Prep High School in South Los Angeles. She drew parallels between the racism she'd encountered during the Vietnam War era and the de facto segregation of the Obama age. Girls like Ms. Crisostomo were not supposed to go to college. Homemaking, caregiving, becoming a maid in a white household on the Westside—these were the common life expectations for young Latinas. Forty-five years later, young women like my former student Ronmely Andrade are not among the Talented Tenth who are expected to go on to college. Ronmely was headed to the military after graduation, swayed by the Marines' relentless on-campus recruitment campaign. A gifted speaker and presenter, at the end of her senior year she expressed misgivings about going to boot camp and training for a career as a mechanic. After we discussed her options for withdrawing from boot camp she enrolled in her first year at community college.

For Paula Crisotomo's generation, the military was pervasive. Youth of color died in disproportionate numbers fighting and killing other dark-skinned peoples in Vietnam because college was not an option in the "ghetto." Despite an increase in the number of students of color in college, aggressive military recruitment continues to be a reality for black, Latino, and Native American students. For many, college preparation and equitable college access are still a distant dream. For some, simply graduating from high school at campuses where less than 50% of the entering freshman class makes it to graduation is an accomplishment. This has become the standard in an era in which the Education

Trust estimates that only "one of every 20 African American kindergartners will graduate from a four-year California university" in the next decade.[5] While predominantly black and Latino schools in South and East L.A. are besieged by military recruiters, the more affluent white schools get the college recruiters, college prep classes, and highly qualified teachers. The Americana fever pitch of the Army, Navy, Air Force, and Marines is unheard of on predominantly white campuses in Los Angeles. It is a given that these students will be going to college, not dying on the frontlines.

But faced with a school-to-prison pipeline that offers no way out, more and more girls like Ronmely are eyeing the military as a viable path to college and careers. As one of the many fierce youth in my Women's Leadership Project (WLP) program, Ronmely and her peers define what culturally relevant humanism looks like in an age of educational apartheid. In 2002 I founded the WLP, a feminist civic engagement and mentoring program, after being frustrated by the absence of explicitly anti-racist, feminist programs for girls in the community. The program was piloted in two South L.A. middle schools during a period in which the black and Latino communities were becoming increasingly intertwined. Sensationalist language about "endangered" black males and feral super-predator young men of color was the order of the day. In a 2004 article entitled "Feminist Pedagogy and Youth Advocacy" I wrote:

> In a cultural climate where the crisis of black boys and young black males has been used as a metaphor for urban dysfunction, scant attention is paid to the special social circumstances of girls of color…many girls of color have little consciousness of how gender inequality shapes their lives. While race solidarity runs deep, they often fail to see the connection between the use of misogynistic language and violent imagery in their favorite videos and the way they are treated in everyday life, at school and in their relationships. Many girls assume a "blame the victim" stance about the rampant sexual assault and verbal abuse of young women that is a staple of American popular culture.[6]

The core curriculum of WLP is humanist, focusing in part on the nexus between organized religion and gender hierarchy. We train students to understand how heterosexist gender roles shape racist/sexist cultural expectations for women of color. Becoming critical observers of the media, public policy, and their local communities, they develop a critical consciousness about how misogynist violence is normalized in their everyday lives. Students spearhead school-community advocacy projects of their own choosing, sharpening their critical thinking, writing, collaboration, public speaking, and leadership skills. WLP's four-year college-going rate for graduating seniors is significantly above that of the schools where our programs are based. The majority of our girls are first generation college students like Ronmely.

Ronmely is an agnostic from a Catholic family. She is a natural born leader who exudes a steely poise and control in front of students that are often hostile to hearing about sexual violence from assertive young women of color. When I was her age, no one ever came to our classrooms to talk to us about sexual violence or sexual harassment. Even though many of us were being sexually harassed or assaulted daily by peers, predatory teachers, and relatives there was no engagement with the role this played in our sense of self-image and life expectations. There was no feminist youth movement to address misogyny and internalized sexism in communities of color. Demonized as "ho" super-sluts women of color weren't true victims of sexual violence. It was accepted that we should remain silent about our victimization, lest we be smeared as uppity castrating bitches detracting from the "real" issue of the brutalization of men of color.

Women of color who refuse to remain silent about misogynist violence are traitors in this culture. Girls of color learn very early on that allegiance to boys and men of color supersedes their allegiance to their own sense of selfhood. But black girls are still profiled by police, followed around in stores like potential criminals, demeaned by teachers as low-achieving, and over-suspended in public schools. For centuries, racism, sexism, white supremacy, and capitalism have "defined" our (sub)humanity in public discourse. In her landmark book *Their Eyes Were Watching God*, freethinker and author Zora Neale Hurston describes black women as "de mules of de world." It is a cautionary truth voiced by the grandmother of Janie, the novel's lead character. Janie's grandmother is a deeply religious woman and former slave who is the moral pillar of her life. Janie's struggle to self-determine in a culture in which black women's bodies and destinies were not theirs to fully control has become a classic metaphor for women of color in white supremacist America.

As a religious skeptic, Hurston nonetheless understood the seductions of god for a people whose humanity was still violently contested centuries after the first Africans came[7] to the United States.[8] Culturally relevant humanism is informed by this seeming contradiction. Embracing godlessness requires critical consciousness of how the tyranny of the unsettled past is a living breathing legacy in the present. For my students, coming of age in a country that has blighted their history, the lie of American exceptionalism is as deadly a national opiate as blind faith in fantastical gods.

CHAPTER ONE

American Terror

A little white boy, a cherub with an impish grin, earnestly clutches a microphone before a church congregation in a blurry video of the Apostolic Truth Tabernacle in Greensburg, Indiana. He begins to belt out a ditty, "I know the Bible is right, somebody's wrong…Ain't no homos going to make it to heaven," in a playful schoolboy lilt. The crowd erupts, rising to its feet, fists pumping, high fives extended, roof raised. The pastor beams proudly from the pulpit, deliciously pleased by this home team display of American Idol precocity.

The video generated thousands of hits and comments online, some praising, many condemning. Christians were slammed as hypocritical and un-Christian; detractors were piously directed to Bible verses smearing homosexuality. The mantra from tolerant Christians was that God doesn't endorse hate, especially from the mouths of babes. Biblical condemnation of homosexuality was a remnant of antiquity, inapplicable to the complexities of the modern world, a distortion of God's unconditional love.

Eavesdropping on the red-blooded zeal of the Tabernacle's come-to-Jesus audience, it's clear that the cherub has renewed its wilting faith. The straight backs of dark-suited men frame the furtive glances of silent little girls in frilly dresses peaking around the camera as whistles and applause ripple through the sanctuary. With the womenfolk tucked away, giving praise to Jesus is just another alpha male sporting event. The wisdom of heterosexual solidarity will not be lost on more tolerant corrupted generations. The cherub is no more than five years old. Soon, he will be new to elementary school, new to the savage dance of peer pressure and the playground rituals of gender. He is "innocent," yet fully initiated into the culture of violence, permissiveness, and patriarchy that says "boys will be boys." Western civilization revolves around this unbreakable sacrament. From the nameless, faceless American military drone victims of the Middle East to the expendable Jezebels of American inner cities, to be American is to always be innocent against the global backdrop of otherness. It is to accept as gospel that "they" hate us because of our freedoms while "we" are free to pillage the globe with American war machines and pipeline youth of color into prisons. Historically, conquering and "democratizing" savage foreign lands has been part of the U.S.' foreordained Christian mission as an "exceptional" civilization. American exceptionalism was a key theme for the GOP and Religious Right in the 2012 presidential race.[1] Former Republican congressman and presidential candidate Newt Gingrich amplified this theme in his book *A Nation Like No Other: Why American Exceptionalism Matters:*

> The ideals expressed in the Declaration of Independence and the unique American identity that rose from an American civilization that honored them form what we call today "American Exceptionalism"…President Obama, for example, simply does not understand this concept. In the past he was outright contemptuous of American Exceptionalism, deriding Americans as "bitter" people who "cling" to guns and religion…If the ideas in the Declaration were not new or particularly radical, then why did this single document fundamentally alter world history? The answer is this: no nation had ever before embraced human equality and God-given individual rights as its fundamental organizing principle.[2]

Caricatured by the right as a socialist revolutionary, Obama sought to burnish his Americana credentials by trotting out the rhetoric of exceptionalism.[3] In 2009 he maintained that it's a "core set of values that are enshrined in our Constitution, in our body of law, in our democratic practices, in our belief in free speech and equality, that, though imperfect, are exceptional." Yet, Obama's identification with exceptionalism was not enough for GOP ideologues like Gingrich, who insist that Judeo-Christian might and right makes the U.S. superior to other nations. Predictably, Gingrich's summary of the U.S.' exceptionalist path contains only passing reference to slavery. For Gingrich, slavery was only a minor deviation from this "nation like no other's" ascent to global leadership. If the Declaration of Independence invokes "unalienable rights" of liberty and equality granted by God, then the U.S.' unique righteousness lies in this contract.[4] According to this view, American civilization, as the most religious superpower on the planet, means God—white, Christian, straight, and pure. And even though the U.S. is the fount of freedom and individual liberty, God cannot be expected to bend to the whims and cultural relativisms of modernity. To do so would be a betrayal of his will, as manifest in "natural" law.

The little white boy of Apostolic Truth Tabernacle is the unofficial face of Americana, the spiritual inheritor of God, mom, and apple pie. This holy trinity was sorely tested by President Obama's landslide victory in the 2012 presidential campaign. The GOP's anti-government message of lower taxes and shiftless welfare queens, coupled with its attacks against birth control, abortion, gay rights and undocumented immigrants, was repugnant to many voters. Yet, although a majority of the electorate rejected the party's Christian fascist rhetoric, those that would write the political and cultural obituary of fundamentalist Americana are premature. God has always been one of the U.S.' primary afflictions. The performance of American national identity is steeped in this cancer. The right-wing backlash against democratic citizenship is fueled by it. Unleashed from its YouTube moment, the cherub's folksy performance deep in the heart of this small Midwestern church reverberates in hundreds of so-called gay conversion therapy sessions throughout the nation. It provides the backdrop for the monster popularity of alpha male toys that give little boys license to prey and pillage. It fuels the suicides that claim the lives of hundreds of lesbian, gay, bisexual, and transgender youth every year. It drives the she-asked-for-it rape culture that says women's bodies are dirty, shameful, sinful, and always there for the taking.

Since time immemorial, religion and science have battled over the boundaries of the natural. Black people were closer to the primitive and thus more natural. Whites were closer to God and his image and thus more supernaturally intelligent. Because blacks were closer to animals, the great proponent of liberty Thomas Jefferson believed that they were more likely to sleep, and less apt to reflect. In his *Notes on the State of Virginia*, Jefferson mused that "(blacks') griefs are transient. Those numberless afflictions, which render it doubtful whether heaven has given life to us in mercy or in wrath, are less felt, and sooner forgotten with them. In general, their existence appears to participate more of sensation than reflection. To this must be ascribed their disposition to sleep when abstracted from their diversions, and unemployed in labour. An animal whose body is at rest, and who does not reflect, must be disposed to sleep of course." Jefferson's commentary reflects his era's mingling of faith-based conjecture with "scientific" analysis. There were certain "knowns" based on rational, scientific observation. Black inferiority was one of these "knowns." *Notes on the State of Virginia* represents Jefferson's wrestling with the implications of this fact. If black people were largely untroubled by and unreflective about the mysteries that heaven/God gave humankind, then there was something deeply lacking in their claim to human sentience.

Throughout much of American history, miscegenation or race-mixing was viewed as being against God and nature. Even though race mixing and interracial offspring were widespread, Anglo-American social discourse branded "mulattos" as unstable, tragic individuals whose ticking time bomb biology would doom them to obsolescence.

"Difference," Jefferson wrote, "is fixed in nature. And is as real as if its seat and cause were better known to us." For Jefferson and his peers, the divide between black and white was not only jarringly real but unbridgeable. Nonetheless, as a wealthy, propertied white man of class privilege under the regime of slavery, Jefferson had been given moral and social license to rape enslaved black women and father mixed race children. The license to commit great acts of barbarism in the name of civilization made white men human. This paradox of violent "intimacy" in the face of unbridgeable difference was centered on the belief that blacks were not fully human. If blacks were slumbering animals incapable of higher-order thinking and reflection, they were closer to the primitive. But if whites were moral and intellectual exemplars, how could American society justify white barbarism?

In his 1852 address "What to the American slave is your 4th of July?" Frederick Douglass critiques the paradox of American liberty in the midst of slavocracy:

> What, to the American slave, is your 4th of July? I answer: a day that reveals to him, more than all other days in the year, the gross injustice and cruelty to which he is the constant victim. To him, your celebration is a sham; your boasted liberty, an unholy license; your national greatness, swelling vanity; your sounds of rejoicing are empty and heartless; your denunciations of tyrants, brass fronted impudence; your shouts of liberty and equality, hollow mockery; your prayers and hymns, your sermons and thanksgivings, with all your religious parade, and solemnity, are, to him, mere bombast, fraud, deception, impiety, and hypocrisy—a thin veil to cover up crimes which would disgrace a nation of savages. There is not a nation on the earth guilty of practices, more shocking and bloody, than are the people of these United States, at this very hour. Go where you may, search where you will, roam through all the monarchies and despotisms of the old world, travel through South America, search out every abuse, and when you have found the last, lay your facts by the side of the everyday practices of this nation, and you will say with me, that, for revolting barbarity and shameless hypocrisy, America reigns without a rival.[5]

Chafing under the yoke of British tyranny and "enslavement," the colonists crafted a nation based on the principles of natural rights and sovereign citizenship. The new republic was to be a paragon of human enlightenment and self-government; a radical experiment unlike any in the history of humankind. For Jefferson and his peers, this radical experiment meant they could lay claim to both godly and natural rights in one breath, with blackness as backdrop.

Patriotism and nature are the last refuge of scoundrels enforcing a moral code in their own image. National discourse about whether or not the U.S. is a "Christian Nation" is a prime example of this insidious contradiction. Claims of Christian nationhood come amidst a significant increase in the number of Americans who don't identify as either believers or religious. According to the Pew Research Center, greater numbers of Americans are identifying as so-called Nones. These individuals say organized religion doesn't speak to their world views or interests. A goodly share of so-called Millennials, or young people between the ages of 16 and 30, identify as Nones. Some have been turned off by the medievalist propaganda of the Religious Right. Many of the Nones describe themselves as "spiritual," averse to the vengeful hellfire and damnation Old Testament God or fundamentalist Allah who rain thunderbolts down onto drooling sinners. Some of these folks believe that God should be lower-case; a matter of individual taste. These spiritualists hew to a designer supernaturalism where each person can tailor god(s) according to their individual needs and desires.

For some, designer supernaturalism is an antidote to the oppressive fundamentalisms of Christianity, Judaism, and Islam. "God made me this way," some gay, lesbian, and transgender folk say, and "God is love." Or, alternatively, "God doesn't make mistakes." For LGBT people of faith, belief in "God's" essential benevolence is a prerequisite for sustaining a healthy self-identity. In her book *Invisible Families*, Mignon Moore notes that "some in the Black gay community use religion to validate their identities as same-gender loving people."[6] Rejecting the Bible's condemnation of gay sexuality, gay African American Christians focus instead on what they believe to be the loving, compassionate, universalist message of Jesus. As one respondent in Mignon's book says, "I do believe God loves me and even though they may not agree with what I am I think that this is between me and God."[7] For many African American LGBT folk, faith is intimately tied to cultural identity and is not easily shorn even in light of the social conservatism and heterosexism of mainstream black America. Indeed, according to a study by UCLA's Williams Institute, when compared with their white counterparts, African American LGBT folk are more likely "to attend religious services, to engage in prayer, and to self-identify with a religious affiliation."[8] Straight and gay African Americans live together in segregated communities where racism, white supremacy, and criminalization shape their shared lived experiences. Save for the drumbeat of white normalcy portrayed in TV, film, and advertising, our worlds are overwhelmingly black and brown. Thus, it's not surprising that gay African Americans are invested in the same religious cultural traditions that prop up straight normalcy yet may afford them with a sense of community. Despite the overall increase in secular Americans, people of color have not embraced secularism in significant numbers. In some instances, faith communities have been far more proactive in creating safe cultural and social spaces for LGBT people of color. Gay-friendly activist congregations like the Unity Fellowship church in Los Angeles (an early leader on HIV/AIDS activism) have enabled gay people of color to reconcile the contradiction of worship and acceptance in homophobic religious traditions like Christianity.

Yet "nature" is the dirty alibi behind the young Indiana church boy's "God and homos" ditty. In the battleground of the schoolyard, the classroom, and the bathroom, "nature" is the regime of boys will be boys. As writer Derrick McMahon notes:

> One of the ways we induct our young boys into manhood is through the toys we allow them to play with. Boys are usually given toys like guns in order to prepare and teach them how to be tough and aggressive. Toys like baby dolls that encourage nurturing behavior are denied to young boys. Boys who wish to play with baby dolls are seen as punks, sissies, and weak. Parents are quick to tell little boys that they have no business playing with baby dolls and little boys are thus conditioned into patriarchal masculinity. To be a man is to be tough. A man has no business wanting to be tender, caring, nurturing, a man has no business with babies. Given the way that we raise our little boys and girls, why is anyone shocked or surprised when the little boys we raised to only be tough and hard grow up to be men who are only tough and hard? They grow up to be men who lack relational skills like compassion, tenderness, love, and the ability to be nurturing.[9]

The most powerful way that this induction occurs is through the language of what is "natural." When I talk with teenage boys about gender and social messaging, one of the first things they say is that their fathers or male relatives snatched dolls and other "feminine" toys away from them as little boys. This intimate policing at the level of average ordinary play and discovery represents the frontline of enforcing conformity. For the little boy still learning about his place in the world, this prohibition means multiple things. First, it sets up a hard boundary between him and girls. Because they are forbidden, "girl things" are mysterious, other, illicit; the "dark" continent that God cursed. Banned from girl things, boys are initiated into the male world of violence and denied access to the full range of human emotion. They are told that displaying vulnerability in this male world of violence is an act of gender betrayal. American boys must toe the line in the shadow of an intense media machine that promotes violent masculinity as religion and creed. In the testosterone-drenched marketplace of mainstream gender roles, God is firmly on the side of guns, sports, tools, Legos, and building blocks. These are the banal everyday paraphernalia of initiation festooning the gender-segregated Walmart toy aisles. They reassure boys that they are not a sissy, punk, fag, or bitch "nigga" dangling in the netherworld between real men and girls. When boys express interest in G.I. Joe or Grand Theft Auto they are only doing what comes "natural." It's accepted that violence will be a defining part of their identities. And so much of that acceptance is based on training boys to be straight.

Many Christians point to homosexuality as a violation of the natural. Nature is a proxy for God. According to Genesis, "So God created man in his own image, in the image of God created he him; male and female created he them." Conservative, liberal, and progressive Christians alike rationalize that God hates the sin and loves, or is willing to forgive, the sinner who repents. God is cool with everybody who accepts him as their personal savior; thus the popular bromide "God is love." Fundamentalists protest that liberal Christians soft-pedal the Bible's condemnations of homosexuality, substituting them for tortured interpretations that justify same-sex relationships and "deviant" sexuality.

Gay conversion therapy providers are on the frontlines of this homophobic assault. Conversion therapy bottom feeders like Atlanta-based pastor D.L. Foster's, the "IM Free Project" claim to liberate gay men and lesbians from homosexual urges. In an IM Free Project video, one participant speaks of how being molested as a child steered him toward same-sex attractions ("attraction came from perversion" not his natural desires). He stereotypically equates being gay with being "flamboyant." A female participant reflects on an early encounter with a woman and the trauma of being rejected by her father. The majority of these stories pathologize homosexuality. Here, gay identity is the result of abuse and neglect, and "broken relationships with the male parent" are often identified as the catalyst for "descent" into gayness. Turning gay is portrayed as the culmination of a series of traumatic personal/family events. Foster and his acolytes maintain that the church should play an active pragmatic role in "compassionately" steering LGBT folk toward heterosexuality: "God delivers people from their sin and he brings people to Jesus Christ and sanctification." On his website, Foster characterizes himself as a "personal witness after experiencing deliverance from homosexual sin over twenty two years ago."[10] Foster is also the founder of the so-called Overcomers Network, a predominantly African American collective of "team-leaders" who conduct seminars to liberate believers from "homosexuality, lesbianism, transgenderism, bisexuality, gender confusion, pornography and other forms of sexual immorality that inhibit the glory of God from shining through their lives."[11] Foster's outfit is part of a global web of faith-based conversion therapy or "pray away the gay" scam enterprises. These bastions of quackery have been discredited by the medical community, elicitingd fierce political opposition from the California State Legislature. According to Andre Banks of AllOut.org, "This isn't just a problem in California or even only the United States…American religious extremists are bringing these dangerous practices to more than 30 countries all over the world, despite their overwhelming rejection by the medical community."[12]

Banks' comment speaks to the global threat posed by the conversion therapy movement. Led by American Christian evangelicals, the conversion therapy movement exploits homophobic hysteria, superstition and, often, ethnic identity in its quest for legitimacy amongst people of color. Masquerading as anti-colonialists safeguarding authentic African identity, the American Religious Right has been able to establish a stronghold in countries such as Uganda, Malawi, Nigeria, and Zaire. According to Political Research Associates, "Anti-gay legislation has passed in Malawi and Nigeria and violence against sexual minorities is on the rise. Increasingly, anti-gay politics is wrapped in African colors with church leaders and politicians alike charging that homosexuality—rather than the Christian right—is a Western neo-colonial project."[13] As in Africa, anti-gay sentiment amongst African Americans is strongly tied to notions of gender and ethnic identity. Homosexuality is not only believed to be a violation of God and natural law, but is viewed as undermining black masculinity and male dominance in an already precarious black nuclear family unit. In this regard, homosexuality ranks with slavery, Jim Crow, and mass-incarceration as key factors in the destabilization of black families. But "former" gay converts like Foster and self-proclaimed "ex-lesbian" Janet Boynes believe that God's love can conquer the sinful lure of the gay lifestyle. As the head of another conversion-based ministry, Boynes also exploits vulnerable LGBT folk seeking salvation with the bankrupt message of we shall overcome.

* * *

Antebellum ideology constructed blacks as naturally savage, primitive, and ineducable. From "zip coon" to Rastus to Sambo to Mammy, the black primitive was further from God but naturally superstitious. The black primitive was incapable of higher-order thinking about cosmology but was deeply spiritual. The black primitive was sexually insatiable, but essentially docile. The black primitive was the antithesis of Puritan sexuality (partly because Anglo-American gender roles were more clearly defined). As rapacious Jezebels, black women were more similar to black men than they were the so-called fairer sex—she of the flowing hair, porcelain skin and "delicate" constitution. Black sexuality, black gender roles, and black families were policed by heterosexist gender norms. With the advent of racial slavery, these norms shaped the dominant culture's belief in Jefferson's notion of the unbridgeable gap between whiteness and blackness. Even though straight men in the antebellum era had open, emotionally intimate same-sex relationships, heterosexist America constructed gay sexuality as debauched and immoral. To be gay was a perversion of God's will and God's design. Centuries later, the fiercest opponents of same-sex marriage claim no less authority for their inhumanity than God's will. Believers who support same-sex marriage and LGBT equality insist that this is a bootleg un-Christian version of God. Trust us, they say, to rescue God from the flat-Earth fundamentalists. Liberal Christians and spiritualists alike insist that the "real" God—their god—is a loving, kind, benevolent, New Testament friendly patriarch (or matriarch). Their god is a fount of inspiration, a benign spirit for good that moves and grooves within everyone and embraces all comers regardless of creed or deed. The good believers assure us that this is so. But they are always looking over their shoulders at the corrupt, fire-breathing believers nipping peskily at their heels like night-of-the-living-dead zombies. They are subject to the same gyrations and justifications as fundamentalists for why their version of God is good, just, and right, worthy of the prizefight and fitting of the title.

Good believers know the tyranny of "God"; God as a means of enforcement, policing, and censure; God(s) as artificial boundary between self and other, a black felt-tip equatorial line between the just or moral and the unjust or immoral. Reference to God in pop culture, political discourse, public meetings, high-profile tragedies, and at sporting events has reached a manic level of lazy trendiness. Depending upon the region of the country one is in, it's impossible to stumble through the day without an "I'm blessed" or "have a blessed day" bleated insipidly by complete strangers. Basking in certainty and the outward trappings of faith, some believers betray their agitation, their insecurity, their feverish unease with the colossal god-forsaking they see all around them in the chaos of everyday life viciously rutting in pig shit.

So radical atheists of color ask why benevolent gods are necessary. Why, given the welter of gods and competing belief systems that have been used to justify barbarism, squelch human rights, and demonize gay people of color as less than human? Why is it necessary to establish supernatural beings as arbiters, intermediaries, and custodians of humanity? And if radical non-believers of color reject God belief as liberatory, what is the moral and political imperative of godlessness? What does freedom from God mean in an era in which the contradiction between mainstream American visions of democracy and the socioeconomic crisis confronting communities of color is starker than ever? What will it mean for a radical humanist vision of social justice that is explicitly anti-racist and culturally responsive?

For the most part, serious humanist thinkers and activists of color came from a 20th century civil rights context. Public intellectuals like A. Philip Randolph and W.E.B. DuBois worked with the black faith community while critiquing it. They left a towering legacy of activism and secularist inquiry that has been unmatched in the late 20th and early 21st centuries. It is for this reason that secular organizing amongst people of color is still nascent. This is largely due to the titanic influence of faith organizations in both religious and secular life. Randolph recognized that secularism would have limited appeal for working-class African Americans because of the intractability of racial and residential segregation. Then, as now, the absence of racially-integrated secular institutions and community spaces buttressed the centrality of the Black Church. From scholarship resources to prisoner re-entry to voter registration and political candidate's forums, African American religious organizations are often intimately involved in every aspect of community organizing and service provision. Similarly, Latino religious organizations provide community members with a broad array of services ranging from undocumented immigrant rights advocacy, job training, and counseling. Non-religious and non-believing people of color may receive services from and/or participate in these institutions because of the dearth of secular alternatives. Deep cultural traditions and the lack of community-based secular humanist alternatives are two reasons why many LGBT folk of color are invested in faith-based organizations.

For example, at LGBTQ[14] youth conferences it's common to see sunny-faced volunteers from gay-friendly ministries hovering by tables stocked with attractive promotional literature. Their message is simple: God is merciful, forgiving, and accepting of difference. Each ministry claims to offer sanctuary from the draconian storm of Christian fundamentalism. At the Los Angeles Unified School District's (LAUSD) 2012 annual queer youth conference Models of Pride, there were three featured workshops with religious/spiritual themes, from shamanism to a session entitled "God knows My Orientation and is Good with It." As a visible and vocal faction in the LGBTQ youth movement, these faith-based organizations fill a moral, cultural, and social void that humanist organizations have yet to proactively address.

A summit on improving the visibility of LGBTQ issues in K-12 curricula, instruction, and faculty training within the LAUSD highlighted the gaping void in humanist outreach. During the summit, the San Francisco-based Family Acceptance Project screened a film called Always My Son, which chronicles a Latino family's journey toward acceptance of their gay son. Finding a church that welcomed queer youth was crucial to their transition. In the film, the boy's father spoke eloquently of how he struggled to come to terms with his own hypermasculine identity as a tough ex-Marine. The relationships the family developed in their new gay-friendly church inspired them to open their home to other families with LGBTQ children looking for community support. In the summit's breakout sessions, representatives from the faith community touted ministries that were accepting of LGBTQ families and youth. They maintained that the model of an angry, punitive God was inaccurate. Several condemned the Religious Right for perpetuating the view that being gay and Christian was incompatible. They stressed involvement opportunities for LGBTQ youth struggling to come out. They also spoke of providing a bridge for religious families seeking to reconcile their faith with the dominant culture's heterosexist notions of morality.

Humanist voices are rarely included in these dialogues for several reasons. First, for better or for worse, social acceptance of LGBTQ youth often hinges on family. Second, it's often assumed that making organized religion "kinder and gentler" is the end goal for affirming disenfranchised queer youth hungry for moral acceptance. Since religion is a big influence in many American families, it stands to reason that educators and resource providers who work with queer youth develop culturally-responsive approaches to engaging families around homophobia, LGBT identity, and religious belief. Third, and perhaps most importantly, humanist organizations that do this kind of work are few and far between. One exception is the American Humanist Association (AHA), which has LGBT Councils.[15] As part of its efforts around LGBTQ inclusion, the AHA was a co-sponsor of a Mississippi-based LGBTQ "second chance" prom. Proms and other life-transition rituals can be important social vehicles for coming out. Humanist organizations can bridge the gap for questioning and non-believing youth grappling with the authoritarianism of some religious traditions.

Yet, countering the homophobic dogma of organized religion is only one aspect of LGBTQ enfranchisement. And it is for this reason that existing humanist organizations are inadequate for queer youth of color. The needs of LGBTQ youth of color can't be adequately addressed by culturally homogeneous or colorblind approaches that don't acknowledge the intersection of heterosexism, white supremacy, and racism. For example, queer youth of color are especially vulnerable to becoming homeless. Family economic instability, sexual abuse, religious dogma, and discrimination at school and in local neighborhoods often cause homelessness amongst African American queer youth. The nexus of foster care and mass incarceration has also dramatically increased homelessness amongst youth of color. Youth who age out of foster care have few resources to fall back on, putting them at risk of becoming homeless.[16] Youth who come out of the juvenile or adult prison systems may be unable to find jobs or housing due to employment applications that require criminal felony disclosures.

With its illusion of glamour and accessibility, the city of Hollywood is a popular magnet for runaways and homeless youth. The majority of Hollywood's homeless youth are African American. Forty percent of all homeless youth in the community identify as LGBTQ.[17] Floating spectrally in the hills above the workaday traffic, the old Hollywood sign, recently repainted bright white, is nonetheless still a faded beacon and gilded promise for the klieg lit dreams of youth everywhere. It's purported that thousands of young people used to dam up at the now desolate Vine Street Greyhound terminal off of Sunset Boulevard every year. Many sought refuge from personal trauma and upheaval, hungry for a new beginning, a semblance of family, home, and, true to the cliché, a shot at fifteen minutes of fame. Hollywood is home to a network of homeless youth shelters run by organizations like the L.A. Gay and Lesbian Center and Covenant House. As the largest privately-funded homeless youth shelter in the nation, the faith-based Covenant House has historically been averse to the needs of LGBTQ youth.[18] After years of discrimination against trans and gender queer youth, Covenant House Texas implemented culturally-responsive policy that specifically addressed the targeting of trans youth.[19] According to Houston's *Out Smart* magazine: "Since the leaders who followed its founder were Catholic nuns, its service has always included a religious component. With little official acceptance of gay people coming from the Catholic Church, Covenant House has not been encouraged to focus on LGBT-specific programs and training."[20] One young lesbian complained that she felt pressured to go to church. After she objected to a staff member's heavy proselytizing "they sent the pastor to talk to" her.[21] Promoting a new book about several inspirational homeless teens, the head of Covenant House has said that "we are each made in the image and likeness of a loving God."[22] But having been despised and demonized by "God" for so long, when the script is flipped and an authority deems that God is suddenly loving and forgiving, why is God necessary at all?

When my colleague, Josh Parr, and I ran a homeless youth leadership group at Covenant House California in Hollywood from 2009 to 2012, some youth struggled to be housed according to their gender identity. Conflicts about sexuality and gender often played out in our group. "Amber", one of our female transgender interns, got into fights with a cisgendered female youth leader who had "problems" with having her as a roommate. In the general population of the facility there was clear tension between the "hard" bangers and so-called gang-related males (who had come directly from the juvenile system) and openly queer and questioning youth. Both groups navigated public identities that had been demonized as criminal, other, and threatening. Being both homeless and of color already made them vulnerable to racist police, who often roust and profile homeless people of color on the streets with impunity. According to the Center for American Progress, of the "approximately 300,000 gay and transgender youth who are arrested and/or detained each year (more) than 60 percent are black or Latino."[23] Carrying on the charade of hyper-masculinity, some of the hard boys were conflicted by their own inability to be truly free, to be comfortable in their own skin as bi or gay young men. Most of the residents had not gone through any training or focused discussion on homophobia and gender identity. The faith-based culture of the organization could not address, much less affirm, the multiple layers of queer of color lived experience. What also became apparent with our youth interns was that the generally conservative culture of Covenant House could not help them reconcile the deep divide between their elusive dreams of TV, film, and music industry stardom and the reality of crushing poverty that homeless youth face. Although the facility provides some job search resources, the more important long-term goal of college access is a major stumbling block for permanently transitioning youth of color out of homelessness. Because their lives are marked by constant physical, social, and emotional upheaval, homeless and foster care youth have lower college-going rates and higher attrition rates.[24]

These issues were a perfect storm in the life of "Todd", one of our most dedicated interns. Bright and well-spoken, Todd had come to Covenant House from a background of sexual abuse and prostitution. He seesawed between wanting to go to nursing school and cosmetology school. Speaking to high school students about his experiences on the streets trading sex for food, pocket change and shelter, he emphasized the dangerous options queer youth have after being rejected by their families. At home and in the street, trans and queer youth are more likely to experience sexual abuse and sexual assault. Lacking meaningful job skills, resources or education, Todd and many other youth at Covenant House were forced to rely on survival sex to stay afloat.

Racialized stereotypes about black and Latino gender roles also place trans youth at high risk, both on the streets and in schools. The brutal 2008 murder of gender non-conforming teen Lawrence King by a male student at an Oxnard middle school shone a national spotlight on transphobia and violence. But the fact that King was a working-class boy of color, possibly grappling with racist cultural misperceptions about what his "rightful" gender identity should be, was not examined in mainstream discussions about the tragedy. The 2009 suicides of Carl Walker Hoover and Jaheem Herrera, eleven-year-old boys of color who had been harassed at school because they were suspected of being gay, did not make headlines. At the same time, bullying-related suicides involving white gay youth were more widely publicized and seized on as national calls to action.[25] These cases were highlighted in magazines and on cable TV and network news. Town halls were convened, experts were tapped, and bullying prevention became the mantra in public schools. But the mainstream view that youth of color aren't deserving victims prevents them from getting the mental health intervention and social reinforcement that they need. Layer on being queer in a homophobic culture that demands hyper-masculinity from young men of color and feminine submission from young women of color (vis-à-vis heterosexual relationships, physical contact with males, caregiving, and life aspirations), and gender non-conforming youth of color are doubly and triply victimized.

Although many homeless youth have to resort to prostitution and survival sex, the issue is especially acute for women of color. Racist/sexist notions of black female hypersexuality and pure white womanhood influence the way black women are perceived in the dominant culture. As I argue throughout this book, women of color have never had the luxury of looking down on white women from pedestals or plantation houses.

The legacy of the dirty rapacious black Jezebel or spicy "bitch in heat" Latina shapes the way young women of color are perceived as naturally sexual and, hence, born prostitutes. Lesbians of African descent are triply stigmatized by cultural demands for racial, sexual, and gender respectability. For *all* American girls, conventional gender mores emphasize sexual purity and unswerving allegiance to men. Narratives of home, hearth, and romance are supposed to enflame every girl's desire. From an early age, girls of color are socialized with the heterosexist script that being desired by a man and having children should be their authentic destiny in life. Nowhere is this message more fiercely promoted than in the global toy industry. Shoehorning girls into dolls, domestication, and dress-up, the global toy industry rigidly polices gender roles, reinforcing heterosexual conformity. More insidiously, big box retailers and toy store conglomerates from Middle to urban America explode with princess merchandise. With its emphasis on dressing up, hooking up, melodrama, pink power, and pageantry, the rise of the Disney princess industry has made hyper-femininity (laced with token displays of "girlish" spunk and "independence") the national creed for millions of girls. Consequently, there is little space in American culture for young queer women of color who are not perceived as "femme" or actively seeking male validation. Out lesbians like Wanda Sykes, or those who are rumored to be lesbians such as Queen Latifah, get "dyke-baited." As a result, all straight and gay children see in the media are chic, gender-conforming, white lesbians (ala those featured on shows like the *L Word* and the *Real L Word*) or ubiquitous images of glamorous "bi-curious" girls making out to give males a voyeuristic thrill.[26]

Homelessness among queer youth is not only driven by media, abuse, and socioeconomic factors. The absence of out queer faculty, administrators, and staff on school campuses exacerbates homophobia for LGBTQ youth of color. In 2011, California passed SB48, or the Fair Education Act, a bill that required new textbooks and high school history courses to include the contributions of gays and lesbians. The bill's advocates hoped that it would provide greater visibility for the connection between LGBTQ communities of color and the struggle for social justice. However, although SB48 looks good on paper, there is no evidence that most California high school curricula are being revised to include examples of prominent gays and lesbians. And what few textbook LGBT portrayals there are rarely acknowledge multiculturalism, multiple identities, intersectional politics, and coalition-building across race, gender, sexuality, and class. Currently, representations of gays and lesbians of African descent rarely go beyond Langston Hughes. In the mainstream K-12 imagination, Hughes has been sanitized, his body of work reduced to the universalist metaphors of the now canonical poem *Dreams*. High school students are far less familiar with his political radicalism and early Communist alignment, his withering critiques of organized religion, and his struggle to achieve visibility as a black gay artist in the midst of Harlem Renaissance-era black male identity politics. In much of his writings about politics and religion, Hughes espoused a humanist vision of queer selfhood and masculine identity. His 1932 poem *Goodbye Christ* was a blisteringly apostate critique of religious hucksterism and God pimping by charlatans like revivalist Aimee Semple McPherson.[27] In the poem Hughes tells Jesus to "beat it," suggesting that he should "make way" for the masses, who, inspired by Karl Marx and company, bow to "no religion at all."[28] In 1940, McPherson and her followers picketed a scheduled presentation by Hughes at a hotel in Pasadena, California.[29] As a result, Hughes cancelled his appearance, leading one nationalist anti-Communist journalist to proclaim that "queer ideologies and strange ideologists who appear to be half-human, half-ape seem to fascinate the sophisticates of the high society realms of Pasadena."[30] Hughes' hostile encounter with one of the giants of 20th century Christian revivalism in sunny "liberal" Southern California is an ironic footnote in American social history. Many early African American migrants viewed Southern California as an antidote to the moral hypocrisy and racial terrorism of the fundamentalist South. But their American dreams of prosperity and equality were crushed by the reality of de facto segregation and racially restrictive covenants—often buttressed by good white Christian "separate but equal" moralizing or appeals to scientific racism.

There is no room for these moral and political nuances in most K-12 histories. Education about Hughes' vision as a radical black gay freethinker could not only reshape young people's views on his poetry but might elicit a different reading of democracy and African American belief systems. It might motivate young people to question why the most Christian nation on the planet has also been the most insidiously white supremacist and heterosexist in the name of democracy. Rather than viewing blackness and gayness as distinct and oppositional (ala the propaganda of the Religious Right and reactionary Black Nationalism), there could be recognition of how they have historically been woven into the narrative of alien-ness, immorality, and anti-Americanism in ways that have both advantaged and disadvantaged straight people of color and white gays.

As an educator and mentor in South Los Angeles schools, I try to infuse this sense of critical consciousness into all of my work. Talking openly about homophobia during a workshop facilitated by my Women's Leadership Project and Gay/Straight Alliance (GSA) students at Washington Prep High School, some of the male students pushed back when asked whether or not they had an obligation to defend a gay friend who was being harassed. Predictably, the football players in the group were the most vehement. They felt that there was a clear line between the way gay and straight males behaved. With its rigid culture of hyper-masculinity and big endorsement deals tied to alpha male and All-American girl superstardom, organized sports have long been a stronghold of anti-gay discrimination. According to the *Los Angeles Times*, there are virtually no *active* professional sports figures that are out[31]. So if a gay male was acting "gay" (i.e., flamboyant) at school then he was asking for a beat down. I don't want to seem homophobic, one student said, but that's not "natural." Nature determined what was moral. "Gaydar" (being able to tell who was and was not gay largely based on stereotypes about gay male effeminacy) was a truism that even the most conscious students believed in. The girls in the GSA asked whether the ball players would feel the same if someone tried to jump them because they were black males. Would it be okay for racist police, white supremacists, or other men of color to target them for simply "being while black"? That's different, some said, but others were silent, letting the analogy sink in. If we had had the space for debate most would've talked about the physical fact of their bodies, arguing that blackness is an indelible biological fact, a magnet for every storeowner, cop or teacher who views black youth as guilty until proven innocent. Pastors, community leaders, and other adults have drilled it into them that equating gayness and blackness is sacrilegious, a ruse manufactured by elite white gays to claim oppressed status and mooch off of African Americans' civil rights legacy. As the students thought about their allegiances, a teacher who has been a leader on social justice issues at the school challenged them to speak out. He likened their moral complicity with homophobia to society's indifference to the racism and sexism they experience every day. Several years ago the school was slapped with an anti-gay bias discrimination suit that led to a settlement.[32] Since then, district policy around bullying and harassment has become more stringent, mandating that teachers and administrators report bias incidents and attend anti-bullying trainings. Though important, mandates and anti-bullying trainings are ultimately band-aid correctives that don't disrupt heterosexist American gender norms, identities, family structures, and cultures. Similarly, simply including Hughes, Bayard Rustin, Gloria Anzaldua, Audre Lorde, Adrienne Rich or other LGBT literary and historical figures in a textbook without the cultural context of their struggles and vision is a variation on the charismatic great man/woman one-trick pony. And setting untrained teachers adrift in the classroom without culturally responsive professional development makes these policies virtually worthless for affecting long term change in classroom pedagogy.

* * *

In the cold light of day, many of us experience school as a place of intimate terror, the gauntlet for policing and conformity, the original fount of gender-coded rules, rituals, regimens, and friendships. It's where we learn to line up as opposite genders, arms at our sides, quiet, obedient, role-playing "ladies" and "gentlemen." It's where we learn that order—in speech, gender, behavior, intelligence, skin tone, and dress—is moral. It's where "play" is empire, incubator for the crippling fear of ostracism or the warm milk of acceptance. Roughhousing behind the schoolyard gates we imbibe sacred prohibitions of the playground. After a certain age, hopscotch, football and double dutch must become foreign lands, forbidden fruit, sexual boundaries that rope off daddy's little girls from mama's boys. In the military hierarchies of the classroom, the world of the apple-cheeked white boy, his church, his God, his flag, becomes the unspoken norm.

Because segregated, post-industrial, capitalist America allows few authentic cultural spaces in communities of color, churches are ambiguous "sanctuaries." Some of the students in our GSA say that their churches accept everyone without judgment. But when we probe more deeply they cannot recall open embrace of LGBT families or relationships from the pulpit. Nationwide, gay African Americans and Latinos are more likely to be raising children in same-sex relationships.[33] Thus, for many, "acceptance" means silence. In its article "Black Churches May Be More Friend than Foe to Gay Congregants," the Center for American Progress challenges the dominant culture's belief (amplified during California's landmark 2008 anti-gay marriage initiative Proposition 8) that black communities and churches are more homophobic than their white counterparts.[34] The article contends that gay folks' "relationship with black churches in fact provides safe spaces and a steadfast social network that helps them deal with societal oppression at large."[35] It quotes the Reverend Delman Coates of Maryland, "who…says he has seldom come upon the anti-gay vitriol that black churches are alleged to promote (and) that, at most, some churches may employ a code of silence around sexuality, but few actually preach division and hate from the pulpit."[36] But Coates' distinction between explicit anti-gay sentiment and "benign" silence is a disingenuous one. Lesbian activist and writer Reverend Irene Monroe is critical of the view that the black church is a more welcoming space for queer and same-gender loving African Americans. Although a number of black pastors followed President Obama's lead when he finally declared his support for same-sex marriage in early 2012, Monroe points out that:

> Church doctrine throughout African-American denominations hasn't changed on the topic of homosexuality, keeping the church tethered to an outdated notion of human sexuality and a wrongheaded notion of what constitutes civil rights…Many African-American ministers still believe the institution of marriage, at least within the black family, is under assault, and that LGBTQ people further exacerbate the problem. For these ministers, some of whom support LGBTQ civil rights broadly but draw the line at same-sex marriage, espousing their opposition to same-sex marriage is a prophylactic measure to combat the epidemic of fatherlessness in black families. In scapegoating the LGBTQ community, these

> clerics are ignoring the social ills behind black fatherlessness, such as the systematic disenfranchisement of both African-American men and women, high unemployment, high incarceration, and poor education, to name a few.[37]

The explosion of gay families of color in the South has highlighted the contradiction between Bible Belt bigotry and gay-friendly faith. According to the *New York Times*, Jacksonville, Florida is "home to one of the biggest populations of gay parents in the South" as well as several gay-friendly churches.[38] The article profiles an African American lesbian family who sought out a black church after feeling disconnected from the predominantly childless congregation at a white gay church. One of the women became a pastor at the new church and developed a youth program. The couple's experiences attest to the important role parenting and creating safe space play in the lives of black lesbians. Lesbians of color are more likely than white women to be parenting dependent children. Thus, finding a culturally responsive, supportive community is paramount for gay families of color. For many African Americans, this void has historically been filled by the church, but to what end?

Gay-friendly faith organizations dangle the promise that being queer, moral, and "good with God" are compatible. But like the original sin of sexual temptress Eve and other dirty reprobates soiled with the shit of the Fall, this goodness comes with caveats and conditions. For example, after working with Zion Hill Baptist Church on a community forum to address homophobia in the Black Church, I was informed by Pastor Seth Pickens that the church leadership was opposed to holding it at their facility. Pickens had been struggling to address homophobia amongst his own parishioners, after some of them opposed a lesbian couple having their partnership blessed at the church. Over the past two years, my group, Black Skeptics Los Angeles, has held forums at Zion Hill on black atheist and Humanist perspectives. Pickens has expressed his acceptance of LGBT parishioners, but ultimately conceded to the demands of the church community.

Tolerant pastors always discover that it's one thing to be tolerant in word and another to be moral and just in *deed,* given the inhumanity of the Bible. Being part of the regime of Christian goodness requires constant vigilance against the fundamentalist barbarians at the gate who police whether or not "homos" get into heaven.

Decades from now, faced with a radically different America, the little white boy from Apostolic Truth Tabernacle church may be repulsed by his fifteen minutes of YouTube infamy. He will be in good company. Some of the most indelible images from the civil rights movement are of young whites jeering and spitting at black students desegregating Central High School in Little Rock, Arkansas. This ugliness captured the pivotal role young white America played in the performance of Christian racism. But the beauty of god(s) as a human invention is that they are everything and nothing. Forgiveness is in the eye of the beholder. Depending upon who's looking, iconic serial killer Ted Bundy and a Good Samaritan both get the same e-ticket to redemption if they accept Jesus as their personal Lord and savior. For the average schlub trying to make it through the dead of night, there must be wrestling, groveling, and whoring after God's favor, wisdom, and omnipotence. There must be surrender to the "godliness" inside oneself when frail naked piddling humanity just won't do. In the face of blood-running-in-the-streets carnage there must be props given to his/her/its benevolent stage-managing. Smacked by the brute force of aging, pissing at the seams, stuffing down meds on a stopwatch and clawing for every scrap of memory, there must be crippling terror over the body's "ugly" mortality. God means bargaining back from the precipice of sagging flesh and invisibility, no limit per buyer.

To be good with God is to always be in a state of negotiation and surrender. One of the most popular expressions of this mentality is the ubiquitous Alcoholics Anonymous creed, the "Serenity Prayer," which was cobbled together by Protestant theologian Reinhold Niebuhr in the 1940s.[39] The lines "God grant me the serenity to accept the things I cannot change, the courage to change the things I can and the wisdom to know the difference" is a lament on human frailty and humility in the face of the divine. It extols the virtues of surrendering to God's will when confronted with the natural world's "sinfulness." Like a used-car salesman screeching "just trust me" to wary customers in a lot of old shit boxes, Niebuhr's "God will make everything right in the afterlife" appeal is a deadening view of life on Earth. If the world is such a cesspit why let heaven wait? Over the past several years, apocalyptic hysteria about cultural otherness has dominated fundamentalist Christian discourse with end-of-the-world ghosts through 21st century Americana nightmares about queer racialized bodies, breeder women of color and the criminal inner city welfare queen. Going against the prison of the divine and the fickleness of gods means rejecting supernaturalist moralities from the mouths of babes, demagogues, used-car salesmen or prophets. There is no justice in surrender.

CHAPTER TWO

God's Body, Science's Brain

It's a good time to be Christian in America. The dark, dirty era of persecution has receded and being Christian—shouting it loud and balls to the breeze proud without the possibility of rebuke—is sexy. Ads from Internet dating sites like Christian Singles beckon during primetime, the Christian catch phrase "I'm blessed" has become a national bromide, and pop culture serves up Americana holiness in one big 14-carat crucifix. The hippest chicest celebs don't leave home without megawatt crucifix bling, network TV dramas crown wayward white women "Good Christian Bitches," and superstar mega preachers command 24/7 branding platforms on slick cable TV shows that hawk their latest motivational pap. Of course, there is nothing new about the latter. In the 1980s, prosperity pimps like Jimmy Swaggart, Jim Bakker, and Pat Robertson parlayed TV evangelism into a multi-billion dollar industry. But 21st century pimping is distinguished by its ubiquity, fueled by the Internet and a glut of religious cable stations that are more accessible to mainstream viewers. In the age of Barack Obama, the brute-force revivalism of the Religious Right has made once-benign issues like birth control partisan and even gotten the yellow-bellied mass media shrieking about the right's "war on women."

Still, the Religious Right has been practically virtuosic in its 2+2=5 mass doublespeak, convincing mainstream America that Christians are the new minority and that commie pinko "secular progressives" (Fox News talk show host Bill O'Reilly's preferred "smear") are at the helm of a socialist conspiracy. During the 2012 presidential race, GOP candidate Rick Perry repeatedly played the Christian victim card in a desperate bid to remain relevant with the very same white evangelicals that courted him in the early stages of his candidacy. After flubbing the presidential debates his numbers plummeted and white evangelicals ditched him for Rick Santorum. Prior to the Iowa caucuses, Perry ran a series of ads boldly declaring that he was not "ashamed" to say he was a Christian. The most campy one was entitled "Strong" and featured Perry striding through the grass in full-blown alpha male mode, inviting viewers to admire his impeccably feathered '70s soap-star helmet hair and Iron John jaw. Perry blasts Obama's "war" on religion, the indecency of allowing gays to serve openly in the military, and the prohibition on prayer in schools. Tellingly, the narrative that Christianity and Christian values are under siege by the first Black president is one of white evangelicals' favorite fairy tales. Because of his blackness, Barack Obama could no more be a legitimate Christian than Fidel Castro. During the campaign Rick Santorum even went so far as to vilify Obama as a suspect Christian touting a "phony theology not based on the Bible." None of this vitriol accompanied Bill Clinton's presidency. Clinton could be as raunchy a philandering cracker as he wanted to be and still be God's child and a good Southern Baptist with only a symbolic connection to his faith.

When it comes to religion and faith, white outsider status can't compete with the black "Other." I was reminded of this legacy when an African American and a white teacher got into an argument about whether or not the U.S. is a Christian nation during one of my teacher training sessions. The school where the workshop was being held is predominantly black and Latino, with a high dropout rate and a low four-year college-going rate. After a high profile incident in which a gun in a student's backpack accidentally went off in a classroom, the school was widely stereotyped by the local media as a dead end repository of lawless black and brown youth. Nonetheless, there are many students at the school who are achieving and showing leadership, contrary to the stereotype. During the discussion, the African American teacher staunchly defended the notion that the U.S. is a Christian nation. The white teacher, who is notorious for making racist, paternalistic comments about students (as well as homophobic slurs about a colleague), swaggeringly proclaimed his non-belief and declared that the U.S. has always been defined by the separation of church and state. It was clear that the "outsider" white man had no fear about being ostracized for his renegade views in a fight with a preachy black teacher. The reality is that even the most abject disreputable white non-believer doesn't suffer any racial consequences for his non-belief. There might be political consequences, but even disreputable white men don't surrender their universal subject status over a little matter of heathenism. You might be a Godless "freedom-hating" flag burning pinko commie infidel but you are still human and still a citizen until proven otherwise. And this has been the paradox for African American non-believers. Historically, being Christian has been a de facto pathway to becoming moral, to becoming American, and to becoming a provisional citizen. American Christianity and capitalism marched in lockstep. Citizenship, as the framers envisioned it, was embodied by private ownership, specifically the democratic right of white males to own and control land. Twentieth century social discourse promoted owning a single family home with a yard as a moral aspiration. It a national standard that set the U.S. apart from every other industrialized nation on the planet, where urbanism was the symbol of modernity. As Herbert Hoover noted in 1931, "To possess one's home is the hope and ambition of every individual in this country. The sentiment for home ownership is embedded in the American heart [of] millions of people who dwell in tenements, apartments and rented rows of solid brick. . .This aspiration penetrates the heart of our national wellbeing."[1]

Hoover's love letter to the single-family Americana home was reflected in automobile manufacturer Henry Ford's declaration that "we shall solve the city problem by leaving the city."[2] As the white working class and white immigrant homebuyers benefited from generous postwar federal programs to move out of inner city slums, the city problem swiftly became the Negro problem. White flight was simply another form of manifest destiny, a fulfillment of the Christian God's bequeathal of land to a new nation of bootstrapping white citizen immigrants.

The Citizenry & Ghetto Loans

A black son asks his mother what democracy means. Her response, "Well, son, that be when white folks work every day so us po' folks can get all our benefits."
"But mama, don't the white folk get mad about that?"
"They sho do, son. They sho do. And that's called racism." (joke told by Arkansas Tea Party official)

White people have started to return to South Los Angeles. They can be seen watering lawns, walking dogs, and frequenting local restaurants. Legend has it that there are a few white families that never left during the post-war mass exodus that magically transformed what was once Southwest L.A. into "South Central"—the notorious, mythic den of drugs, drive-bys, and destruction that launched a thousand gangsta rap careers and corporate parasites rolling to the bank on the backs of "bitches" and "hos".

Back in the day, all of the "bad" black and brown schools in Compton, Watts, and Inglewood were teeming with whites. Americana *Leave it to Beaver* mom icon Barbara Billingsley even graduated from Washington Prep High School, a local 'hood school, in the 1930s. But these new white transplants are merely symbols of the turbulent real estate market, not inner city missionaries slumming for an ethnographic high. They're canaries in the coalmine of negative equity. Priced out of the "better" (read white) areas of the city, some white homebuyers have been forced to venture back into the hood. Snapping up Spanish or Craftsman-style bungalows, they're rediscovering the "quaintness" of Southwest neighborhoods that their forebears escaped decades ago courtesy of government programs like the GI Bill and FHA mortgage lending. Touring the streets, some register surprise at the area's suburban aura, the tidiness of the houses, and pride in ownership that the natives demonstrate. Having the luxury to move back to the "ghetto" is part of their democratic birthright. White American democracy has always meant the bliss of segregation and willful ignorance to who gets displaced. It's ladled out in cultural initiations like being warned to keep the car windows up when driving through black areas or having a nifty cell phone app nicknamed

"Avoid Ghetto."[3] Even in the era of rampant "Main Street" foreclosure and negative equity, white American democracy still means the privilege of mobility. When whites move into neighborhoods that residents of color have been forced to leave due to plummeting home values and high unemployment it's called gentrification. It's only cause for national political action and reform when white middle-class homeowners are impacted by housing bubbles. Bipartisan political rhetoric that fixates on the "middle class" (as the default category), with no attention to disproportionately *asset poor* working-class people of color, merely reinforces a colorblind class myth where struggling white people have it "just as bad" as people of color.

For the party of the Religious Right, poor people don't work and they don't pay taxes. God's pecking order does not favor being on the dole and accepting handouts. The muscular Jesus extolled by demagogues like Christian broadcaster Bryan Fischer, head of the American Family Association, which is "to the right of Fox News," is a bad ass who is all about self-reliance and rugged individualism and doesn't take any shit.[4] Fischer, an influential right-wing radio talk show host and virulent Christian fascist homophobe, has argued that "government social welfare programs violate the Bible and the Constitution."[5] According to Fisher, the Bible cautions that welfare can become a form of lifetime dependency. The association of free enterprise with biblical morality and Christian values marks poor people of color as other, as beyond redemption. Christian nationhood and the belief in black socioeconomic dysfunction go hand-in-hand. In the minds of many whites, black "ghettoes" and the persistence of black poverty are in and of themselves clear evidence that African Americans just can't cut it when it comes to "real" Christian values of hard work, thrift, and sacrifice. So perhaps there is something to the Children of Ham curse. The curse of Ham launched a thousand cross burnings and civil legislation designating due process as for whites only. As descendants of Noah's son Ham, blacks were doomed to inferiority and underachievement because Ham caught Noah lurching around naked in a drunken stupor. Other than underscoring the Bible's value as one big incestuous soap opera, the myth also links blackness to sexual depravity and "indecency."

Historically, white morality, ethics, and justice were framed within the context of black immorality. As Toni Morrison says, "it is no accident that immigrants understood their American-ness in opposition to the resident black population" because black otherness was enshrined in the Constitution with the "three-fifths" person "compromise" clause, re-inscribed with Jim Crow, and regurgitated in 20th century welfare discourse. American exceptionalism is validated by the specter of the Black ghetto as den of immorality. According to this narrative, African Americans have squandered the advantages of living in a democratic society in which everyone has an equal chance at economic mobility. Black poverty is only immoral insofar as it reflects a certain cultural indolence and pathology on the part of shiftless blacks. While "cultures of poverty" corrupt, cultures of success, based on capitalism, free enterprise, and hard work uplift and moralize. Systemic discrimination has never been deemed immoral in the American mainstream. For the Right, systemic discrimination is a quaint oxymoron, a vestige of a primitive era when the U.S. was presumably less evolved. The moral universe consists of getting ahead in pure Darwinian terms (the way God wanted it) free of the fetters of restrictive public policy that rewards the sloth of homeowners of color.

In 2011, former mortgage giant Countrywide was found guilty of engaging in predatory lending which targeted black and Latino homebuyers. In 2012, Wells Fargo settled a lawsuit after it was accused of steering over 30,000 black and Latino homebuyers to subprime loans. The class-action suit stemmed from a Baltimore city lawsuit in which former employees alleged that Wells Fargo "loan officers referred to minority borrowers as 'mud people' and called subprime mortgages 'ghetto loans.' "[6] During the lending boom, Wells Fargo officials regularly conducted "wealth building" seminars in communities of color, often headlined by talk show host Tavis Smiley. Officials secretly peddled predatory loans at these events.[7]

So, while homebuyers of color were essentially taxed for being black or brown, white homebuyers "bootstrapped" their way to the American dream with lower interest rates and better terms handed to them by the big banks. "Homebuying while white," many of them had the same credit scores and incomes as applicants of color. What they didn't have was the same capital and asset holdings. Not only is black and Latino wealth a fraction of white wealth, the vast majority of it is based on home equity, home equity that has been pillaged by Wells

Fargo, Countrywide, Bank of America and other lenders. As Yuan Miu of the *Washington Post* argues, the housing bust has "left a scar on the finances of black America…(it) has not only wiped out a generation of economic progress but could leave them at financial disadvantage for generations to come."

Yet, mainstream narratives on the housing meltdown tended to revolve around irresponsible homebuyers lapping up variable mortgages they couldn't pay off or vulnerable homebuyers sacrificed on the altar of Wall Street's credit default swap morass. After President Obama finished bailing out the big Wall Street banks, his rhetoric turned to shoring up Main Street. To hear Obama tell it, the brunt of the crisis was squarely centered in Middle America. Urban neighborhoods devastated by the TKO of predatory lending, foreclosure, job discrimination, and mass incarceration barely registered on the radar of the administration or the mainstream media. There was little mass outrage over the systematic disenfranchisement of black and Latino homebuyers by the banking crooks. Neither GOP lawmakers nor prominent Democrats, other than those in the Congressional Black Caucus, rushed to criticize the lending industry's white affirmative action policies. Nor did they condemn the racist practices of bankruptcy attorneys, who refer debt-ridden black consumers to more costly Chapter 13 bankruptcy filings.[8]

Being against big government intervention or social welfare for working-class communities of color has always been about morality. It is reflected in right-wing venom against public employee unions and health care reform, both overwhelmingly supported by people of color. And it is amplified in racist discourse around illegal immigration. As the white population and white births continue to decline, nativist propaganda against undocumented immigrants has become more unabashedly Christian fascist. It's no accident that Bible Belt and/or heavily evangelical states like Alabama, Georgia, and Arizona have passed the toughest anti-illegal immigration laws in the nation.

But before the serpent of Revelations descended, the GOP and the Religious Right tried to channel compassionate conservatism in the run-up to the 2012 presidential election. During George W. Bush's administration, compassionate conservatism was supposed to boost GOP support amongst "moderate" constituencies alienated by Reagan-Bush's trickle down policies and welfare queen rhetoric. Bush's faith-based initiative was a key part of the drive to rehabilitate the GOP's hard-line image. After months of aping white supremacist Minutemen with a hard-on for dangerous illegals, Mitt Romney tried to appease Latinos with a "kinder, gentler" message. Romney's pivot was hastened by Barack Obama's pledge to grant work permits and temporary freedom from the threat of deportation to undocumented youth under 30. When Romney mounted the podium at a meeting of the National Association of Latino Elected Officials he didn't dare reiterate his infamous demand that undocumented Latinos "self-deport." Instead, in a blizzard of limp paternalism, he trotted out bromides about keeping "strong families" together. Romney's evolving stance mirrored that of some white evangelicals. Like the corn-fed Mormon missionary boys who ritualistically descend onto the third world/inner city, some evangelicals are bug-eyed over the prospect of fresh meat from the "barrio." The smartest among them have been reading the tea leaves and checking the collection plates. They see the future and it is brown. For the past several years Latinos have been the fastest growing segment of the evangelical population. Latino parishioners are fueling a resurgence of Pentecostalism in the U.S. and filling in the gaps of an aging white demographic in decline. Taking a nativist stance on immigration is political suicide for the GOP and the Religious Right. Coasting into the 21st century with the same stale smorgasboard of guns, gays, ghettoes, and "gov'ment" will only seal its doom with a Latino electorate that overwhelmingly supports social welfare and government spending. Yet, as the Right continues to pirouette on immigration policy, it will ratchet up classic divide-and-conquer narratives tied to bootstrapping, a racialized mythos of hard work, and so-called family values. These messages ultimately turn on an implicit contrast between immigrants and African Americans.

This contrast—between the immigrant trajectory of seized opportunity (and earned citizenship) versus the resident black population's essential otherness—is a subtext of the GOP's anti-government platform. Every school-age child of color has been indoctrinated into the Statue of Liberty shtick declaring that somewhere back in the mists of time white people were poor, backward immigrants clawing tooth and nail to make it on America's gold-paved streets. Every child of color is supposed to know that whites who work every day achieve upward mobility against great personal odds. That's why they don't see white people living in their neighborhoods or going to their schools. That's why some of my students associate white masculinity with Donald Trump caricatures of wealth and privilege. The white immigrant narrative is privileged as the most authentic version of personal ingenuity and achievement. Exposed to textbook stories of heroic white historical figures that triumphed against adversity, students of color are taught to believe that all white work is hard work. Dirt poor whites whose ancestors grew up in log cabins escaped pogroms in Eastern Europe, potato famine in Ireland, and bubonic plague in England made America the proud beacon of democracy and free enterprise that it is today. In the late 20th century Asian and (legal) Latino immigrants picked up the torch. The blaring message to blacks is, if "those tired, poor, huddled masses did it, why can't you people?"

As nativist and xenophobic as the GOP's opposition to the Dream Act is, it's still mediated by the perception that immigrant workers are hardworking.[9] Much of GOP presidential primary messaging about work—from Newt Gingrich's racist slurs about blacks waiting for food stamps, to Rick Santorum's "I don't want to make black people's lives better by giving them other people's money" comment—evoked the myth of black welfare dependency and white industriousness. Thus, even though immigrants of color will always be perpetual outsiders, their citizenship is viewed as hard fought, hard won, and richly deserved. For example, golden boy Republican senator Marco Rubio has become the right's Hispanic du jour because his autobiography seems to fit neatly into the narrative of American exceptionalism and immigrant enterprise. This narrative being of mixed black, Asian, Indian, and European ancestry, the majority of Latinos in the U.S. identify racially as white.[10] Clearly the ambiguity of Latino racial identity was a significant factor in white Middle American solidarity with George Zimmerman. Jewish Peruvian-American "white Hispanic" Zimmerman's initial $200,000 defense fund was bankrolled by white fears of the criminal black welfare leeching other. Had Trayvon Martin been "white Hispanic" and Zimmerman black, not only would there have been no defense fund but Zimmerman would have been arrested, charged, and tried in due course. The cold reality is that while the brown-skinned Zimmerman would have surely been hauled in and interrogated under the terms of racial profiling legislation like Arizona's SB1070, he is, at the end of the day, not black.

Race: the Power of an Illusion

> A person from the Congo and a person from Mali are more likely to be different genetically from each other than either is from a person from Belgium. Yet, if everyone from this region got up and moved to the United States, we'd call them all African Americans and see them as members of the same race.
>
> --Joseph Graves, *The Race Myth*[11]

There is a great scene in the 2002 documentary *Race: The Power of an Illusion,* in which a young white runner muses that black running prowess might be due to blacks having an "extra bone." She smiles sheepishly as testimony from other runners and media clips bear out the stereotype that black runners are somehow genetically "blessed" with supernatural superhuman athletic talent. The myth of the superhuman black athlete (excelling in football, basketball and track, and not so much in hundreds of other sports) has always been a sexy, multi-million dollar global commodity. Back in the heyday of Michael Jordan Inc., little white kids gushed that their life's ambition was to "be like Mike." Being like Mike didn't mean being racially profiled or Jim Crowed in urban public schools. It didn't mean being dark-skinned or being more likely to die from a gunshot wound in an emergency room with no health insurance. It didn't mean being given a subprime loan by Wells Fargo or Countrywide. Being like Mike meant being cool, hip, successful, and filthy up by your bootstraps rich—the epitome of the colorblind American Dream. It also meant being irreproachably male and manly, having the feral yet controlled hetero male charisma that black men are supposedly so good at exuding. The filthy-rich black basketball player is white America's ultimate racial aphrodisiac. White America likes its raw black ball players, its inner city savage hip hop, its soulful R&B, its funky black dance moves (Norman Mailer captured this cultural imperialist lust in his paean to the hip abandon of the "White Negro"), and shrieking black gospel singers. It's a bottomless pit for black exotica. White America fetishizes the black ball player's blackness, natural grace, soulful masculinity, and Dionysian athleticism resonates but still viscerally recoils at the prospect of multiple blacks in its neighborhoods, churches or schools.

Be that as it may, *Race: The Power of an Illusion* forcefully reminds the viewer that race is just a mirage. It deconstructs the biological basis for race by tracking the experiences of a group of high school students decoding their mitochondrial DNA. The series deftly yokes the history of race construction with imperialism, white supremacy, and racism. Race may be an enduring fiction, but esteemed evolutionary biologist Joseph Graves puts to rest any colorblind we-are-the-world homilies when he breaks down the hard reality of being a black man who is constantly mistaken for an athlete or a criminal at the predominantly white university where he teaches.

Graves (the first African American to have earned a Ph.D. in evolutionary biology) is in an elite group of internationally-renowned African American scientists who have struggled with entrenched institutional racism in academia. For example, studies have shown that African American scientists are widely discriminated against when it comes to research funding by the National Institutes of Health. Grant funding is a major part of an academic's resume. As Earl Smith notes in the article "Gatekeeping in the Halls of Science: the Continued Significance of Race," applicants who do not have federal funding are "less likely to be offered a job…If African Americans are less likely than their White counterparts to exit graduate school and/or a post-doc with grants they will be less likely to be offered a position."[12] Institutional bias excludes African Americans from achieving tenure in the science disciplines. Smith notes that this vicious cycle also extends to publication—if black academics don't have major funding they may not be able to conduct field research. This would limit their ability to generate publishable material. In 2007, MIT medical professor Frank Douglas resigned in protest over the university's refusal to grant tenure to an African American colleague in the Biological Engineering department. Explaining his decision, Douglas stated, "I did so because I perceived unconscious discrimination against minorities and because my colleagues and the institute authorities did not act on my recommendations to address these issues."[13] Douglas' resignation on principle was somewhat similar to that of legal scholar Derrick Bell, who resigned from Harvard Law School in 1990 in protest over its failure to hire a black woman.

Conservative propaganda says that meritocracy would automatically mitigate hiring and retention bias. In 2003, former University of California regent Ward Connerly sponsored the so-called Racial Privacy Initiative, which would have prohibited racial classification in the public sector. Supporters of the initiative claimed racial categories were obsolete and that continuing to categorize individuals by race only perpetuated racism. Connerly (a leading opponent of affirmative action and architect of California's destructive landmark Proposition 209) is of African descent and frequently condemns race-based remedies as discriminatory towards whites and Asians.[14] Under the regime of the one-drop rule, anybody with known black ancestry is black. Right-wing ideologues like Connerly, who foam at the mouth about race cards and identity politics, are fond of blaming the one-drop rule's long shelf life on militant blacks who supposedly police the boundaries of blackness like the Stasi. Empirical data on the persistence of racial disparity amongst African descent populations never make it into right wing diatribes against racial categories. The fact that the U.S., alone among nations, has always had its power structure firmly rooted in the one-drop rule also never makes it into these diatribes. When dark-skinned, African-descent immigrants from Latin America, South America or the Caribbean come to the U.S., they express surprise at their newfound black "identity." In their native countries they were more defined by social class and cultural background. Blackness was something that folk in the race-obsessed U.S. fixated on. In her book *Volunteer Slavery,* journalist Jill Nelson reflects on this dichotomy, acidly noting that "many such immigrants often have a hard time relating to and understanding African Americans… ignorant of our history (they) pass judgment: African Americans…are lazy, cynical, always looking for a hand-out…Denying the role of race, they mouth the prejudices of white immigrants in blackface. Forget racism, history, the brutalization of the African American psyche from the middle passage on down, they holler. America is a nation of immigrants, and we are just like the Irish, Polish, Japanese and Jews…They conveniently forget that African Americans, unlike them, unlike any other immigrants, did not come here voluntarily; we are, all of us, the children of slaves." But America "the amnesiac" says that legacy should be forgotten.[15]

Twenty-first century blackness has only become more "rigid" in the context of ever expanding vistas of white supremacy and white social capital. One need only turn on American television for an initiation into the normalization of whiteness. On TV, any illusion of racial progress is ritualistically shattered by the steady parade of new shows featuring young white upwardly mobile protagonists who range from psychotic to level-headed. Black, Latino, Asian, and Native American actors may get a few more cracks at the exotic slut or neo-mammy caregiver sidekick but lead protagonist roles are still in the Jim Crow zone.

White supremacy has a peculiar genius for appropriating and defanging racial identities. Take the phrase "We are all Africans" for example. White conservatives never invoke a scientific view of the social construction of race. The idea that blacks and whites are united by genetics is heresy for even those that aren't rabid creationists. Yet their rhetoric on colorblindness and meritocracy holds that racial differences don't matter when it comes to progress. For the right-wing conservative, racial difference on the phenotypic level may be set in stone but it's hardly a barrier to individual achievement and progress because American institutions facilitate upward mobility for all. The only real barriers to upward mobility come when an individuals fail to work hard. Acts of racial (or gender) prejudice are unfortunate but never indicative of a systemic pattern.

A similar mentality exists amongst whites in the atheist movement who are fond of reminding people of color that "We are all Africans," as though the regurgitation of this statement nullifies their white privilege and investment in white supremacy. Over the past few years progressive non-believers have pushed for greater cultural diversity in the atheist movement. Writing about the subject in *The Guardian*, Alom Shaha said:

> While black and Asian people may not be actively excluded from atheist and skeptic gatherings, the lack of black and Asian people as speakers or audience members might be one reason why many black or Asian people feel such events are not "for them." So, even if there's no deliberate exclusion, there is accidental exclusion. Perhaps some people are genuinely unaware of this, but perhaps others are just hoping the problem does not really exist.[16]

Shaha goes on to identify the movement's lack of focus on cultural issues that are important to people of color. However, the eternal debate about whether white-dominated movements are intentionally or unintentionally exclusionary can be obfuscating. As Canadian atheist writer and health economist Ian Cromwell observes, "The face of atheism is, or at least has been, a white one. It's intimidating for a member of any visible minority community to walk into a room and be the only dark face in the crowd. Whether or not people actually *are* staring at you (and, yes, people do stare), it's tough to get over the feeling that you don't fit. Many black people, particularly those in the sciences, are used to being outnumbered, and have figured out a way to deal with it." As a leading young voice on Humanist social justice, Cromwell has been an outspoken critic of institutional racism within the secular community. Commenting on the Canadian context, Cromwell notes that "Blacks are about 3% nationally. We don't have entrenched black infrastructure, colleges, black caucuses or an NAACP because the population isn't large enough and hasn't been here long enough. Canada is far more secular than the U.S. and much more suspicious of shows of overt religiosity."[17] The reality is that in both the U.S. and Canada, most mainstream institutions of power, privilege, and political influence are white-dominated. Since racial segregation is the ironclad norm in residential communities, employment, education, and the art/literary/media establishments, atheist enclaves are simply a microcosm of the dominant culture. But Cromwell believes that "it's more shocking to hear racist talking points from people who pride themselves on rationality and evidence-based decision making. When race comes up as a topic, I'm often mildly amused/horrified to hear the kind of 19th-century 'scientific racist' slogans that come out of the mouths of my confreres."[18] The shock only lies in the balls-to-the-breeze boldness that some "We are All Africans" white atheists exhibit in their defense of the status quo.

One such outburst involved skeptic writer and academic Michael Shermer. Shermer was rightly criticized by writer Ophelia Benson after suggesting on a talk show that being a big dog in the secular world (i.e., being alpha enough to speak at conferences, go on shows, stand up and be an intellectual, bay at the moon, etc.) was a "guy thing" and that women just didn't have that kind of proclivity.[19] In a response to Benson he also insisted that the dearth of people of color in the secular community didn't mean "that all of us in the…community are racists, implicitly or explicitly."[20] Here, racism is caricatured as third-rail extremism which ultimately comes down to intent not effect. Since white atheists are all good liberals, and not foaming at the mouth evangelical Bubbas toting guns 'n religion, they can't be racist. In a blog post slamming Shermer, writer/biologist PZ Myers retorted, "You are making an implicitly sexist/racist remark when you blandly insist that what ought to be a truly catholic movement to improve humanity is just fine if it somehow fails to engage the concerns of non-white non-male people as much as it does us."[21]

At the end of the day, the absence of in-your-face Klan-style racism does not absolve social movements, academic departments or places of employment from accountability for patterns of exclusion and marginalization that systematically privilege white people and males. This ignores the very real racial/class and gender advantages that have historically accrued to whiteness, a dynamic that I will discuss in greater detail in the next chapter. Several years ago, as an instructor at the esteemed California Institute of the Arts, I was constantly getting the Kumbaya "we're boho artists that embrace everyone with patchouli-scented open arms" party line from the faculty and administration. "Cal Arts" was supposed to be a liberal arts oasis. African Americans and Latinos were a small minority on a campus that was already small, insular, and nestled in a notoriously conservative reactionary community. When racist anti-black graffiti was discovered in the campus art gallery and dorm of an African American student there was handwringing and denial. While students of color pushed for accountability the administration deflected with "this is an isolated incident" platitudes. At a school assembly convened to address the issue, the school president cried and invoked Martin Luther King. In the immediate aftermath of these incidents there were public relations pleas for healing and calm but no meaningful engagement with the need for institutional change. With barely any black or Latino faculty, no mentoring programs, and no connection to local communities of color, the retention rate of struggling students of color was poor.

When whiteness is the default standard for success and visibility in any academic program then only the most motivated and/or extensively supported students of color will succeed. Success often comes at the price of emotional and psychological well-being. Students who resist the status quo are frequently worn out with resentment and anxiety, often balancing activism, school work and the isolation of being "the first" and "the only." It's no accident that people of color in general and African Americans in particular suffer from disproportionate rates of depression due to racism and perceptions of racial discrimination.[22] The rigors of white-dominated academia are especially stressful for students of color that come from high school backgrounds where they were not prepared for the competitive and often isolating culture of higher education.

Racism, Sexism, and the Science Pipeline

In the mainstream imagination, science and God are united in mystery. Both are contested terrain whose authority is defined, governed, and controlled by powerful elites. Both promise transcendence, a taste of the immortal, a swipe at redemption. Religious promotion of the God concept is premised on enlightening and uplifting the sinful masses. Science illuminates the inner workings of the unknown; religion glorifies the inscrutability of the unknown and makes the sinful masses wallow in it. There is a popular African saying that the white man stole Africa's vast riches of raw materials and left the natives his Christian religion in return. It is at its core a commentary on the science of colonialism. As one of the most heavily evangelized regions in the world, Africa's poverty is a reflection of the dialectic between Western progress and "third world" superstition. African wealth allowed the West to innovate and build empires; evangelism kept Africa compliant, balkanized, and perpetually embroiled in internecine strife. It's commonly accepted that the "West has dominated world politics and economics with the power of science."[23] Science is the linchpin of modernity, progress and, by extension, moral betterment. It's what distinguishes the West from the technologically primitive and morally backward third world—Christian, Muslim and all points in between.

Historically, American science traditions have been portrayed as the domain of enterprising whites striding fearlessly across the global stage advancing knowledge and enlightenment. Although the right wing bellows about "our" freedoms coming directly from God—science and scientific innovation are still the U.S.' ace in the hole. Science, military might, and the supposed moral superiority that the two confer are the engines of empire. When Christian fascists like Missouri Congressman Todd Akin rant about women's bodies being able to "shut down" impregnation after a "legitimate rape," they are vilified as aberrations (if it's an election year) rather than representatives of the backwardness of white culture and white religious beliefs. When the white "natives" speak in tongues about the Earth being 6,000 years old they're not primitives they're patriots. Whites are not collectively stained by the taint of being anti-science or anti-modernity. Their culture is universal, timeless, rational, immortal. Hence, individual whites will never be called to account for the dangerous delusions of white evangelicals and the havoc they've wreaked on the lives of American women. They will never be smeared as a people besotted with superstition and paralyzed by prayer, a role that is colorfully fulfilled by the black Other. As cultural and political propaganda, cinematic scenes of praying, shouting, dancing Negroes getting a witness in church are a feel good staple of American pop culture. This cinematic shorthand gives American audiences access to the authentic rituals of African American communities. It's also a window into what white America is not—namely backward looking and complacent, waiting for God to give it a sign. Scenes of devout black folk are the cinematic equivalent of comfort food, an artery clogging dollop of macaroni and cheese, meatloaf and chicken pot pie all rolled up into one. Thus, the pious darkies of the 1940 Lena Horne/ Ethel Waters musical *Cabin in the Sky* are a window into an earthy wondrously mystical culture, in which the "Good Colored Boy…leaves… the Christian Good Woman to take up with the Bad Black Girl."[24]

The flipside of blubbering black piety is white scientific ingenuity, popularized by the mad scientist icon. Throwing propane on the church pews, the mad white scientist encapsulates the restless genius of the first world, "trespassing into the territory of gods," flirting with apocalypse.[25] From *Frankenstein* to *Dr. Strangelove* to the megalomaniac scientists of Marvel Comics, the conflict between dystopia and utopia have always informed depictions of white scientific ingenuity. The mad scientist might be evil or virtuous, goofy eccentric (ala Doc Brown of the 1985 film *Back to the Future*) or a raving Nazi-esque Strangelove. Regardless, he is a genius who generally starts out with good moral intentions and a whiz-bang invention that will transform the universe. However, when people of color are depicted "doing science" their goals are generally less ambitious. Isolated from communities of color, they are either the rare, rugged individualist (the exceptional credit-to-his-race Negro) or the white male genius' self-effacing minion. Mastery, heroism, and world-saving nationalism are not their currency and the neutered geek Negro generally bites it long before the credits roll.

Gender and racial politics, couched in themes of masculine mastery, are always at play in the representation of science as an elite domain. Decked out in a white lab coat straight from central casting, the African American science teacher featured in Target's 2012 "Back to School" commercial is a cartoonish reminder of the dearth of images of black scientists in American popular culture. Riffing about school supplies to the tune of Thomas Dolby's *She Blinded Me with Science*, the teacher whimsically declares, "Parents, this year I'm going to teach your kids that magic does exist. It's called science" Unfortunately, his whimsical classroom is filled with mostly white students doing quirky lab experiments. When youth of color see scientists in mainstream film, TV or advertising, it's usually the lone wolf, trailblazing, bulletproof-Einstein white male (or the sexualized white female variant, typically buried behind thick attitude glasses ready to be whipped off before a sex scene) peering through a microscope with furrowed brow. Mainstream representation codes heroism, scientific discovery, scientific genius, and rationality as white. This bias is also reflected in science textbooks in which the vast majority of scientists are white males or white females.[26] Media coverage of the Mars Curiosity rover's ecstatic, predominantly white Jet Propulsion Lab (JPL) crew was yet another affirmation of this link. A few weeks after Curiosity's successful landing on Mars, Nobel prize winning chemist Ahmed Zewail wrote that "Curiosity—the rover and the concept—is what science is all about: The quest to reveal the unknown. America's past investment in basic science and engineering, and its skill at nurturing the quest, is what led the Mars triumph and it is what undergirds U.S. leadership in today's world."[27]

The belief that African Americans and Latinos are averse to "science" because of their religiosity is a mainstay of secularist discourse. The belief that the religiosity of African Americans and Latinos inhibits their embrace of science, hindering their representation in the science field, is expressed in the following syllogism: People of color are overly religious. People of color are underrepresented in science. Hence, religiosity is the driving factor in the low levels of science achievement amongst people of color. Here, people of color are the victims of their own magical thinking. But, as I will argue, this convenient fiction is not borne out by research on African American girls' experiences with science education.

U.S. leadership in the STEM (science, technology, engineering and mathematics) field remains stubbornly segregated. As an aspiring oncologist enrolled at a South Los Angeles high school not far from JPL, college-bound twelfth grader Karly Jeter's role model is African American surgeon Ben Carson. He is the only person of color in the medical science field that she looks up to. She says that this is partly because he "made it on his own" and partly because she doesn't know of any other examples. Karly's desire to be an oncologist stems from being a cancer survivor herself. She describes finding a cure for cancer as her biggest passion. On the other end of the college spectrum, planetary geologist Devin Waller has a Bachelor's in Astrophysics from UCLA and a Master's in Geoscience from Arizona State University (ASU). As a graduate student her concentration was in planetary remote sensing on Mars. At ASU she was also a research analyst for projects involving the predecessors to Curiosity. Although they are at two different stages in the science education pipeline, these young women both represent the challenges that confront African American women in science and technology.

In her book *Swimming Against the Tide: African American Girls and Science Education*, Sandra Hanson explodes the myth that black girls are somehow disinterested in science due to hyper-religiosity or "culture." Hanson found that, despite significant institutional and societal barriers, there is greater interest in science among African American girls than in other student populations. She frames this seeming paradox in historical context, stressing that "Early ideologies about natural inequalities by race influenced the work of scientists and scholars as well as the treatment of minorities in the science domain. Racism is a key feature of science in the United States and elsewhere. This has a large impact on the potential for success among minority students. Early work on science as fair has not been supported."[28]

Hanson outlines some of the obstacles that confront budding African American women scientists from elementary school to the postgraduate level. Stereotypes about girls of color lacking proficiency in science, the absence of nurturing mentors, the dearth of education about people of color who have contributed to science research (i.e., culturally responsive science instruction), and academic isolation often deter youth who would like to pursue science careers. Science researcher Diann Jordan, author of *Sisters in Science*, notes that her study of black women scientists helped her combat the sense of isolation she felt in a field where she was often perceived as an interloper. Nonetheless, Jordan, Hanson, and other researchers have found that "African American girls in particular are very positive about science."[29] In an interview on encouraging black girls in science, stem cell scientist Valerie Johnson McCullar stressed that, although black girls begin with high interest in math and science in elementary school, they begin to lose interest in quantitative subjects around the fifth and sixth grade. McCullar attributes this to the fact that, "if there is not someone around you to constantly show you the beauty in certain things you get channeled in certain ways." Hanson notes that black girls, as opposed to white girls, are actually more inclined to stay engaged with science throughout their K-12 careers. In elementary and middle school girls tend to outperform males in math and science. However, the "trend tends to reverse itself in the white but not the African American communities as the young people enter high school." Indeed, "African American girls have been found…to be in more advanced math classes, to get better science grades, and to participate more in science than their male counterparts."[30] But Hanson emphasizes that greater participation amongst African American girls does not necessarily translate into high achievement. Academic outcomes for students of color still lag behind their white counterparts. Indeed, the presumption of underachievement that dogs even the "best and brightest" African American science students underscores the depth of educational apartheid in the U.S.

Karly Jeter's desire to be an oncologist developed in spite of the culture of her school. Similar to the magical Target classroom, Karly is typically only one of two or three black students in her Advanced Placement classes. Reflecting back on her junior year, she bitterly recounted when her AP English teacher excluded her from a list of students (all Asian and Latino) he predicted would pass the mock AP exam. When she was one of the few who passed he accused her of cheating. In her chemistry class she and other African American students were routinely criticized by their black teacher as having no other ambition in life besides playing sports.

Although there have been small gains, the abysmal number of African American students who successfully pursue college degrees and careers in science is a national disgrace. From K-12 to college, African American youth who are passionate about science education often face an uphill battle. President Obama's Master Teacher STEM initiative is ostensibly designed to address these disparities. It would develop a core of fifty educators to assume leadership in instruction, training, curriculum development, and mentorship in their school communities. Though the unveiling of the new plan provided a nice photo-op, Obama's vision doesn't address the culture of institutional racism that defines under-resourced schools. As Hanson argues, "research on African American women's experiences in the science education system shows the critical role of teachers. Unfortunately, African American women are often marginalized because of their race and gender. Science teachers tend to overlook these young women as a source of science talent...Textbooks and teachers focus mainly on science knowledge and inventions created by white scientists. Hence (students) are seldom made aware of the contributions of African Americans (much less African American women) in science."[31]

Karly's experiences illustrate how the nexus of low expectations, as well as college preparation and course programming barriers, can derail the most motivated science students. She regularly battled with her school counselor to be programmed into the elite AP Biology and Physics courses that have become virtual gatekeepers for future college science majors. She remarks that "some counselors believe that you might not succeed. They say maybe it might be a little too hard for you." As a result, parental intervention is mandatory for black science students at every step of the way. Although conventional wisdom holds that class status and income dictate interest and academic success in science, Hanson concluded that social capital such as family support and investment in the community were the most compelling factors. Girls whose parents (regardless of income levels, education and family composition) were supportive and engaged in their education were more likely to pursue science. In addition, girls who had higher levels of community involvement, volunteerism *and* participation in religious activities were also more likely to pursue a science major and have high achievement in science.[32]

The absence of quality college prep instruction at the high school level is often one of the most significant roadblocks to college access. Initiatives like the Latino and African American High School Internship Program for students in South and East Los Angeles highlight how low expectations can deter youth of color from careers in science and technology. Based at Children's Hospital Los Angeles, the program recruits high school seniors from "underrepresented" schools. According to an article in the *Los Angeles Times*, the program has struggled to attract African Americans because:

> Some area schools are not receptive and fail to see the potential in their students [the program's founder said]. "I get responses like, 'You know, the type of students you're looking for, we just don't have…That is just not right.' Chuck Uzoegwu, 19, participated in the program in 2010 and is now studying business and is pre-med at USC. He first noticed a slow attrition of fellow African American classmates when attending King Drew Medical Magnet High School. In the summer program, he was one of only a few African American students. He returned to the hospital this summer to volunteer in the lab and said he has yet to meet a role model there who looks like him. 'It disturbs me. It's nice to come into a place and see other people that are like you,' he said. 'It definitely feels like the higher up you go in education, the higher up you go in any organization, the less African American males you see.' "[33]

Uzoegwu's experiences reflect the hard reality of many high schools where the number of African American students who are encouraged to pursue science is criminally low. At the elite level of enrollment in Physics and Advanced Placement (AP) science courses, the numbers thin out even more. Nationwide, African American students are underrepresented in AP course enrollment and exam taking. At 14% of the U.S. student population they comprise only 3% of those enrolled in AP courses or taking AP exams. Native American students are also underrepresented. With the exception of a few states like Hawaii and South

Dakota, there has been greater success in closing the AP gap for Latino students than black or Native American students.[34] In addition, some schools don't even have AP courses, placing students who want to go to college at a major disadvantage.[35] According to the Harvard Education Press, "students who took AP math or science exams were more likely than non-AP students to earn degrees in particular physical science, engineering and life science disciplines."[36] Jacqueline Hernandez, a Watts resident enrolled in the Children's Hospital internship program, decries the lack of AP classes at her school. Hernandez once feared her college dreams would be derailed by teenage pregnancy like those of her three sisters. In 1999, students from the Inglewood Unified School District in Los Angeles successfully sued to get more AP courses at their schools. The suit charged that black and Latino students were systematically denied access to college preparation courses that were standard fare at white schools in Los Angeles County.

When AP courses *are* provided in so-called inner city schools, part of the enrollment gap comes down to inveterately low expectations for African American students. Most national studies on student on student performance confirm that teacher quality is perhaps the single greatest factor in student achievement and that teacher expectations are of paramount importance.[37] In her book *Culturally Relevant Teaching*, educator Geneva Gay argues that "positive and negative teacher attitudes and expectations have profound effects on student achievement."[38] Often African American students are perceived as defiant, unwilling to learn, criminals in training, saddled with dysfunctional family and cultural backgrounds that make them "bad" candidates for accelerated, gifted or college prep classes.[39] According to the College Board report, "The vast majority of Black high school graduates from the Class of 2011 who could have done well in an AP course never enrolled in one because they were either 'left out' or went to a school that didn't offer the college prep courses."[40] "Left out" is a euphemism for being viewed as underachieving, a theme that is consistent with my experience as a student in the L.A. Unified school district during the late '80s. In my senior year I was one of a small handful of black students in AP English and AP Biology classes. There were few black males in these classes. The ones that were enrolled were frequently marginalized, targeted for goofing off then bounced out of class (while the white students who engaged in similar behavior got warnings). As the most disproportionately suspended, expelled and special-education assigned group in the nation, black males have targets on their backs.[41] Numerous studies have shown that high rates of suspension and expulsion often lead to drop-out and incarceration.[42] In this regime, youth like Jarmaine Ollivierre have already been criminalized as expendable. During the 1990s, Ollivierre, a NASA aerospace engineer and former special education student from Philadelphia, participated in a tailored college preparation program that was designed to redress the 26% college-going rate at his high school. He went on to receive degrees in physics and aeronautical engineering. Unlike most special education students, Ollivierre had the benefit of strong mentors who saw his promise and provided him with resources and reinforcement.

While rigorous yet nurturing teacher-mentors of any kind are pivotal, the small number of African American science instructors is another factor in the marginalization of black science students. Unless Karly Jeter goes to a historically black college or university, she will have few African American science professors as mentors. According to the National Science Foundation, "Black faculty with SEH (science, engineering and health) doctorates differ from most other racial/ethnic groups in that a lower percentage were employed in RUVH (Research Universities with Very High research activity) institutions and a higher percentage were employed in master's-granting institutions." In 2008, African Americans who'd received Science and Engineering doctorates were only 4% of the faculty at U.S. colleges and universities.[43] At Cal Tech, one of the leading science and technology institutions in the country, African Americans are less than 1% of the faculty. They are 4% of the faculty at MIT. In her report "Barriers for Black Scientists," chemistry professor Donna Nelson found that "Blacks represented 8.8 percent of chemistry B.S. recipients in 2004 and 1.3 percent of all chemistry professors at the FY2005 'top 50' chemistry departments. The ratio 8.8 percent to 1.3 percent—versus a corresponding ratio of 37.7 percent to 77.5 percent for white males—indicates that black chemistry majors do not enjoy the supply of same-race faculty role models and mentors that majority chemistry majors do."[44]

Conservatives who disdain "liberal multiculturalism" in higher education dismiss such concerns about diversity in hiring as handwringing.

According to this view, there is only one standard academia should use: Objective and unbiased, untainted by affirmative action. Yet white students are beneficiaries of cradle-to-grave affirmative action. As I stated earlier, white students grow up seeing the dominant image of rational, trailblazing scientific discovery spearheaded by courageous, rugged, individualist white males. They are socialized to believe in a template of "purely" meritocratic success and individual achievement. Meritocracy becomes gospel and lucre. They can take it to the bank and use it to repel the less-qualified savages. Racial or gender others who make it into science's inner sanctum are either interlopers scrounging for handouts or shining exceptions bootstrapping up from the inner city wilds. At the insular level of college Physics and Engineering, white male dominance is perpetuated by "boy's club" peer groups, networks, faculty, and administrative support systems that facilitate access for the racial majority. While she was at UCLA, Devin Waller was the only African American woman in the Astrophysics department. On the first day of her upper division classes she recalls being asked by male students befuddled by her presence whether or not they "were in the right class." Since peer networking and study groups in science departments are largely white and male, white academic success and scholarly legitimacy in science become a self-fulfilling prophecy. For black women in white male dominated professions, showing vulnerability and experiencing any kind of public failure are simply not options. Like many women of color, Devin's approach was that "You kind of go in there and set a precedent. Everything you do is watched. You have to establish yourself as intelligent. There were no black women in my classes. No one who looked like me."[45]

In her autobiography *Find Where the Wind Goes: Moments from My Life*, Carol Mae Jemison (the first black woman astronaut and first woman of color in space) reflects that after professing an interest in becoming a scientist to one of her teachers she was told to think about becoming a nurse instead. As a sixteen-year-old undergraduate at Stanford University, Jemison was practically shunned by her physical science instructors. Although her experiences occurred during the '60s and '70s, the dominant view of who is a proper scientist has not changed. Nursing is still a more acceptable aspiration for black women who are culturally expected to be self-sacrificing caregivers for everyone in the universe.[46]

Ironically, a major inspiration for Jemison was Nichelle Nichols' character Uhura from *Star Trek*. Uhura was the first black woman astronaut ever portrayed on TV. Decades later, Jemison's experiences are still being played out in science classrooms across the so-called post-racial U.S., where the contributions, struggles, and leadership of scientists of color continue to be as "exotic" as the Starship Enterprise.[47]

Thus, as the data on racial disproportionality in discipline, special education, AP and gifted class placement bear out, the presumption of black underachievement cuts across class boundaries. Black middle-class students are only nominally viewed as being better academic performers than their poor and working-class peers. Indeed, teachers may even show "particular hostility and rejection to the brightest black students."[48]

Speaking to a group of college students in 2010, world-renowned astrophysicist Neil deGrasse Tyson recalled a conversation he had in graduate school with a fellow student who believed high-achieving African Americans should pursue more overtly sociopolitical careers, and not science. The conversation exacerbated Tyson's feelings of ambivalence about science's relevance to black uplift. Years later he pondered the absurdity of this dichotomy when he was asked to provide commentary on atmospheric issues for a local newscast. It was "the first time" he'd ever known an African American to appear on a newscast to comment on something other than race. Throughout his distinguished career, Tyson has been the kinder gentler face of science on PBS, popularizing an abstruse field that most Americans know little about. As arguably one of the most famous scientists in the world, Tyson negotiates the racial politics of visibility and invisibility that shapes the reception of any person of color in a white-identified and white-dominated field. But, as I have argued throughout this chapter, science is unique because it has been defined by narratives of white Western genius and objectivism, narratives that are intimately connected to the construction of the racialized body. The universal truths and discoveries of Western science relied in part on the fiction of the racial other. Nowhere was this more evident than in traditions of medical experimentation. As Harriet Washington notes in *Medical Apartheid*, "Historically, African Americans have been subjected to exploitative, abusive involuntary experimentation at a rate far higher than other ethnic groups."[49] Because of racist perceptions of black vulnerability and invincibility, black bodies were earthy *and* supernatural, primitive *and* otherworldly, able to withstand intense heat, cold, and pain while at the same time being sickly and fragile. Writing about the racial politics and legacy of medical experimentation, Washington notes:

> The culture of American medicine has mirrored the larger culture that encompassed enslavement, segregation, and less dramatic forms of racial inequality…Enslavement could not have existed and certainly could not have persisted without medical science. However, physicians were also dependent upon slavery, both for economic security and for the enslaved "clinical material" that fed the American medical research and medical training that bolstered physicians' professional advancement.[50]

Washington's reflection on the role barbarism and enlightenment played in medical science echoes Toni Morrison's view of how Africanism was invented within the context of the liberated New World. African American scientists exist in this space of contestation. This dynamic is embodied in Tyson's belief that his visibility as one of the most famous physicists in the world is itself a blow against racism and racial stereotyping. Commenting on white people's perceptions on ubiquitous black squeegee men, he says "One of the last stereotypes that prevails is that black people are somehow dumb. The squeegee man could have been this (a brilliant scientist) but for lack of opportunity and supporting institutions." The dominant culture's passion for the supernatural Negro only permits a few shining exceptions into the corridors of science. While Tyson is a beacon for other scientists of color, the Talented Tenth effect is still a strong current in mainstream American perceptions of mobility and intellectual achievement. Here, so-called colorblindness—not appreciation for cultural difference or acknowledgment of the institutional barriers and supports that Tyson alludes to—becomes the default "explanation" for the success of Neil deGrasse Tyson. If there were simply more brilliant blacks who studied hard, applied themselves, had fewer "baby mamas and daddies," stopped snorting crack for breakfast and took advantage of America's God-given freedoms, then there would undoubtedly be more Tysons.

As Barack Obama's re-election has demonstrated, the prominence of superstar leaders or academics of color (regardless of whether or not they bleed Christian gratitude) in American society does not automatically humanize average everyday black people. Twinkling black superstars don't magically eliminate the institutional barriers that exist within American education. In fact, superstars can often be used to undermine justice. The inward gazing capitalist ethos of the prosperity gospel, which fetishizes personal relationships with Jesus as the ultimate star fuck, bottles super-individualism, and touts the cult of personal responsibility, deepens American apartheid. It's no surprise that right-wing ideologues have wrapped themselves in the flag and the Bible while declaring racism dead. This marriage has been America's special theatrical genius—to smite out unreason, wallow in supernaturalism, and beat back the savages within its own shores in one fell swoop.

CHAPTER THREE

Straight to Hell: Christian Fascism and Americana

"Show me a population that is deeply religious and I will show you a servile population, content with whips and chains…content to eat the bread of sorrow and drink the waters of affliction."

--Hubert Harrison[1]

The Judgment Day billboard sprawls luminously below like a big, tricked-out index card over Memphis. The Rapture is coming, a worldwide crucible spreading death and destruction to the unrepentant of Graceland and beyond. One month before the Christian zealots' judgment day and the Memphis airport vibrates with the ant flow of disembarking passengers and carnivores getting down to the serious business of waiting in line for ribs. There are rib joints bulging with impatient customers every few feet, underscoring why the Bible Belt struggles with epidemic obesity. Torrential rains and a tornado watch in

Alabama, where I am scheduled to give a talk at the University of South Alabama, have delayed planes and stranded hundreds. Passengers pace, prattle into their cell phones, and slump morosely onto the floor, eyes scanning the horizon anxiously for any sign that the clouds will part, disgorge a plane, and free them from the finger-licking blitz of Neely's Barbecue.

But this is God's country, and deliverance is all in good time—his time. As only the fifth most religious state in the U.S., Tennessee bows to its neighbors, Alabama and Mississippi, in nationalist fervor and divinely-ordained racist splendor. Decades after the passage of the Civil Rights and Voting Rights Acts, the Southern states have risen up in a spasm of anti-undocumented immigrant xenophobia. Following Arizona's lead, Alabama, Ole Miss and Tennessee passed legislation that either encouraged or mandated criminal profiling of undocumented immigrants and their families—a most Christian ethos. What kind of judgment day will there be for racist, xenophobic states and neo-Confederate policy makers? Harold Camping, geriatric mastermind of the now faltering California-based Christian radio empire that launched 2011's doomsday cult, offered no clue. For fundamentalist Christians, racism—disguised as "America first" patriotism, bootstraps free enterprise or any number of claptrap euphemisms—has always been a badge of honor. Writer Chris Hedges, author of *American Fascists*, has defined Christian fascism as the Christian fundamentalist belief that every aspect of government and public policy should flow from the Old Testament. In 2007, Hedges opined that this impulse was precipitated by the decline of the middle class, high unemployment, and the looming recession. Dominionist backlash was driven by "stories of…failure—personal, communal and often economic; despair that would empower dangerous dreamers—those who today bombard the airwaves with an idealistic and religious utopianism that promises, through violent apocalyptic purification, to eradicate the old, sinful world that has failed many Americans."[2]

The performance art of millennial Christianity requires epic Red Sea parting plagues. Certainly the election of a black president, the ascent of gay marriage, feminist "ball-busters" pushing for abortion on demand, and Orwellian big government jackbooting its way into the lives of law-abiding hard working white citizens qualify. It's no accident that doomsday scenarios elicited such sheep-like furor from masses of white Christians across the heartland. The Rapture fit comfortably into the Tea Party's swoon of apocalypse: A sinful world woefully unrecognizable to the lily white forefathers tending slaves and savages in a battle for the soul of American Manifest Destiny.

The pageantry of Main Street Mobile is half holy-roller, half Americana retail—a visual ode to the thousandth Subway sandwich shop and the millionth check cashing place hawking predatory loans to poor people. The University of South Alabama is a largely commuter school mired in the backward racial politics that characterize most of mainstream academia. The college has few tenured faculty or administrators of color. Often, critically-conscious, permanent faculty of color must bust their asses mentoring, supporting, and apprenticing undergraduate and graduate students of color, leading to frustration and burnout. This factor has contributed to low retention and graduation rates for African American and Latino students. Nationwide, the script is the same for students of color—higher tuition, nonexistent or shrinking tenured faculty of color, vanishing classes, negligible financial aid, and skyrocketing student loan payments. It's a bleak landscape compounded by a racist, irresponsible media fond of bloviating about the declining value of a college education vis-à-vis jobs and wages. This vogue in college bashing is a white phenomenon that omits the crushing reality of downward mobility for both uneducated and educated people of color. In the current climate of postindustrial malaise and endless recession, there is no way in hell that my black and Latina female students can ever expect to earn a living wage for most of their adult careers without a college degree.

At the end of my talk, at the university, a white woman springs up from her seat, her voice quaking with rage as she scolds me for not spreading the "good news." Doth the errant Negress not know that linking racism, lynching, and Jim Crow to good Christian traditions that promote love, tolerance, and charity is a grievous error? The rattle of slave bones, of black homeowners rousted from their beds in the middle of the night, of black towns burned to the ground, overtake her voice. During the late 19th and early 20th centuries, the leading activist against lynching terrorism was Ida B. Wells. Wells' forerunning work as a journalist, publisher, orator, and touring mother embodied the kind of "intersectionality" radical feminism reveres. Wells traveled the globe lecturing and agitating about the U.S. government's endorsement of domestic terrorism against African Americans. Lynching as a form of "outlaw justice" was central to the maintenance of States Rights. As Earl Ofari Hutchinson notes in *Betrayed: A History of Presidential Failure to Protect Black Lives*, "Between 1880 and 1920 more than three thousand blacks were burned, shot, and mutilated by lynch mobs. During those years, a succession of presidents and attorneys general repeatedly rebuffed black appeals to intervene. They claimed it was the job of the states to prosecute the murderers. However, less than 1% of the murderers were ever tried in state court."[3] The absence of federal anti-lynching laws allowed local jurisdictions and municipalities to murder black people and pillage their homes and communities with impunity. Wells' activism exposed the gender and economic nexus of lynching. She highlighted how lynching was not just used to violently suppress black men but to validate the institutionalized rape of black women by white men. This form of social control had a powerful economic motivator. In the post-Reconstruction era, free black Southern labor undermined white capitalist dominance. Further, the creation of the "black beast" rapist "kept restless white women…[out] of the public sphere, and helped to bring whites of opposing class interests into a one-party political system."[4] And although black men were targeted more frequently by lynch mob violence, black women were also lynching victims. Motherhood and childrearing were linchpins of good American womanhood but they were informed by a white supremacist rape culture. In this dyad of terrorist occupation, white morality and the universality of white personhood were reinforced. There was no concept of the "fairer sex" or "feminine honor" where black women's bodies were concerned.

Quiet as it's kept, there was no judgment day for lynchers, slavers, or rapists. No apocalyptic tide looming in red whiplash wrath to still the cameras of America's own blockbuster horror show. No 20th century Harold Camping or assault rifle-toting millennialists foaming at the mouth about the end of civilization. Instead, Christian president after Christian president, from the cipher Warren G. Harding to the profane nigger-spewing Lyndon Baines Johnson, kowtowed to the divine power of the states, allowing my Alabama questioner to find her righteous sea

legs a century later in an auditorium crammed with the rubber-necking descendants of slaves, slavers, savages, and infidels.

But it's folly to single out Dixie on lynching when it was a nationwide phenomenon, an eminently democratic sport and faith-based enterprise that the most talentless white kid could excel in. As Scott Malcomson observes, lynching allowed whites to "g(ive) meaning to their whiteness by committing ultimate acts of animal transgression, which was exactly the behavior they attributed to their victims, rather, to their victims' blackness…A white man or woman or child would take this fragment of a black body home as trophy—keep it there, possibly display it."[5] In her short story *The Flowers*, Alice Walker chronicles the horror of a young girl who discovers the decomposing corpse of a lynching victim while she is out picking flowers. Walker's two-page story powerfully exposes the savage contradiction of a nation that has always portrayed itself as a fount of freedom and justice while erasing its legacy of racial terrorism and disenfranchisement. After the magnitude of her discovery sinks in, the story ends with the salvo "and then the summer was over." By contrasting the idyllic lightness of the girl's quest with the weight of her discovery, Walker suggests that to be a black child is to never be innocent. The summer is not just "over," but the brutality of a nation in which black children are already othered, racialized, and criminalized has begun to be a reality for the girl. The summer's end speaks to the impossibility of a black girl in America being considered innocent simply because she is a member of the "fairer" sex. It reminds that even "exceptional" black female icons like Michelle Obama, and the recently deceased Whitney Houston, are never exempt from the association of black femininity with savagery and hyper-sexual otherness. In the parlance of racist white America, Michelle Obama becomes a henpecking Sapphire with a "big bottom" and Whitney Houston a dead "crack ho." Walker's Southern story illustrates how the violence of lynching—as a cornerstone of Southern culture, of Southern comfort—relied on a Southern hospitality that black women were entrusted with caretaking while their own bodies were being ravaged.

Northerners are trained to revile the "primitivism" of the South. It's a reflex borne of the legacy of slavery as well as an American gothic of trailer parks, inbred cousins, moonshine swilling troglodytes, toothless Klansmen wielding Confederate flags, and redneck police brandishing fire hoses. In the newsreel of the unconscious, the South becomes the face of drooling, unvarnished Bible-drenched racism, the North's demonic double. It is envisioned as the site of original sin, even though one of the first and largest slave strongholds was in 17th century Manhattan. But the black Northerner has a complex, ambivalent relationship to this narrative of opposites. In the early-to-mid 20th century, Southern terrorism and economic inequity spurred the Great Migration of African Americans to Northern cities of "opportunity." The Northern drive was the stuff of legend and lore, firing the prose of writers as generationally diverse as Richard Wright and Toni Morrison. Black church denominations like the African Methodist Episcopal (AME) church played a big role in helping African Americans transition to deeply-segregated Northern black communities that were often hostile to Southern transplants. Yet kin and communal ties kept black migrants spiritually and emotionally wedded to the South. As much as the South was the primal scene for black slavery, it was also a source of close-knit black community, culture, and linguistic traditions. It was a space where African Americans were segregated yet provisionally self-sufficient, forced by necessity to establish their own businesses, schools, banks, medical practices, and cultural centers.

Zora Neale Hurston notoriously rejected the antidote of "Northern" integration. In much of her work she extolled the virtues of black self-sufficiency and rugged individualism. For Hurston, these values were best embodied by her adopted hometown, Eatonville, Florida. Reflecting on the 1954 Brown vs. Board of Education decision, Hurston wryly noted that "it is a contradiction in terms to scream race pride and equality while at the same time spurning Negro teachers and self-association."[6] Southern black cultural traditions were an example of that venerable heritage of self-association. Hurston disdained what she perceived as blacks' tendency to grovel for white moral and social validation. Not only was integration a smokescreen but it falsely absolved whites of their complicity in institutionalizing white supremacy. In the 21st century, contemporary platitudes about the increase of multiracial relationships, expanded U.S. Census categories for multiracial people, and the alleged decline of racial identification amongst the "Millennial generation" disguise the folly of post-racialism. Indeed, according to a 2011 survey by *Colorlines* Applied Research Center, millennials don't believe that racism has magically receded in the age of Obama.[7] Race and racism are very much relevant to them, especially when it comes to issues like mass incarceration and employment discrimination.

From where many of us living in areas that have been demonized as ghettoes, inner cities or urban jungles sit, the social construction of the black and brown other is still a vital part of white Christian nationalist solidarity. It's no accident that the majority of those petitioning to secede from the Union after Obama's re-election are Bible Belt states in the lap of the former Confederacy. One of the most vociferous petitioners was a Texas GOP treasurer who squealed, "Why should Vermont and Texas live under the same government?" casting Obama's reelection as influenced by "maggots" voting on an "ethnic basis." Poll after poll has shown that the Tea Party (even though dealt a resounding blow by Barack Obama's re-election) and white evangelicals speak with the same voice. Historically, much of this sentiment emerges from the same kind of white supremacist and class-based resentment exemplified by Richard Nixon's Southern Strategy. The Tea Party's antipathy toward the Occupy Movement demonstrated that it's not really interested in upending the status quo but in exploiting anti-establishment rhetoric to maintain white supremacy and capitalist disparities in wealth and power. During the 2012 presidential campaign, all of the Republican candidates heeded this call to Manifest Destiny. From former House Speaker Newt Gingrich's attack on shiftless black folks on food stamps to Senator Ron Paul's reputed warning about a black-driven "race war," the politics of black-baiting will never go out of date or become unprofitable when it comes to appeals to white nationalism.

Only in America could Barack Obama, the mild-mannered Black Other, morph into the all-purpose godless, communist, anti-family, heathen of right-wing wet dreams—affiliations that stigmatize white individuals but don't permanently cast them out of the fold or make them forfeit the wages of whiteness (or WOW). WOW is the sheer privilege, the naked abandon, the ghostly disembodiment of being able to walk around in any Middle American mall and belong there as a citizen of the world. It's the performance art of buying a pretzel, slurping on an Orange Julius smoothie or shopping at an Old Navy store safe and smug in the knowledge that if a "terrorist" bomb or enemy drone got dropped on that mall the whole world would know about it and be made to care about the loss of American lives. Even though the federal government has always been in the bloody business of suppressing radical revolutionary movements led by people of color, these federal acts of terror have never been publicly framed as a mortal threat to American individualism and liberty. During the Clinton administration, the stand-offs in Ruby Ridge, Idaho and Waco, Texas elicited backlash against the federal government. They spawned a wave of pro-gun, States Rights sentiment amongst disgruntled whites. Yet this backlash never veered into right-wing vilification of Clinton's cultural identity, religion or allegiance to America. Backslapping philandering good old boy Bill Clinton was, flawed though he was, all too much a part of white Middle America's dysfunctional family to be demonized as a seditious traitor.

Christianity will not immunize or protect the black other because Thomas Jefferson's analysis about the unbridgeable moral and intellectual gulf between African Americans and whites still resonates centuries later. For the right, Obama's fireside God bless America's have about as much purchase as Phyllis Wheatley's paeans to the moral purity of Africans did for Virginia slaveholders like Jefferson. All God's children may have wings, but in the post-racial U.S. a "nigger" with a Bible, a Harvard degree, and the biggest seat on Air Force One is still just that.  The smears against Obama illuminate the connection between white supremacy, morality, and Christian religiosity in the U.S. But in the midst of a renewed right-wing focus on exceptionalism they also raise the question of why the U.S. is so religious in comparison to Europe.

According to some researchers, the U.S.' deep religiosity stems in part from its unique relationship to the Enlightenment. In their book *Religious America, Secular Europe*, authors Berger, Davie and Fokas hold that the American Enlightenment—unlike that of France, where the Enlightenment assumed an anti-clerical, anti-Catholic bent—embodied the so-called "politics of liberty":

> The French Enlightenment was epitomized by Voltaire's famous cry: 'Destroy the infamy'—the infamy being the Catholic Church. The French Revolution made a valiant effort to do so. It did not succeed but what followed it was more than a century of struggle between two visions of France—one conservative and Catholic, the other progressive and anti-clerical…The American Enlightenment was very different indeed… the authors and politicians of the American Enlightenment were not

> anti-clerical—in any case, there was no clerisy to be against—and they were not anti-Christian. At worst (from a conservative Christian point of view), they were vaguely Deist. Thus the American Enlightenment could not serve as a legitimation of secularity in either state or society.[8]

Whereas the U.S. has always been characterized by the "politics of liberty," France has embraced the "ideology of reason." The U.S. never had a state or national church. There were no parishes. No one was "born into" a church. The power of American churches lay at the level of the congregation. And the framers' commitment to the separation of church and state facilitated religious pluralism and the intersection of Judeo-Christian ideology with the emergent capitalist state.

Yet, in order to understand the role religion plays in American politics, it's important to understand the way race has historically shaped American religiosity—especially when it comes to the tacit rule of hypodescent (the identification of mixed race individuals of African descent as black and thus lower caste), aka the One-Drop rule. Early colonial law prohibiting the enslavement of Christians presented the white ruling class with a quandary: If black "heathens" converted to Christianity then their enslavement was unlawful. So how could good Christians justify enslaving their brethren? When blacks converted, the colonists simply moved the goal post. Thus, "in 1639, Maryland became the first colony to specifically state that baptism as a Christian did not make a slave a free person."[9] Earthly freedom wasn't the desired goal to strive for, but an afterlife in the Kingdom of Heaven was. Moreover, 17th century Virginia law stipulated that the status of all children be defined by the condition of the mother, thus bolstering the emergent slave regime.[10] Only black women could birth and produce slaves, while white females—be they indentured servants or freewomen—could not. American racial slavery was institutionalized on the backs and in the wombs of black women. Although the One-Drop rule was formalized in response to Jim Crow in the 20th century, the requirement that children be *legally* classified through the condition of the mother effectively imposed a one-drop rule on the social construction of race and enslavement in the colonies. This edict absolved white men with black offspring of their legal responsibilities as fathers. The black offspring of white fathers were, by definition, ineligible to lay claim to property or inheritance rights, ensuring that the categories "slave" and "black" were virtually synonymous. The line of demarcation between "Christians" (i.e., whites) and blacks became very explicit, such that "If any Christian shall commit fornication with a Negro man or woman, he or she so offending shall pay double the fines imposed by the former act."[11] As "counterfeit" Christians, black converts would never again be exempt from bondage. As a reward for their Christian piety they were given Sunday worship and a blue-eyed Jesus with flowing locks patterned on massa's image. Hence, the advent of racial slavery was facilitated by the prohibition of blacks from the rights and privileges of Christian conversion.

At a talk I gave in Tucson, a white man approached and asked if African Americans "self-identified" with the One-Drop rule. The U.S. is the only country in the world that assigns black or lower caste status to all individuals of "known" African descent. Historically, this rule was never applicable to Asians, Native Americans or Latinos. Thus, "not only does the one-drop rule apply to no other group than American blacks, but apparently the rule is unique in that it is found only in the United States and not in any other nation in the world. In fact, definitions of who is black vary quite sharply from country to country."[12] In 2000 and 2010, the government revised the U.S. Census to allow individuals to check more than one race or to mark the box "some other race." Nonetheless, the legal, social, and cultural residue of the One-Drop rule still persists. A survey by Harvard University researchers James Sidanius and Arnold Ho concluded "that one-quarter-Asian individuals are consistently considered more white than one-quarter-black individuals, despite the fact that African Americans and European Americans share a substantial degree of genetic heritage."[13] Christian religious dogma buttressed the One-Drop rule and the anti-miscegenation bloodlust that characterized Jim Crow. Responding to the 1954 Brown v. Board decision, Circuit Court Judge Thomas Brady "maintained that God opposes racial mixing and that Southern whites had a God-given right to keep their blood white and pure."[14] In *Religious America, Secular Europe?"* the authors underscore the contradiction between the U.S.' vaunted modernity and its hyper-religiosity. They note the irony of a country that constantly disparages the rest of the developing world as a backward cesspit of superstition yet is itself politically dominated by fundamentalist zealots. America exceptionalism is nourished on the belief that the U.S.

is the most modern country in the world. But it exists uneasily with deep traditions of American anti-intellectualism, anti-science bias, and right-wing hostility to basic human rights. It's this paradox that secures Christianity and the specter of Christian nationhood as the moral template for American culture.

So what's race got to do with the imperial business of manufacturing God-fearing subjects? Hollywood always offers useful cultural insight into the psychology of American white supremacy. It is one of the most powerful mechanisms of national identity, initiating global audiences into the perverse racial code of Americana while lulling white Middle America into a narcissistic stupor. When white America settles down into its seat at the local multiplex on the weekend, it's generally met by the comfortable image of Middle American heroism, romance, adventure, and drama—safely scrubbed of black, brown, Asian or Native American realities.

One of my favorite movies on this score is the 1997 film *The Apostle*, which stars Robert Duvall as a Southern Pentecostal preacher and murderer on the lam seeking redemption. Duvall founds a small church in the backwoods of Louisiana whose backbone is elderly black women. The film is replete with vivid images of devout black people. In one pivotal scene, Billy Bob Thornton (a redneck trailer park escapee from central casting) threatens to bulldoze the church because Duvall is consorting with "niggers." Duvall, through his sheer come-to-Jesus magnetism, subdues Thornton's neo-Nazi venom by leading him in prayer with an old King James Bible. Thornton's redemption scene is punctuated by the knowing incantations of a black woman congregant. The serviceable figure of the God-fearing black woman helps the white Southern preacher/hero/savior/redeemed sinner come into sharper focus. White male moral authority, heroism, and rationality achieve special reinforcement when set against the backdrop of the primitively-spiritual other.

This is one of the reasons why millennial movements like Camping's 2011 extravaganza are strategically marketed to people of color. It's also why on a clear day you can see bright-eyed, bushy-tailed white Mormon boys moving briskly through "inner city" streets for their next conquest. Over the past few years, Millennialism and Mormonism have been joined by Scientology as revivalism du jour. In Hollywood film it's the specter of Southern black working-class communities redolent of the shrieking fury of the black choir, the bellow of the Negro preacher's sermon, and the rhythm of black women fanning themselves—all familiar film tropes from the 1943 *Cabin in the Sky* to the 2010 mammy-fest *The Help* to Queen Latifah's 2012 film *A Joyful Noise*.

Hijacking Public Morality

During the 2012 presidential campaign, the right-wing assault on public morality took ever more Gothic turns. Pimping the ghost of Ronald Reagan, each GOP candidate pledged to uphold the Christian Right's anti-abortion, anti-gay marriage, and anti-family planning platform. Perhaps more than any other issue (besides an anti-taxation position), a rigid stance against abortion and family planning have become the most important litmus test for GOP candidates. It was not always so. As Jill Lepore notes in her article "The Politics of Planned Parenthood and Women's Rights," GOP patron saint Barry Goldwater was an "active supporter" of family planning, as were George H.W. Bush, Richard Nixon, and Dwight Eisenhower.[15] In 1970 Nixon signed Title X into law, mandating federal funding for family planning. Title X has been at the epicenter of the right-wing assault on family planning, contraception, and abortion services.[16] But abortion was critical to Nixon's infamous Southern Strategy because it was a wedge issue that enflamed Southerners and conservative Catholics who voted Democratic. Hence, "abortion wasn't a partisan issue until Republicans made it one."[17] Nearly four decades later, the GOP's assault on abortion rights is a cornerstone of its extremist vitriol against the welfare state. Whereas Republicans in the seventies and early eighties were "more pro-choice than Democrats," the current GOP orthodoxy recognizes no inconsistency between its strident anti-government rhetoric and its authoritarian call for more government control over women's bodies. The 2012 GOP campaign saw the resurrection of welfare queen iconography—with Newt "are there no prisons are there no workhouses" Gingrich smearing President Obama as a "food stamp president" who has (further) socialized black people to settle for handouts and not jobs. During the second round of Republican primary voting in South Carolina, the white nationalist appeal of Gingrich's Christian fascist message sharpened. Indeed, his marital infidelities and alleged appetite for "open marriage" failed to faze Bible Belt voters in South Carolina. Far more important than his fidelity to the Ten Commandments was his relentless demonization of shiftless blacks and lazy poor children from families with no work ethic. In this regard, Gingrich set the moral tone for the presidential race, figuratively mooning the Occupy Movement and flaunting GOP allegiance to the 1% with explicitly racist classist imagery. Gingrich successfully married "American exceptionalism under siege" rhetoric with down home appeal to white economic resentment, mining the same territory that fueled Hillary Clinton's pandering to "good working white people" during the 2008 presidential campaign. After Gingrich's comments, liberal pundits quickly pointed out that the biggest ethnic/racial group on food stamps was white people. But naïve liberals fail to grasp that facts and empirical evidence are never deal breakers for the GOP. So, for example, while white voters in South Carolina rail against "government hand-outs", South Carolinians scooped up more government funding from public programs than did liberal Californians. Medicare and Social Security top the list of government programs white conservatives disproportionately benefit from. When GOP demagogues like Rick Perry and Paul Ryan railed against Medicare and Social Security, they were immediately faced with backlash from the very red-blooded heartland voters they were trying to court. Not to be outdone, eventual nominee Mitt Romney mined this territory well at a crowd of private donors when he berated the laziness of the 47% who don't pay taxes. After his resounding defeat, he went on a rampage against all the errant blacks, Latinos, young people, and women who voted for Obama because they'd received "gifts" (i.e., handouts) from the administration.

But poor God-fearing white people are poor because they simply had the bad luck to be swindled out of a job by an affirmative action black or illegal immigrant Latino. Those that don't work hard—the substance abusers, grifters, and criminals that dam up in Jerry Springer, Maury Povich, Dog the Bounty Hunter train wreck reality shows—are aberrations. They don't reflect the cultural failings of the white race because a robust work ethic is the linchpin of white national identity. The real culprit in the small Southern burgs and Midwestern hamlets devastated by the economic meltdown is not a rapacious capitalism fueled by the surplus labor of under-educated workers but a secular socialist machine manned by a closet Muslim

Revelations

In the verdant Louisiana backwoods of the *Apostle*, Duvall's holy man sets up a Jesus bus to take his parishioners to church. Certain as a sunset, a group of admiring black women flock like bees to honey, moths to a flame. The narrative suggests that they are his for life, talismans warding off the long arm of the law. When non-believers bemoan the need for "church-like" community amongst non-believers, it is with sibling rivalry-esque type envy. How can secularists compete with the ecstatic velocity of the Charismatic movement, where speaking in tongues, miracle healing, divination, hoofing, writhing, laying on of hands, and non-stop revelry entice the wayward, the wanting, and the wishful? Where is the secular world's safe haven of scientism as antidote to the 24/7 bonanza of Missouri's International House of Prayer? The end of the world furor that gripped the nation and sucked up endless airtime in the mainstream media was a function both of the anxiety elicited by the global meltdown and the racial/cultural unrest exemplified by the Obama age. At the height of the Judgment Day frenzy, young white families interviewed by the press said that they had quit their jobs and begun hunkering down for apocalypse. Some tortured souls sold all their earthly possessions and then hit the road to evangelize, making crucial last minute donations to Harold Camping's charlatan empire. Eleventh-hour converts haunted the pews, looking for an adrenaline boost of Holy Spirit baptism, the Pentecostal money-shot long scorned by mainline Protestants as unorthodox, seedy, and borderline heathenish. Non-believers gleefully contemplated a world without a certain brand of Christian. And in the wreckage of non-destruction, mainstream media had a feeding frenzy with all the head-scratching believers who woke up on May 22nd to idle another day away.

But, of course, apocalypse is especially alluring when a black president is in office and "illegals" are massing at the border. In the spring of 2011, after many of the most racist anti-Obama caricatures had been confined to the far corners of the Web, an Orange County Republican official circulated an email depicting the President as a baby chimp. The email's punch line said "now we know why no birth certificate." A national firestorm ensued, and the official immediately trotted out her solid Christian family values background to deflect criticism about her racism, noting that many of her good friends were black. White

Christian racists invariably have plenty of black cronies with whom they break bread, swap intergenerational primate stories, and share cartoons that compare blacks to monkeys. Orange County is home to the Minutemen anti-illegal immigrant hate group and more megachurches than you can shake a stick at. Despite the media image of "the OC" as a haven for white suburban debauchery it's a predominantly Latino and Asian county. Indeed, the OC played a forerunning role in civil rights history when several Mexican American families became the lead plaintiffs in the landmark 1947 Mendez vs. Westminster Ninth Circuit Court case outlawing segregated Mexican American schools. Mendez laid the groundwork for Brown v. Board. As lead attorney for the NAACP, future Supreme Court Justice Thurgood Marshall worked on the Mendez case and would go on to successfully argue Brown in the Supreme Court. Like Mendez, Brown rested on the Supreme Court's invocation of the 14th amendment's equal protection clause.

The shared history of black/Latino struggles over school desegregation and Jim Crow is illustrative when considering how white nationalists have coalesced around demonizing undocumented immigrants and the (black) welfare state. For example, Gingrich has condemned bilingual education programs, exhorting Latinos to stop speaking the "language of the ghetto" and learn English, "the language of prosperity." During the Florida Republican presidential primary, Romney and Gingrich sparred over who was more "anti-immigrant." While Gingrich advocated a kinder, gentler paternalism that would limit the Dream Act to those who serve in the military, Romney opposed the Dream Act outright. According to the Service Employees International Union, Spanish language ads for the two candidates often downplayed or omitted their extremist positions on immigration reform. In an election year where the "Latino vote" was critical this gambit wasn't surprising. But the GOP candidates' attempts to soft pedal their racist pandering to scoop up a few Latino votes didn't appease Latinos or the far right electorate that was so galvanized by welfare queen revivals.

As far back as Bacon's Rebellion of 1676, the white "giddy multitude" has consistently shown how race/class allegiance trumps the alleged class solidarity of all working-class people. Bacon's Rebellion was an uprising of disaffected un-landed poor whites and blacks against Jamestown's ruling elite. The insurgents believed Virginia Governor

William Berkeley was conspiring with Native Americans to deprive them of land and resources.[18] Many historians view the uprising as a turning point for instituting racialized class divisions between the white working class and African Americans.[19]

While racial distinctions were still in flux, white elites' fear of class collaboration between blacks and poor whites led them to make more concessions in the interest of white solidarity.[20] As Howard Zinn notes, "In the early years of slavery, especially, before racism as a way of thinking was firmly ingrained, while white indentured servants were often treated as badly as black slaves, there was a possibility of cooperation."[21] According to Ira Berlin:

> Bacon's Rebellion (leads to) the consolidation of a planter class. The planters had not been able to control this rowdy labor force of servants and slaves. But soon after Bacon's Rebellion they increasingly distinguish between people of African descent and people of European descent. They enact laws which say that people of African descent are hereditary slaves. And they increasingly give some power to independent white farmers and land holders. That increased power is not equality. Dirt farmers are not elected to the House of Burgess in Virginia; the planters monopolize those offices. But they do participate in the political system. In other words we see slavery and freedom being invented at the same moment.[22]

The simultaneous "invention" of slavery and freedom signified a turning point for racial categorization. It was necessary for elite planters and lawmakers to facilitate white working-class mobility in order to neutralize the threat of interracial class solidarity. As Theodore Allen, author of the *Invention of the White Race*, notes, by "establishing a system of social control…whereby the mass of poor whites was alienated from the black proletariat and enlisted as enforcers of bourgeois power," the aftermath of Bacon's Rebellion laid the foundation for racial slavery. Centuries later, the lessons of Bacon's Rebellion can be found in the 21st century white working class' complicity with the ruling elite.[23] This historical dynamic informs contemporary paroxysms of race/class strife, reinforcing the tyranny of the One-Drop rule. In the still uncertain colonial brew of free black and black indentured servants transitioning to slavery, a sharp cleavage between whiteness and blackness was desirable for the economic growth and stability of American empire. In many regards, the new republic's "commitment" to the universal rights of man softened white working-class resentment. If all white people were free, and promised mobility based on shared racial membership, then there would always be a serviceable black or, later, Latino, racial other/scapegoat to pin white downward mobility on.

It is little wonder, then, that some of the staunchest defenders of anti-undocumented immigrant legislation come from the Christian white working class of the Southwest and the Bible Belt. For example, a 2011 *Los Angeles Times* article on the impact of Alabama's anti-undocumented immigrant law chronicled a small, predominantly-white church congregation's struggle to reconcile its embrace of Latino congregants with the realities of the new legislation. Alabama has elicited national outrage over legislation that sanctions profiling of suspected "illegal immigrants" in schools, employment, and traffic stops. According to Riverside Baptist Church pastor Randy Billingsley, "illegal immigration poses a national security threat."[24] Nonetheless, the pastor conceded that "They're humans. We want to minister to them regardless of what legal status they have."[25] Of course, ministering has always been a linchpin of Christian missionary conversion of heathens of color. New Latino congregants mean more tithes, more membership, and, ultimately, an infusion of younger constituents to compensate for aging white populations. So, what about the connection between supposed traditions of Christian charity and notions of fairness for the disenfranchised? Alabama Governor Richard Bentley, a good Southern Baptist, was one of the main power brokers behind getting the legislation passed. Bentley is trying to revise the law after a backlash from growers and other employers who complained that the exodus of Latino workers has hurt their bottom line. As Riverside congregant Tommy Graham noted, "I'd hate for them to go back to what they came from... All of them are good workers, and not working jobs that white people would take." The notion of the "hardworking Latino" who happily does shit work that no one else will do is a convenient stereotype that has been evoked by the right to both justify worker exploitation and pimp racist notions of the American dream. Graham's statement floats the specter of Bacon's Rebellion. Undocumented Latinos are good workers. They are worthy of staying in the U.S. and tasting our great freedoms.

But white workers who won't do shit work even in light of soaring unemployment are not lazy, shiftless, free-loaders but merely protective of their birthright to living wage jobs.

American whiteness, the whiteness of Newt Gingrich and exceptionalist America, wouldn't exist without under-compensated surplus black and Latino labor. Lazy black workers are the underside, the cultural double of the hardworking Latino. This is despite the fact that black women have the highest workforce representation amongst all women of color. But renewed fervor over immigration and Obama's presidency underscores how corrosively deep the legacy of Bacon's Rebellion runs. Without the illusion of free enterprise, unlimited economic opportunity, and our Americana creed of bootstrapping to success, the cesspit ghettoes of GOP lore (in which very poor children "never see anyone working") wouldn't have such a powerful hold on the white mainstream imagination. Gingrich's nationalist rhetoric was a shot in the arm for a disaffected white electorate poised to reap the reward of the "take back our country" clarion call of the 2010 midterm elections.

Under future Republican administrations, mass deportations would be a kinder gentler ethnic cleansing. Then, perhaps, the good Christians of Alabama, Georgia, Arizona, and the rest of Jesus' America can sleep soundly at night knowing that there are fewer very poor children with no work ethic sucking up welfare in their fair hamlets, burgs and Main Streets. After all, to paraphrase one of the true believers from Riverside Baptist, even if the undocumented devout are deported they can always score new converts in their native lands.

CHAPTER FOUR

White Picket Fences, White Innocence

There is a great difference between Christianity and religion at the south. If a man goes to the communion table, and pays money into the treasury of the church, no matter if it be the price of blood, he is called religious. If a pastor has offspring by a woman not his wife, the church dismisses him, if she is a white woman, but if she is colored, it does not hinder his continuing to be their good shepherd.

--Harriet Jacobs, Incidents in the Life of a Slave Girl [1]

What was Carrie Butler's relationship to the public and private sphere? Her reproductive and productive labor were rendered invisible by the privileged status of her white employer's right to privacy. The rights to privacy enabled white Southerners to ignore multiple forms of labor in their own households. It also allowed them to violate black women's bodies without recognizing the unthinkable consequences on black women in the public sphere.

--Alex Lubin, *Romance and Rights: The Politics of Interracial Intimacy*[2]

Belatedly then, I say a little prayer to you, in the hope that this time, the bloody din of crickets won't drown out my plea for a mammylicious Aryan nation refugee; a hair flipping anti-diva who's wicked with a wooden spoon and the arcane funk of cooking oils, a maven empathetic who's only got the fear of you, Crisco, sweaty make-the-crippled-walk-and-the-blind-see tent revivals and wayward baby dust weevils plotting in the bottom of a mint julep glass. Of course God, this prayer, this petition is only a humble salvo in support of the sistahood, the intimate ties that bind all women regardless of the long dusky shadows of Tara and the mutant bones of Monticello slave cabins.

There he stands, hale, hearty, and über-masculine, peering majestically down onto traffic. On the campus of the University of South Carolina in Columbia, a statue of the late white supremacist Senator and native son Strom Thurmond frames the square. "Ol' Strom," a decade-gone, is still a living breathing throbbing presence in this picturesque college town. The mammoth school gym evokes his blitzkrieg obsession with physical fitness. His steely visage and sculpted physique have been memorialized down to the last quivering pectoral, soldered into the built landscape, his mythic presence a beacon to every casual visitor.

Thurmond was a prominent member of the Christian fundamentalist cabal The Family.[3] He conducted the longest Senate filibuster in history against the Civil Rights Bill of 1957, serving in Congress up until his death in 2003. Shortly thereafter, it was revealed that he was the father of a retired African American educator from Los Angeles named Essie Mae Washington Williams. At the time of her birth, Williams' mother, Carrie Butler, was a 15 year-old girl who worked as a maid in the Thurmond household. My sister-in-law Maria Hutchinson is the great granddaughter of Thurmond and Butler. Her children, my nieces and nephew, are his great-great grandkids. In 2013, Ms. Williams passed away at the age of 87 after an extended illness. She was warm, sharply intelligent, giving, and deeply involved in the local Los Angeles civic community.

Though there has been much speculation about Carrie Butler; virtually no pictures remain of her. No trace of *her* image, writings or letters, no definitive document that would respectfully memorialize her voice, lived experiences or personal history. Maria and her mother Monica Hudgens have long deplored the grand narrative of forbidden love and youthful abandon that's swirled around Butler and Thurmond's relationship. As Monica notes, "Carrie Butler was the cook. What do you say to the person who you're indebted to for your employment? When I was a child I recall a relative using the word 'wrassling' to describe their so-called encounter, suggesting that he used force. She was only 14 years-old when she became pregnant with my mother."[4] Thurmond was older, wealthier —a privileged white son in a world where the rape of a black woman was an impossibility.

As a black feminist, Hudgens believes it is important to honor Butler's silenced voice as a metaphor for all of the black female domestics for whom sexual violence was a fact of life. But in a book entitled *1948*, white author David Pietrusza implicitly places Butler in the Harlequin romance ranks of heaving bosomed temptresses, a closet overstuffed by the likes of Sally Hemings and other comely "concubines" that "massa" just couldn't keep his hands off of. Butler's sphinx-like status gives her entrée into the prurient sisterhood of black women whose motivations for "becoming involved" with powerful white men will forever be "unknown." These women are always dusky, yet Europeanized airbrushed beauties: she of the flowing hair, the whippet thin waist and hour glass figure is always the ambiguously culpable party. The Song of the South lore of happy banjo strumming darkies and tragic mulattos makes it understandable why a white man would be driven to distraction by such impudent wench-ness seething and simpering under his own roof. On the other hand, African features, dark skin, and natural hair are more incriminating attributes, more indicative of the collapse of civilization Europeans prophesied if miscegenation became the norm. What does it say about the civilized to yearn for the savage, other than that the civilized has always been the savage leering from the catbird's seat?

When my mother found out about the family connection after Thurmond's death in 2003 she exclaimed, "My babies are contaminated!" Contaminated is an interesting word choice, given Thurmond and his ilk's monstrous obsession with the illusion of racial purity. Over the past decade, the explosion of DNA testing has officially debunked historical notions of a genetic basis for racial difference. White people strut around with t-shirts proclaiming their African-ness. Marinating in white privilege, some atheists have begun to wield common African ancestry like a weapon against "minority" claims of institutional racism and white supremacy. So now the contamination of which my mother speaks is supposedly more abstract, more theoretical. The latter generations of "Thurmonds," the ones who are identified as African American, those who are prohibited from sharing his legacy due to the regime of the one-drop rule, are surely contaminated with the residue of civility and racial terrorism that he represents.

In her 2005 memoir *Dear Senator*, Ms. Williams relates their first encounter with the anticipatory flutter of the young school girl that she was.[5] Descending from his law office perch, Thurmond was the perfect Southern "gentleman"—circumspect, businesslike, professional, aloof, and (in her view) ruggedly handsome. Williams' feelings of ambivalence toward Thurmond consume her, plunging her into a lifelong quandary about her role in his life and his role in hers. The absence and early death of her mother brands her as a space of projection, a vessel for all of Ms. Williams' fantasies and wish fulfillment. The Carrie Butler that appears in the book is a maternal cipher, a question mark devoid of flesh, heft or desire other than her achingly forbidden love for Thurmond. Official history denies women of color the right to narrate their own stories. Their bodies become re-territorialized as a result of racist sexist assumptions about black women. There is no space for anger, vengeance or public airing of sexual terrorism; only shame, forbearance, steely caricatured strength, and silent suffering. For women of color, this burden is intensified by the presumption of hyper-sexuality and amorality that communities of color often reinforce with uncritical acceptance of, if not reverence for, million dollar-selling hip hop, pop culture, and TV/film artists that promote dehumanizing images of black and Latina women.

In 2011, white feminists initiated the Slut Walk campaign to protest the normalization of sexual violence against women. The campaign was designed to bring attention to the blame-the-victim hysteria, shaming, and demonization that re-victimizes sexual assault victims. Public demonstrations were held nationwide and many younger (mostly white) women dressed in "provocative" clothing to challenge the objectification of scantily clad female bodies. Some feminists of color questioned the racial politics of this move, criticizing a young white protestor's decision to parade around with a sign that said "woman is the nigger of the world," in homage to Yoko Ono and John Lennon's 1972 song. If woman is the nigger of the world what is the status of the woman who is actually a "nigger?" Such nuances elude bright eyed bushy tailed white fourth wave feminists. White women's ahistorical usage of the term underscores the longstanding racial and class divide within American feminism. Some saw Slut Walk as an opportunity to flaunt their sexuality without fear of reprisal and backlash from men. But others decried the overemphasis on being scantily clad without grasping the historical implications of nudity and exposure for women of color. Historically, American white women have never had the experience of being displayed on auction blocks, of being poked, prodded and searched until every inch of their bodies were assessed for potential commodity value. This emphasis on hypersexuality as "liberatory" has been decried by black feminists as yet another example of white privilege and entitlement. How could all feminists not be united in "reclamation" of women's space as a form of radical protest? An anonymous writer at the blog Crunk Feminist Collective breaks it down:

> The organizers of Slut Walk are genuinely baffled that this happened in the first place. To organize a movement around the reclamation of a term is in and of itself an act of white privilege. To not make explicit and clear the privilege and power inherent in such an act is to invite less-informed folks with privilege (in other words, folks who know just enough to be dangerous) to assume that reclamation can be applied universally. Slut-shaming has particular resonance for white women, whose sexuality has largely been constructed based upon middle-class, often Christian, heteronorms of proper chaste womanhood. The positive referent about chastity against which slut becomes the negative referent has never been universally available to Black women. A Black woman who "freely enjoys hers own sexuality" has been called "jezebel, hoochie, hoodrat, ho, freak, and perhaps, slut." In other words, "slut" is merely part of a constellation of terms used to denigrate Black female sexuality; it is not at the center of how our particular sexuality has been constructed.[6]

The fallen jezebel can never "reclaim" slut as a liberatory status because being promiscuous is only part of the equation. Black female sexuality is constructed as oppositional to the normative model of white innocent virginal femininity. It is the backdrop against which white women of any moral standing transcend sluttiness to embody Western civilization's moral ideal. According to Crunk, "We are always already sexually free, insatiable, ready to go, freaky, dirty, and by consequence, unrapeable. When it comes to reclamations of sexuality, in some senses, Black women are always already fucked."[7] At the high schools where I teach black and Latino girls are told 24/7 that they are hos; amoral, loose, untrustworthy, skeezing gold diggers who anything can be done to at anytime. So reclaiming slut as a form of empowerment would be absurd if not dangerous. In other words, the worst white female "slut" (from bad slut mothers like Casey Anthony to bad slut entertainers like Madonna, Lady Gaga and the list goes on) is significantly more valued in American culture than the most virtuous black woman could ever be. Racial disparities in rape convictions reflect the degraded status of black women's bodies in the criminal justice system. Perpetrators who attack black women are far less likely to be convicted and jailed for their crimes. Indeed, "for most of American history the crime of rape of a Black woman did not exist."[8] Up until the mid twentieth century, the criminal justice system considered raping a black woman to be an oxymoron.

This travesty is chronicled in Danielle McGuire's book, *At the Dark End of the Street*. McGuire notes that sexual violence and exploitation of black women was largely a non-issue for the predominantly male leadership of mainstream black civil rights organizations.[9] In 1963, civil rights activists Dorothy Height and Jeanne Noble of the National Council of Negro Women and Delta Sigma Theta testified on WNEW radio about the pervasive sexual abuse black women protestors experienced in the jails of Georgia, Alabama, and Mississippi. However, "these abuses, which often occurred behind closed doors and were exposed only months later, garnered neither the media coverage nor the organizational support necessary to stop them from happening."[10] As have other historians before her, McGuire documents a culture that was based on the systematic protection of innocent, virginal white femininity at the expense of the degraded bodies of black women. During the 1960s, this ethos was embodied in the racist propaganda against Freedom Summer in Mississippi. Thus, "In order to…shore up white solidarity, state and local officials acted as if the student volunteers were an army of amalgamation hell-bent on forcing the state to allow interracial sex and marriage."[11] As during Reconstruction, the rape of white women by black men was portrayed as both the ultimate moral offense and the ultimate national transgression.

Speaking to the States Rights convention in 1948, Strom Thurmond said, "I want to tell you that there's not enough troops in the Army to force the Southern people to break down segregation and admit the Negro race into our theaters, into our swimming pools, into our homes and into our churches." Essie Williams writes of watching her father morph into a Klansman right in front of her eyes. Disgusted with the "tepidness" and racial concessions of the Democratic Party, he ran for president under the States Rights Party platform in 1948, carrying several Southern states. Thurmond's words were carefully calibrated to exploit the primal dread, horror, and abjection that roiled the South, reinvigorated by a new wave of civil rights initiatives implemented by the Truman administration. But the spaces that he evoked were theatres of white subjectivity. Churches were preserves of white supremacy and Jim Crow, enforcing the doctrine of white female purity and black savagery. Segregated swimming pools reflected white abhorrence of the black body banished from the canvases of scantily clad white bodies cavorting in leisure. Theaters were rigidly divided into floor seating for white patrons and "nigger heaven" (the satirical nickname given it by Zora Neale Hurston) balcony seating for black patrons.

This view of a well-regulated world based on the regime of racial terrorism apparently informed Thurmond's "sponsorship" of his black daughter behind closed doors. Throughout much of her adult life, Thurmond gave Williams money and partly funded her college education. Some viewed this as a ploy to buy her silence. A "Negro in the woodpile" would have sunk his skyrocketing career as the nation's foremost white segregationist. Williams chronicles this period through the prism of her college pursuits and the grinding everyday indignities of Jim Crow. Her ardent belief in the unrequited "romance" of Thurmond and her mother becomes the lens through which she views her identity as a mixed race woman with an unsettled claim to home, family, and community.[12] Acknowledging the considerable privileges of being light-skinned in a brutally rigid race and color caste system, she is nonetheless aware of how black women's bodies are constantly being policed in the sexualized regime of Southern apartheid. Black women's bodies were (and remain) public space, be it within the context of private homes or public buses. A critical aspect of racial apartheid was the treatment of all black women like prostitutes. As civil rights activist and rape survivor Endesha Mae Holland said:

> It was just part of life and if you...were black, you were always at the mercy of white people...We could just as easily be picking cotton or walking to the store or spending money in the white man's store when the mood would take him and he'd take us—just like that, like lightening striking.[13]

In essence, "Holland understood that black women's bodies did not belong to themselves."[14] Certainly part of Williams' internal struggle was this question of the right of ownership and dominion over one's own body. Thurmond's public disavowal of paternity, his militant States Rights leadership was crucial to this regime of terroristic ownership. Rape and control of black women's reproduction was not only a vital part of the American political economy, it defined white Southern manhood. Unseen and unraced, white men's bodies were the bodies of reason, judgment, and law. True to the brutal myth of the noble Southern patriarch, Thurmond hewed to a particularly noxious brand of rationalization:

> Just as there are in this country two main and quite distinct cultures, a northern culture and a southern culture, so there are in this country two different species of genus segregation...Segregation in the South is open, honest, and aboveboard. Northern segregation is founded on hypocrisy and deceit.[15]

The open, honest, and aboveboard segregation that Thurmond speaks of is the blood price of slavery, a code bred on the ships that etched the Middle Passage, as black men and women lay shackled together belly deep in each other's waste, plowing into the unknown, time meted out into beatings, mutilations, rape, and suicide. Open, honest, and aboveboard, lynchings, public humiliations, and the squalor of separate but equal gave the children's stories captured in the first generation of Dick and Jane grade school primers their ethereal sheen of innocence. Dick and Jane illustrated the racial code of private space. From the 1930s to the 1960s they were America's bright-eyed tour guides through the idyll of green lawns, lazy bike rides down hopscotched sidewalks, and the mystery meat treasure of sandboxes under blue skies that sparkled into eternity. Dick and Jane taught America how to read the American dream. Picture book primers with these two characters snaked through every schoolhouse from the Deep South to the rugged West Coast of African American "Promised Land" reveries. Before the mainstreaming of phonics, the Dick and Jane primers were the first to provide sight reading instruction supposedly grounded in average everyday life. In their sun-kissed freckle-faced average-ness, they schooled America in the cultural literacy of suburbia and the holy trinity of nuclear family, heterosexual marriage, and white supremacy. Neat, well-dressed, eterenally courteous, Dick and Jane established the template for a "normal" childhood of perfect single family homes in segregated subdivisions tethered to the world's largest interstate highway system. Father was breadwinning and boozing. Mother was homemaking and Easy-Off sniffing. Spot, the family dog, brooded faithfully at brother Dick's side, primed to rip off the balls of any intruder. Government subsidized Federal Housing Administration (FHA) loans and GI Bill funded college educations smoothed the pathway for Dick and Jane's nuclear bootstrapping. Black vets and black families needn't apply.

During the 1970s, the anti-busing movement was a major linchpin in ensuring white suburbia was protected from the dark other. Both white Catholic and evangelical communities were at the forefront of these efforts, underscoring the ideological differences between African American religious traditions and that of their white counterparts. In his book, *Reconciliation Blues: A Black Evangelical's Inside Look at White Christianity,* author Edward Gilbreath reflects on what he learned in Sunday school:

> The first thing I learned…was that black was the color of our hearts without Jesus, red is the color of Jesus' redeeming blood and white is the color of our hearts after we accept Jesus as our 'Lord and Savior.' There

> were even visual aids, construction paper cut-outs that demonstrated the red blood washing away the black sin to reveal a brand new white heart.[16]

Bussed to a lily white school in the seventies, Gilbreath got a crash course in what it meant to be a little black boy in a white Christian Nation. Segregation was a naked reality, both outside and inside the pews. God's shield didn't extend very far, as his introduction to the nexus of white supremacy and Christianity came while riding the bus in the Rockford, Illinois of post-Brown v. Board America. Gilbreath was at ground zero in the furor over busing—which became a litmus test for safeguarding white America from the black hordes of public school integration. During the mid-to-late seventies this conflict came to an infamously violent head in Boston when working class Irish Catholics mobilized against a federal school desegregation order. The Boston uprising was partly spearheaded by a coalition of white parents, community activists, and politicians called Restore Our Alienated Rights or ROAR. As the conservative Hoover Institute puts it, the battle to ensure white children were protected from contact with blacks was not only "dominated by women" but signified the white community's efforts to preserve its democratic right of citizenship and individual liberty.[17] White Catholic mothers rallied to protect their children, giving the anti-busing movement a "feminist" bent:

> One day in fall 1975, about 400 Charlestown mothers marched up Bunker Hill Street, clutching rosary beads and reciting the "Hail Mary." They knelt in prayer for several minutes on the pavement between Charlestown High and the Bunker Hill Monument. And then they stood up and walked toward the police line, still in prayer, handbags held high to shield their faces. Soon a scuffle broke out between the mothers and the police. Some women were tossed to the ground. Although the women's movement was on the rise, the feminist establishment had no interest in the working-class woman's struggle against forced busing. They were indifferent to the wailing mothers who were throwing themselves down in front of delivery trucks owned by the *Boston Globe* (the pro-busing newspaper) or fleeing from the dogs that police used to enforce curfews. The same people who celebrated when the Supreme Court recognized a woman's 'right to choose' to have an abortion were unmoved when a

> federal court revoked a mother's right to choose where her children could go to school.[18]

This public performance of Catholic piety and "sisters doing it for themselves" (to use a phrase from the eponymous song by Aretha Franklin and Annie Lennox), must have been an electrifying display of grassroots nationalism. Integration, clearly an act of the devil working through big government, demanded divine intervention. Who better to cash in the God card than Boston's white mothers, the demographic that launched a thousand Southern, Midwestern, and Northern lynchings? White women's leadership of one of the most significant pro-segregation movements in modern education history is a landmark of reactionary activism. But comparing a woman's human right to choose whether or not to have an abortion to preserving segregated schools for white children is yet another example of racist right wing appropriation of civil and human rights. White mothers who fought to preserve segregation were just as "feminist" as antebellum white women who sought to control and exploit their black slaves. In both instances religion played a key role in justifying the maternal right to protect home, hearth, and nationhood. Just as slavery could not have thrived as an institution without white female complicity, so school segregation could not have thrived without the investment of everyday ordinary white women, protecting little Dick and Jane from the black savages menacing white neighborhoods on the school bus. In Boston, white women were at the forefront of the Home and School Associations (a Boston variant of the PTA) which provided the organizational muscle behind the anti-busing movement and a considerable part of ROAR's constituency.[19]

Radical left analyses often attempt to rationalize this brand of white working class racism. The classic white Communist or Socialist rationale is that reactionary poor whites are simply displaying a "false consciousness" influenced by capitalist exploitation. However, as the journal *Radical America* argues: "Because these neighborhoods suffer from high unemployment, poor housing, and lousy schooling it has been tempting for liberal journalists and leftists alike to explain away white working class racism as a product of lower class frustration, backlash or manipulation...but it is wrong to explain racism away by romanticizing the ethnic pride and community solidarity of neighborhoods like South Boston or by resorting to a conspiracy theory that explains racism away as a frustrated response to a ruling class plot in the form of busing."[20] Similarly, working class white women's manipulation of God and country piety cannot be explained away as false consciousness, "mother love" or ethnic solidarity. Instead, it illustrates how the confluence of racist sexist identification shapes white women's sense of self and community.

* * *

In her World War II era novel *The Bluest Eye,* Toni Morrison begins almost every chapter with a bitter homage to the role space, race, gender, and the illusion of suburban tranquility played in the manufacturing of Dick and Jane. The book opens with "Here is the house. It is green and white. It has a red door. It is very pretty. Here is the family. Mother, Father, Dick, and Jane."[21] On the next page the words blur together, spidery and damp, underscoring the brutal contrast between idyllic Americana and the novel's blistering chronicle of incest, racial apartheid, misogyny, and psychic degradation in the life of a black Midwestern family. Subsequent editions of the Dick and Jane primers emphasized overtly Catholic and Christian themes. Good children were obedient to their elders, ever mindful of the specter of sin and temptation lurking around every dark corner. Bad children knew no restraint. Unlike the unruly black pickaninnies of American film the white children of the Dick and Jane chronicles were the picture of restraint. They set the stage for postwar portrayals of red-blooded boys like the Beaver, Dennis the Menace, and the Nelson sons of Ozzie and Harriet—neighborhood icons whose boyish peccadilloes could all be tidily resolved with sage adult intervention by sitcom's end. The emergence of "benign" postwar nuclear TV families bore out Strom Thurmond's admonition about the honest South versus the deceitful North. White picket fence neighborhoods occupied an idyllic zone in which black people were either airbrushed out of the picture or trotted out as the usual motley crew of god-fearing maids (Beaulah), malaprop spewing buffoons (Amos n' Andy), faithful man-servants (Rochester) and bug-eyed urchins (Buckwheat). For mainstream white viewers this universe was a sweet return to a normalcy, balance, and calm torn asunder by the wartime upheaval in gender roles and family norms that saw thousands of American women enter the workforce for the first time. In post-war TV fantasy Rosie the Riveter morphed smoothly back into Suzy Homemaker. For viewers of color, it was an insidious erasure of the terrorism they continued to experience under American apartheid. Mother, Father, Dick, Jane, and Spot were the perfect alibi for the burning streets of the deep Jim Crow South and the teeming slums of the deceitful North, black America's Promised Land.

White picket fence domesticity was a key element of postwar anti-civil rights propaganda. If American white women could be commercially anesthetized through the lure of shiny modern appliances, cleaning products, and newfangled food brands, then American families were safe from the radicalism, race mixing, and godlessness represented by the civil rights movement, Communism, and the Soviet threat. In her book *Redesigning the American Dream*, Dolores Hayden chronicles how 1950s dream houses promoted a culture of consumption and insularity. Streamlined appliances became the antidote to unhappy marriages and unsettled families, buttressing modern womanhood. If the isolated single family home was the man/patriarch's castle it was the proving ground for female domestic enterprise. Indeed, "The dream houses, because of their isolation from society and from each other, often required numerous purchases of appliances such as stoves, clothes washers, and refrigerators."[22] According to Hayden, mass advertising laid a "guilt" trip on women and men about the maintenance of the home front, emphasizing appliances as critical to efficient homemaking. Husbands were encouraged to placate their wives by buying them new gadgets that promised to make busted homes whole. Self-containment and efficiency became synonymous. As a result, the body of the modern 1950s middle class white female was mechanized, streamlined, and unobtrusive—made all the more so by the unseen labor of black female maids and nannies. Focusing on the disillusion of the character Carrie Breedlove, a black mother who is also a maid, Morrison's *Bluest Eye* foreshadows the way these disparities would play out in the postwar era. Imprisoned by the color caste system of racial apartheid Carrie seeks solace in the hyper-white fantasy world of American romance movies. In a gut-wrenchingly painful scene she lashes out at her daughter after she accidentally destroys a freshly baked pie. Blasting her daughter for the mistake, she proceeds to comfort the cowering white child of her employer. The scene underscores how black female domestics must always negotiate a white supremacist space in which the emotional needs of black children are always devalued. Here, black children are never included in the presumption of childhood innocence.

Women like Carrie smoothed the path for white patriarchy to "take back the country." This neat division of labor reinforced the postwar baby boom, allaying nationalist anxiety that birth rates amongst white women had been reduced by wartime increases in female employment. As Alex Lubin maintains in his book *Romance and Rights: The Politics of Interracial Intimacy*, "The ideological project of containment after World War II sought to place all sexual matters in the private sphere. This placement...sought to limit women's opportunities in the public sphere by attempting to contain normative femininity in the domestic sphere. Further, the postwar emphasis on the home as the only appropriate space of female sexuality reasserted patriarchal relations in light of women's wartime participation in the industrial workforce."[23]

God, country and reclaiming white birthrates were a key part of postwar American national identity. This rhetoric was bolstered by the clarion call of American exceptionalism. For example, the rising fame of Christian evangelists like Norman Vincent Peale, Billy Graham, and Fulton Shelton was based on this marriage of exceptionalism, capitalism, and Americana.[24] As Susan Jacoby notes about Peale's influential self-help book the *Power of Positive Thinking*, "Real Americans—Peale's 'own kind'—came not from cities but from the small-town heartland, though, in the Horatio Alger mold, a humble Midwestern boy might grow up to become the leader of one of the wealthiest churches in the richest and most sinful of American cities. 'Everyday people' were not Jews, humanists, or atheists, but Christians."[25] Peale's reveries evoke the notion of the U.S. as a "city on a hill." America, as epitomized by the rugged individualism of small towns and farms, was a global beacon of freedom, democracy, and prosperity; a model to be worshipped and emulated across the globe. Peale and company were clear on the divine right of American empire. Nationhood and godliness were one and the same. In a 1957 Times Square address Graham exhorted his flock to "tell the whole world tonight that we are morally and spiritually strong as well as militarily and economically. Let us...make this a time of re-dedication—not only to God, but to the principles and freedoms that our forefathers gave us."

Graham's bombast has a more militant echo in the venom of former GOP senator and presidential candidate Rick Santorum. With his sweater wearing paternalism, bogus working class hero swagger, and medieval anti-family planning stance, Santorum has come to personify the backlash against women's rights more than any other contemporary political figure. His "father knows best" posture mirrors the 1950s corrupt family values whitewash which pimped American women for the materialist comforts of the dream house. In Santorum's world, birth control is a sinful incursion into God's plan. Women in the workplace ushered in a dangerous era of amorality, family dysfunction, and subversion of traditional authority. Being impregnated through rape is a "gift of human life." And women are inherently unfit for combat because they're too weak and emotional. Despite these views, Santorum has been a big hit with conservative women. According to the online magazine Politico "far from being scared off by Santorum, conservative women are zealously embracing him...he has the highest favorability rating among women of any GOP contender."[26]

Santorum's popularity amongst conservative women highlights the gender nuances of America's Jim Crow era nostalgia. God's body has both religious and secular overtones in the pop culture fixation on and battle over women's fertility. Over the past decade there has been an explosion of super mom reality TV shows featuring tabloid ready teenage mothers, white suburban mothers of multiples, alpha nannies and mega breeders like the ultra Christian fundamentalist Duggar family. The vast majority of these programs spotlight white families and traditional heterosexual two-parent households. The intersection of voyeurism, fertility innovations, and reactionary family values has kept these shows profitable. Similarly, tabloid obsession with the pregnancies, babies and reproductive dramas of (generally) white celebrities have also become an integral part of mainstream discourse. Littering the Internet, the first titillating pictures of celebrity baby bumps have become the prenatal equivalent of porn money shots. Despite all the mainstream media's chest-beating post-feminist rhetoric, it is implied that having a child is still the pinnacle of femininity. Tabloid validation of fertility becomes a female celebrity's most coveted honor as websites breathlessly chart the progress of Beyonce, Britney, Mariah, Tori, Celine, ad nauseum. This theme is amply borne out in the train wreck appeal of popular reality shows like *Teen Mom* and *Sixteen and Pregnant*, whose young white "stars" are regularly featured in the pages of People, In Touch, and US magazines. According to the creators of these shows the tone is supposed to be cautionary. The audience becomes absorbed with the experiences of young girls confronting the life challenges and hardships of premature parenthood. Many of my students confess that watching these shows has become a guilty pleasure. But as young black and Latina women they are quite clear that none of their friends will ever be spotlighted as sexy baby-to-bling Horatio Alger success stories in the tabloids a la teen mother and GOP evangelical poster child for illegitimacy Bristol Palin. By cherry-picking the whitest and most "relatable" teen mothers, the producers of these shows play into the soap opera glamorization of white female melodramas reflected in the tabloids. Moreover, by focusing primarily on girls who decide to continue their pregnancies they also reinforce the notion that abortion is a repugnant decision that no "moral" woman would make.

Teen Mom and *Sixteen and Pregnant* are merely one aspect of a global market that promotes compulsory pregnancy and motherhood. In 2010, a new generation of baby dolls that encouraged young girls to practice breastfeeding hit the market in the U.S. The product's ad campaign focused on white girls, instructing them on the proper way to hold their dolls for maximum exposure. Gender segregated marketing—girls bombarded with an orgy of pink outfitted baby dolls, play houses and appliances; boys directed toward cars, action figures, tools, and science toys—has hardly abated in the post-feminist era. If anything, marketing has become even more aggressively retro. For example, in 2011 the manufacturer of Lego toys elicited a firestorm over its decision to market a line of "girlie" Legos featuring "shapely mini figures that lock into pink, purple and pastel green settings such as a dream house, a splash pool and a beauty shop."[27] The toymaker claimed that it was merely responding to extensive market research about what girls wanted from Legos. And indeed, the new girlie line explodes in an orgy of pink more dreamily diaphanous than circus cotton candy. Sporting cutesy miniskirts, the waiflike Lego figurines are not only gender stereotypical, but, predictably, in a nod to commercial correctness, they include a light-skinned green-eyed girl of color (who, as the resident minstrel of the group, likes to sing and dance) for little black girls that are already indoctrinated into light skinned beauty ideals. Familiar cultural themes linking femininity to domesticity, leisure, and primping evokes a pigtailed sexualization; underscoring how traditional divisions between public and private are still steeped in gender hierarchy. Miniature beauty parlors and dream houses speak to every girl's wet dream of being the perfect little princess, of waiting wistfully above the castle drawbridge to be rescued, knocked up, and devoured by their own children.

In God's Body We Trust

In the reality show era, burning dream houses are more titillating than intact ones. Even though boozing, pill-popping, glue sniffing, incest, rape, and criminality lurk within the walls of the modern dream house, the basic template is still lily white. As the murder of 17 year-old Trayvon Martin in February 2012 demonstrated, there is nothing more viscerally disconcerting to the American mainstream than the oxymoron of black suburbia. The through line between Carrie Butler as jezebel and Trayvon Martin as marauder is the invisible body of white nationhood, one which NRA-backed laws like Stand Your Ground reinforce. Black sexual deviance and black criminality buttress the national narrative of a white innocence perpetually threatened, perpetually under siege, and perpetually in need of defense. Shortly after the Martin shooting, these themes were defiantly trotted out by former National Review columnist and author John Derbyshire in his white supremacist post, "The Talk: The Non-Black Version." Martin's murder elicited a national conversation amongst black parents about how to counsel black youth on public conduct given the realities of racial profiling. But Derbyshire wanted to set seditious black folk straight about who the real victims were. Evoking the image of the scary bestial black spook, the post is a mini-primer on black depravity. It advised whites and other non-blacks to steer clear of black neighborhoods, avoid events with large numbers of black people, and anticipate situations where they could potentially become victims of black violence. Dividing negro-hood into a neat taxonomy of hostile blacks and domesticated intelligent blacks, Derbyshire's post offers rich insight into how the white nationalist backlash centers on preserving space. Even though the majority of white Americans live in predominantly white communities the fantasy of the lurking black criminal *other* still tantalizes. If we arm ourselves to the teeth, make sure those spooks stay in their ghettoes, and neutralize race card-playing black politicians, we'll be able to preempt the "Birth of a Nation" scenarios Thurmond envisioned in his Jim Crow caricature of the deceitful North versus the honest South. The sanctuary of the white neighborhood, the primal site of Americana, depends on it.

Thus, as metaphors for American innocence, Dick and Jane continue to taunt and terrorize. Pink cheeks glowing in the dark, they ghost through the orgy of "white women in peril" stories which dominate tabloid media. People Magazine and carnival barkers pimps like CNN Headline News host Nancy Grace (dubbed queen of the "Missing White Girl" hour) are ground zero for America's missing white women fetish.[28] Screaming from the clutter of supermarket checkout stands and video monitors, they tell us that these are the bodies that matter, that are worthy of protection, that demand the national reckoning with evil epitomized by "our" panting obsession with all the missing Caylees, Jaycees, Lacis, Chandras, Elizabeths, and Natalees. These mascots for American innocence are stolen promises, missed opportunities, squandered birthrights. As potential mothers they are lost yet found, reborn and immortalized with the sulfurous stamp of Lifetime cable network melodramas, martyrs to fallen white womanhood. With the exception of Laci Peterson, the most prized missing white women have either been single and unattached or children frozen in time, suspended in the flower of perpetual innocence. Single and nubile plays better than married and experienced; Persephone is more alluring than Demeter.

But good mothers are hard to find. The so-called feminist assault on traditional family values has made constructing and manufacturing "good mothers" an urgent matter of national security. In this reactionary "post-feminist" climate white America's worst scourge and object of fascination is the specter of the bad white mother. This hysteria was evidenced in the national attention lavished on the trial of Casey Anthony. Anthony was a single middle class young white woman accused of killing her three year old daughter Caylee. The mainstream media's manic fixation on Anthony's trial underscores how much the ideal of white womanhood is steeped in reverence for white motherhood. As many cultural commentators observed during her trial, Anthony was appealing because she was a perverse representation of the Middle American "us." A footloose and fancy free twenty two year-old who continued to indulge her party girl ways after Caylee came up missing, she epitomized the seductive quandary of how seemingly good middle class white girls, good white mothers, could go so colossally bad (a la reality TV). The white masses were transfixed and outraged by the tawdry saga of Caylee's disappearance because she was "every one's child." She was not Aiyanna Jones, a seven year-old Detroit black girl who burned to death after police lobbed an incendiary device in her home. Nor was she Jahessye Shockley, James Lewis Reed or Zakyyah Copeland-Taylor—all African American children who have been missing for several years. In order for the disappearance of a child to elicit swooning national concern there must be emotional investment in and empathy for the plight of the child's mother or parents. When Anthony was identified as the lead suspect in her daughter's disappearance the sanctity of white motherhood was on trial. The trial was featured on Court TV and followed by average citizens with the fervor of a World Wrestling Federation smackdown. After she was acquitted she was universally scorned as a deviant baby killer, a whorish gender and race traitor to the ideal of moral white motherhood.

Casey Anthony morphed into the Salem Witch on national TV. Being marked as bad bitches already, women of color don't have far to fall when it comes to the pathological mother immorality sweepstakes. To paraphrase Gil Scott Heron, the realities of neglectful mothers of color will not be televised. They will not become the object of round-the-clock cable news, Court TV or supermarket tabloid frenzy. They will not elicit thousands of dollars in Internet donations to defray legal expenses. The subtext of the bad black or Latino mother is the good white mother whose children are America's children. For example, fetal homicide laws disproportionately criminalize poor pregnant women of color. Like decades-old legislation that has penalized generations of pregnant black women for crack cocaine use, fetal homicide laws are the new frontier in the anti-abortion backlash. One of the more egregious examples of this involved the case of Rennie Gibbs. In 2006, Gibbs, an

African American Mississippi woman, faced a life sentence for murder after giving birth to a stillborn baby when she was sixteen years- old. The state of Mississippi charged that Gibbs' stillbirth was due to her alleged cocaine use. Although medical reports concluded that Gibbs' cocaine was not a contributing factor in her child's death, the case nonetheless went to criminal court.

In some states, fetal homicide language loosely defines a person as an "unborn child in utero at any stage of development regardless of viability." And it is no accident that the majority of these laws have been enacted in the South and the Midwest, where unrestricted access to safe, legal abortion resources is rapidly disappearing. Thurmond's South Carolina was the first to enact a fetal homicide law. While these laws were initially designed to protect pregnant women and their unborn children against assault by a third party, the National Advocates for Pregnant Women estimate that the vast majority of people charged under these laws have been pregnant women instead:

> Women of color, however, have been particularly targeted for harsh and punitive prosecutorial responses and account for the majority of those arrested for continuing pregnancies to term in spite of a drug problem. While this disproportionality has been true nationwide, nowhere is it more apparent than in South Carolina. In Charleston, South Carolina the Medical University Hospital instituted a policy of reporting and facilitating the arrest of pregnant African American patients who tested positive for cocaine. African American women were dragged out of this predominantly Black hospital in chains and shackles, evoking sharp modern images of African-American women in slavery.[29]

In an amicus brief in defense of Gibbs, several Mississippi health care providers argued that these policies further criminalize drug addiction and discourage women from seeking treatment. Yet, white women drug abusers are far more likely to receive counseling, treatment, and other rehabilitative care than are black women.[30] Nationwide, black women consistently receive harsher prison sentences than white women who have committed similar offenses. Intra-racial disparities are also evident in sentencing patterns. Some research has even shown that lighter-skinned offenders are more likely to be convicted and to receive shorter sentences than are darker-skinned women.[31] Within this context, poor pregnant drug-addicted black women are the ultimate criminal scourge. As Dorothy Roberts notes in her book *Killing the Black Body*, "Prosecutors and judges see poor black women as suitable subjects for these reproductive penalties [like fetal homicide] because society does not view these women as suitable mothers in the first place."[32] The degraded motherhood of black women is part of a legacy in which "a pregnant slave woman was subject to legal fiat centuries ago because the fetus she was carrying already belonged to her master...The prosecutions are better understood as a way of punishing black women for having babies rather than a way of protecting black fetuses."[33] Consequently, racist drug enforcement and sentencing policies, coupled with mainstream assumptions of bad black motherhood, make black women natural targets of fetal homicide laws. Currently, black women constitute over 30% of the U.S. female prison population. They are primarily incarcerated for non-violent drug offenses. A significant number of them are mothers. Increases in black female incarceration coupled with cuts to child social welfare services and reproductive health care will only increase the numbers of black children in the foster care system and amongst the homeless. Dispossessing black women of their humanity, the new cult of true womanhood puts a bulls-eye squarely on communities of color. This backlash is exemplified by the right wing war against contraception, abortion, and health care for poor and working class families.

A Good Mother is Hard to Find

A pure, benign sacrificial motherhood anchors Western God concepts. If black mothers are not sympathetic, are not perceived as sufficiently self-sacrificing, and are viewed as profligate breeders, then black children are not innocent. Reproduction and childhood are prisms through which the connection between race, gender, and nationhood becomes visible. Black women's lack of ownership over their bodies and their children's bodies was a cornerstone of the slave economy. Because black children were already property, forced to work like adults, traditional European American distinctions between childhood and adulthood simply didn't apply. Conversely, there was no separation between white women's bodies and that of their children. As Dorothy Roberts argues:

> Bearing children who were their masters' property only compounded the contradictions that scarred slave women's reproductive lives. It separated

> mothers from their children immediately upon conception. This division between mother and child did not exist for white women of that era. The notion that white mother and child were separable entities with contradictory interests was unthinkable, as was the idea of a white woman's work interfering with maternal duties. Both violated the prevailing ideology of female domesticity that posited mothers as the natural caretakers for their children.[34]

In the shadow of the slave regime, Carrie Butler's "motherhood" was a contradiction. Forced to give up her child and secure another job in a city where she would not be scorned as the unwed mother of an "illegitimate half-breed," she was caught between the enduring symbol of the stalwart mammy and that of the debased Jezebel. While Thurmond rose through the ranks of American politics and played a towering role in shaping Southern political sensibilities, Butler was a historical enigma. But this was simply God's will and God's plan. Thurmond's destiny depended upon Butler's erasure and invisibility. Again, as surrogates for the body of God, white men's bodies were inviolate; they were the law, reason, and universal truth. Fathering illegitimate half-breeds was not only essential to antebellum slave economics, but to a post-bellum nation that revered whiteness as the image of God. There could be no Thurmond without Butler. There could be no barnstorming Dixiecrat statesman and heroic protector of white Southern honor without the specter of black maids scrubbing toilets, wiping white asses, and powering white households despite the pervasive threat of sexual exploitation. The strapping Type A picture of virility that Williams evokes in her most fawning reveries about Thurmond was a function of this dialectic. In her eyes, Thurmond was a principled segregationist, a stern taskmaster whose rejection of her, his black birth daughter, was tragic, even odious, but symbolic of a calculated moral purpose and moral order. This arrangement was merely a continuation of slave regime patriarchy, for "Slave law installed the white master as the head of an extended plantation family…the plantation family ruled by white slaveholders was considered the best institution to transmit moral precepts to uncivilized Africans. Courts reasoned that the slave owner's moral authority over the family was ordained by divine imperative."[35] White men's dominion over home, hearth, and "the Help" was a 20th century extension of this system. And when it came to slave rights and American jurisprudence there was no tension between the secular and the divine. Slave rights—especially those of African American women, breeders at the center of the slave economy—were virtually an oxymoron.

American lore is filled with dark skinned black mammies suckling white children; the sexual and the maternal seared into the otherness of black skin. Thus, "Loving, hating, pitying or pining for the mammy in the twentieth century became a way for Americans to define the character of the nation, the meaning of freedom, and the racial and gender boundaries of the citizenry."[36] The mammy becomes the white child's most intimate adult confidante, tending to her wounded heart, affirming her beauty and worth, guarding her center-of-the-universe princess status. In Kathryn Stockett's 2009 novel *The Help*, the lead character Abilene's son has conveniently been killed before the story begins.[37] This allows Abilene to lavish all of her attention on the young daughter of her white employer. For Abilene, the white child's struggle with potty training becomes the object of intense, near heroic focus. Black children as full-bodied characters are screamingly absent from the novel. They float like apparitions behind the scenes, intruding whenever there is a need to lend domestic verisimilitude to Stockett's noble savages. The expendable black child makes mammy the ultimate symbol of maternal betrayal and sacrifice. Since black women had no binding natal ties to their own children black children were wholly other.

Contemporary images of black children are informed by this legacy. In many American classrooms black children are treated like ticking time bomb savages, shoved into special education classes, disproportionately suspended or expelled then warehoused in opportunity schools and juvenile jails. At a Georgia elementary school in 2012 a six year-old African American girl was handcuffed by the police after throwing a tantrum in the principal's office.[38] Handcuffing disruptive black elementary school students is not uncommon. It is perhaps the most extreme example of black children's initiation into what has been characterized as the school-to-prison pipeline, a phenomenon that has been more accurately dubbed the cradle to grave pipeline. Not surprisingly, many commenters in the blogosphere agreed with the strong arm tactics used on the girl. As with the Trayvon Martin murder, the inherent brutishness of black children was the subtext to how her treatment was perceived by white mainstream America. Stereotypes about dysfunctional violent black children ensure that the myth of white children's innocence is preserved. Nowhere is this more evident than in American schools where education data has consistently pointed to an epidemic of black suspensions.

Nationwide, black children spend more time in the dean's office, more time being opportunity transferred to other campuses and more time cycling in and out of juvenile detention facilities than children of other ethnicities. Conservative critics love to attribute this to poverty, broken homes, and the kind of Bell Curve dysfunction that demonizes "welfare mothers" who have too many babies they can't take care of. Yet there is no compelling evidence that socioeconomic differences play a decisive role in these disparities.[39] The fact remains that black children are criminalized by racist discipline policies regardless of whether they come from "Leave it to Beaver" homes, foster care or homeless shelters. According to researchers Daniel Losen and Russell Skiba, authors of the Southern Poverty Law Center's "Suspended Education" report, "ethnic and racial disproportionately in discipline persists even when poverty and other demographic factors are controlled.[40]

National research such as the Southern Poverty Law Center's study and the Indiana Education Policy Center's 2000 "The Color of Discipline" report has consistently shown that black students do not, in fact, "offend" at higher rates than their white and Latino counterparts.[41] Middle class African American students in higher income schools are also disproportionately suspended. This implies that black students are perceived by adults as more viscerally threatening. "The Color of Discipline" report found that black students were more likely to be referred out of class for lower level offenses such as excessive noise, disrespect, loitering and "threat."[42] According to the Southern Poverty Law Center, "race and gender disparities in suspension were due not to differences in administrative disposition but to differences in the rate of initial referral of black and white students."

Similarly, a 2011 study by the Council of State Governments on suspensions in Texas schools, concluded that black and Latino students were disciplined far more harshly than white students who'd committed similar offenses.[43] Black students were more likely to get off site suspensions and transfers to alternative schools. White students were also more likely to receive counseling and on-site suspension or detention. As a result of these push-out policies, students of color were more likely to drop-out of school.[44]

Things are even more heinous at the middle school level. Middle school has been characterized by some researchers as the gateway for student success. A 2003 Johns Hopkins University study by Robert Balfanz found that poor performance and low attendance in middle school were some of the most reliable predictors of incarceration rates and drop-out at the high school level.[45] For example, during the 2009-2010 school year, black suspensions in LAUSD South Los Angeles middle schools were off the charts. The LAUSD is the second largest district in the nation and is over 70% Latino. At Audubon Middle School, which has one of the last majority black populations in the district, black students were 64.9% of the population yet represented a whopping 85% of those suspended. Latino students were at 33% yet constituted only 15% of suspensions. At that time Audubon had a black principal. Similar patterns exist at district schools with smaller African American populations.[46]

Based on this data, the handcuffing of a six year-old black child is consistent with a national climate in which the innocence of black childhood is itself contested. It has been well-documented that depression, anxiety, and behavior disorders among black children and adolescents are routinely criminalized rather than addressed through a mental health lens. As the suspension data attests, there are deep racial disparities in the use of rehab, therapy, counseling, and other mental health strategies when it comes to dealing with disruptive youth. Disparities in identification, diagnosis, and treatment become a self-fulfilling prophecy. Racial stereotypes promote the view that black children are naturally more threatening and violent. Thus, black children who do act out violently are automatically pathologized and criminalized.

This Catch-22 fuels mainstream belief in an epidemic of out of control black children, bolstering anti-government bootstrapping spare-the-rod-spoil-the-child disciplinary policies. It is no accident that some of the biggest proponents of tough law and order zero tolerance policies which advocate trying juveniles as adults are on the far right. Their views conform neatly with the Christian fundamentalist belief that submission and repression are the best strategies for dealing with wayward children. In public education these agendas dovetail with the view that only neo-liberal education reform policies can redeem otherwise un-assimilable racial others. The new wave of corporatized education spearheaded by billionaire donors like the Broad Foundation, the Gates Foundation, and the Walton Family Foundation promote shopworn themes about Booker T. Washington bootstrapping as the antidote to violence, ghetto dysfunction, and academic underachievement.[47] African American and Latino students are the most heavily impacted by this shift to market driven schools. As the U.C.L.A. Civil Rights Project attests, embrace of "charterization" historically comes during a period in which "civil rights has been given a very low priority in federal and state policy... and civil rights is in retreat."[48] The gross re-segregation that the charter movement has facilitated hearkens back to the Jim Crow era, in which "school choice" was the "clarion call" for white segregationists. High quality charters are far outnumbered by those that exacerbate existing public school segregation. Some even function as "oases" for exurban whites fleeing public schools "overrun" with blacks and Latinos.[49] Indeed, while charters have been perceived by some as the magic bullet for failing neighborhood schools and low achievement among students of color, most of them perform no better (and many actually perform much worse) than traditional public schools.[50] Nonetheless, charters, high stakes testing, and merit pay for teachers have been the cornerstone of the "liberal" Obama administration's public school policy. Insofar as charters re-segregate, operating from a laissez faire model of achievement with little accountability or quality control, the charter movement is actually a conservative throwback to Thurmond's confederate paradise of separate but equal. Decades after Dick and Jane became the standard for teaching elementary reading comprehension in the U.S., American schools are aping their 1950s counterparts, preserving a white picket fence vision of cultural literacy that leaves the vast majority of children of color behind with no boots to bootstrap.

In his 1963 inaugural address as Alabama governor, George Wallace, a good Southern Baptist, infamously called for "segregation today, tomorrow, and forever." Wallace's fiery bombast was dominated by paeans to manifest destiny and American exceptionalism. Alabama's agricultural bounty was a blessing from God. The state was the heart of the "great Anglo Saxon Southland" and its people had spread enterprisingly across the nation to make their fortunes on the Western frontier, in the Midwest, and New England. Segregation represented liberty; integration signified tyranny, economic enslavement, and betrayal of the Confederacy's legacy. The promise of white enterprise, its cultural foundation and national soul, was intimately tied to divine providence and divine will.

Wallace's declaration has become a self-fulfilling prophecy. Now, all God's children, white children and children of color, can drink from the same water fountains, pee in the same antiseptic public bathrooms, and be force fed the same message of capitalist exceptionalism in segregated classrooms and neighborhoods that would make Wallace and Thurmond proud.

My nephew "Aaron" is the great great-grandson of Carrie Butler and Thurmond. A precocious bright-eyed seven year old who loves science and superheroes, he will be perceived as a public enemy just as Trayvon Martin was, crossing white picket fences on that fateful winter's afternoon. Nearly one hundred and fifty years after slavery was abolished, his intelligence and curiosity will not shield him. His sense of empathy will not shield him. And certainly "God" will not shield him from the presumption of guilt before innocence that bound and continues to bind black bodies to the apartheid laws of the South, the apartheid code of the North, and the apartheid legacy of this most Christian Nation.

CHAPTER FIVE

Prayer Warriors and Freethinkers

I found, while thinking about the far-reaching world of the creative black woman, that often the truest answer to a question that really matters can be found very close.

--Alice Walker [1]

The 24-hour prayer sessions are the true test of a warrior for Jesus. They require Herculean stamina, the patience of Job, and the rigor of elite marathon runners hitting the wall in a fiery sweat pit at high altitude primed for God's finish line. In many small, storefront Pentecostal churches, these "pray-a-thons" are women's spaces: Hubs of music, food, caregiving, and intense witnessing. My student, Stacy Castro,* is a bass player in her Pentecostal church's band. She's also the pastor's daughter and a regular participant in the pray-a-thons, a mainstay in some evangelical congregations. Much of her weekends are focused on church activities. And though she is an intelligent gifted speaker, up until her participation in the Women's Leadership Project she thought little about pursuing college and wanted to go to cosmetology school. Stacy's aspirations are not atypical of students at Washington Prep High School in South Los Angeles. In a community that is dominated by churches of every stripe, only a small minority of students go on to four-year colleges and universities.

In my book *Moral Combat: Black Atheists, Gender Politics, and the Values Wars*, I argued that the literature on secularism and gender does not capture the experiences of women of color negotiating racism, sexism, and poverty in historically religious communities. The relative dearth of secular humanist and freethought traditions amongst women of color cannot be separated from the broader context of white supremacy, gender politics, and racial segregation. Harlem Renaissance-era writers Nella Larsen and Zora Neale Hurston are generally acknowledged as pioneering 20th century black women freethinkers. However, what few women's histories of freethought there are celebrate the political influence of prominent 19th white women non-believers, many of whom were suffragists and abolitionists. None contextualize these women's influence vis-à-vis the race and gender politics that informed both the feminist and freethought movements. For example, I have yet to see an appraisal that problematizes the racism and xenophobia of forerunning freethinkers like Elizabeth Cady Stanton or the "curious" absence of women of color from freethought movements.

Susan Jacoby's *Freethinkers: A History of American Secularism* is a case in point. Jacoby devotes a chapter to the connection between anti-clericalism, abolitionism and feminism in 19th century anti-slavery activism. She maintains that "the conjunction of radical abolitionism with early feminism is an important chapter in the history of American secularism because those who came of age in the 1820s and 1830s were the first generation of American social reformers to make the connection between reactionary religion and reactionary domestic social institutions...Religious conservatives today are the ones who are mistaken in their insistence that the anti-slavery movement had nothing to do with Enlightenment values—values that would...be adapted by abolitionist women who wished no less for themselves than they wished for slaves."[2] This passage underscores the deep legacy of paternalist racial politics that informs American feminism. Might it be possible that some of these "abolitionist women" were not just white women but *also* slaves or freewomen of color, individuals who were not trailblazing secularists but religionists who subscribed both to "natural rights" and biblical notions of redemption in the eyes of God? Throughout the antebellum period, white women activists used slavery as an analogy to characterize their subordination under patriarchy. As Louise Michele Newman notes in her book *White Women's Rights*, "white women, the argument went, could empathize with enslaved peoples because they, as women, experienced similar oppression due to their sex."[3] However, comparing themselves to slaves was problematic on several levels. For example, white women were advantaged by their class, race, and ethnic privilege. White women held slaves as property, exercised physical control over them, and profited from their labor and submission. White women topped the hierarchy of women, were the universal beauty ideal, and, unlike women of color, could be protected from sexual violence, abuse or transgression in courts of law.[4] If white women were deemed to be the weaker, fairer, sexually-debased sex, then their status was elevated in comparison to that of female slaves, who were considered to be less than human. Thus, drawing analogies between their experiences as white women and that of African slaves was especially offensive to black women. Black women were workers first and foremost. The slave economy depended on their bodies. They were subjected to sexual and economic exploitation by white women's husbands, brothers, fathers, sons, and uncles. Whereas white feminists' grievances were primarily focused on patriarchy (rather than patriarchy *and* white supremacy), black women were by necessity in racial and class solidarity with black men.[5]

In her book, Jacoby not only implies that anti-clerical secularists were the driving force of abolitionism but also props up white thinkers and activists as its moral compass. Save for a brief appearance by Frederick Douglass, religious humanists or believers of color play a marginal role in Jacoby's tale of the epic battle to restore America back to its vaunted Enlightenment anti-slavery principles. Jacoby situates abolitionist feminism with the Grimke sisters, claiming that "The first female public speakers—(Lucretia) Mott and the Grimke sisters—could hardly have been anything but anticlerical." This account glaringly omits the galvanic influence of orator Maria Stewart, an African American freewoman abolitionist from New England. Stewart delivered a trailblazing round of speeches in the early 1830s and is believed to be the first woman to give a public address to a mixed, or so-called "promiscuous," audience.[6] According to Paula Giddings, Stewart's brief career as an activist encapsulated the divide between white feminism (which was greatly influenced by the example of abolitionist activism) and black feminism. Black feminism emerges from the struggle against white supremacy and white racism. Racial slavery depended on the sexual exploitation of black women and the commodification of black women's reproductive labor. It established an economic and gendered hierarchy of women that advantaged white women and continues to shape feminist politics to this day.

Like most black women of the early 19th century, Stewart came from black evangelical traditions that emphasized the liberatory force of biblical scripture and redemptive suffering. "Evangelicalism both undermined white male privilege and empowered disenfranchised blacks, women, and others because it challenged the social status quo in the antebellum South."[7] Although she drew heavily from the Bible, Stewart's "words straddle the line between secular and sacred address."[8] Given the realities of slavery, and the basic restrictions on mobility, employment, education, free speech, assembly, and social life that kept freewomen and freemen segregated, the Black Church was the most powerful black political institution in the antebellum era. Forbidden to train formally as a preacher because of her gender, Stewart nonetheless looked to the Bible and church traditions as a means of intellectual development as well as spiritual expression. But black women were hardly passive consumers of religious dogma. Cooper notes that "particularly for black women…evangelical conversion had the power to create powerful, new and often liberating social relationships."[9] Even though black women evangelists could not be classified as freethinkers:

> Black women also bypassed the barrier of religious thought that circumscribed even radical white activists until the late 1830s…black women had been able to justify their activism even earlier…A woman who had experienced a religious conversion, Stewart was confident enough to challenge the exhortations of Saint Paul, whose words had long been used to justify slavery and sexism. Stewart…simply went over his head.[10]

Stewart rejected the sexist, misogynist, and racist prescriptions of scriptures like Timothy, First Corinthians, and Ephesians. Instead, she fashioned a powerful nationalist argument for social justice as a moral imperative steeped in biblical ideology. Black women's ability to reconcile Christian traditions with social justice activism grew out of their unique circumstance—as chattel whose bodies were a source of profit for the slavocracy, work was central to how they were defined as less than female and less than human. Black maternity was beholden to the plantation economy and black motherhood (as a supposedly inalienable biological right of women) was an oxymoron. This obscenity is central to Toni Morrison's novel *Beloved*, in which the lead character, Sethe, murders her infant daughter so she will not have to live in slavery. In exposing the violence and terrorism that undermined the "sacred" bond between slave women and their children, *Beloved* asks whether black motherhood could rightfully exist under the slave regime. Under the slavocracy, neither secular nor Christian morality respected the right of a black mother to raise much less protect her children. Since black women's bodies were already part of the public domain, the rigid dichotomy between public and private sphere that defined white women's lives did not apply to black women. Black women worked outside of the home in the homes of white women, raising their children, cooking their meals, and, frequently, being abused by their spouses. They worked in menial, low-wage jobs doing dirty work that white citizen and even immigrant women were not expected to do.[11] These critical differences in expectations have always shaped black women's relationship to feminism, dividing black women and white women on key political priorities. As former Black Panther Party chair Elaine Brown once acidly declared, "White women have always been Miss Ann. We have never been Miss Ann."

Being Miss Ann means being the face of civilized feminine innocence. It means being forgiven and rewarded for "immoral" "sluttish" behavior like Bristol Palin, being the missing white girl who commands all the headlines, or being anointed spokesperson, ala Hillary Clinton, for "women's" issues and concerns, despite racist pandering to the white working-class during the 2008 presidential campaign.

Historically, Miss Ann has been "the lady" to black women's super-tramp mammy welfare queen. Nineteenth century mores enshrined her in the Cult of True Womanhood. Myths of 20th century exceptionalism cast her as the pinnacle of human evolution. In Jacoby's book, Miss Ann shows up as the secular civilizer fighting for equal rights and emancipation on a stage without women of color. Jacoby lauds Elizabeth Cady Stanton for her secular feminist activism yet makes only passing reference to her infamous racist denigration of men of color and immigrant men. Stanton's critique came in the aftermath of ferocious conflicts within the women's suffrage movement over the passage of the Fifteenth Amendment granting black men the vote. As Newman remarks, "Stanton, the intellectual powerhouse of the suffrage movement, held firmly to moral distinctions and discussed them in gendered and racialized terms."[12] After the passage of the Fifteenth Amendment, white feminist discourse shifted more explicitly to rhetoric about white women's moral superiority vis-à-vis people of color and immigrants. White women were positioned as moral beacons standing at the top of the hierarchy of civilization next to white men. Thus, "the feelings of racial superiority that Anglo-Protestants nurtured concerning their own ancestry, heredity, and evolutionary history led them to insist that they shared the white man's inherited capacity for self-government."[13] Indeed, "It is not surprising that white activists had a heightened racial consciousness of themselves as civilized women contributing to and reinforcing dominant religious, scientific, and cultural ideologies that attributed to them unique moral and political roles on the basis of this identity. Blending religious conviction…with science (social evolutionary theories) and political ideology (progressivism), white proponents of women's rights helped create new roles for themselves that explicitly maintained the racial hierarchies that were based on the presumption that Anglo-American Protestants were culturally, as well as biologically, superior to other peoples."[14] In essence, black women did not have the luxury to be freethinkers within a European American context because they were constructed as the racialized sexual other. Their bodies were the backdrop to European American notions of individual liberty, humanity, and natural rights. Their labor was the raw material for European American intellectualism. European American freethought traditions were predicated on the enslavement of the racialized sexual other. Within the context of slavery and Jim Crow, women like Stanton, Ernestine Rose, and early white feminist freethinkers would not have had the license to be secular were it not for the dialectic between the civilized white Western subject and the degraded amoral racialized sexual other.

Black women were not supposed to be geniuses. In the West, genius and Godliness are intimately bound to each other. Black women's lives were too cluttered with the debris of the everyday—the cooking, cleaning, minding, managing, and tending that comes with the earthly terrain of caregiving—to soar to the heavens with geniuses. Small wonder then that the spaces they did find themselves in, that were made available to them, became wellsprings for expressions of Godliness, both subversive and conforming. That the vast majority of black women were only afforded access to the worlds of work, the family, and church meant that their "genius" would by necessity be a reflection of those worlds. In the turbulence of antebellum America, "God" became ordinary black women's medium for expressing genius, creativity, artistry, mastery, and invention. Hence, secularism was a dangerous and untenable position because of the way black dehumanization was institutionalized. Where would black women go to be affirmed as persons? The courts, where their rights were not recognized? The Constitution, where their bodies were vessels? The education system, where their culture was demeaned as savage, primitive, and un-Christian? Government, where their bodies were deep profit for some of the nation's most esteemed legislators and moral philosophers? White churches, where they were debased as Jezebels and amoral Children of Ham? Absent from Jacoby's account of heroic white women freethinkers is an appraisal of how xenophobia, nativism, and racism in the 19th century feminist movement informed secular freethought traditions. The civilized liberated freethinking white woman of the late 19th and early 20th centuries could not have existed without the specter of the debased Jezebel of color.

* * *

Jezebel continues to have a powerful influence on the self-image and self-policing of women of color. In her article "Guadalupe: The Sex

Goddess," Sandra Cisneros reflects on the ease with which white women own and occupy their bodies in the locker room:

> In high school I marveled at how white women strutted around the locker room, nude as pearls, as unashamed of their brilliant bodies as the Nike of Samothrace. Maybe they were hiding terrible secrets like bulimia or anorexia, but, to my naïve eye then, I thought of them as women comfortable in their skin. You could always tell us Latinas. We hid when we undressed, modestly facing a wall, or, in my case, dressing in a bathroom stall. We were the ones who still used bulky sanitary pads instead of tampons, thinking ourselves morally superior to our white classmates.[15]

White women strut, reveling in their liberty. Latinas retreat, private, and prudish, the antithesis of cultural stereotypes about spicy hot-blooded vixens jiggling around spewing broken English to horny white men. Cisneros' passage highlights why religious mores and racial politics continue to be key in shaping gender norms amongst women of color. White women are the cultural, moral, and aesthetic standard against which all women of color are judged. White femininity is the global beauty ideal that all girls of color grow up aspiring to emulate. At the Disney store, mecca for young capitalists in training, girls like my ten-year-old niece flock like honey bees to Disney princesses with long, lustrous, Rapunzel-esque blond hair. Tiaras with platinum blond tresses beckon from the shelves. Snow White dresses wait to transform some lucky girl with thirty dollars. Only a doll modeled on the "spunky" uber blond character from *Tangled* can satiate the raging goldilocks lust of tween girls. Despite the market savvy multiculturalism of the 21st century Disney princesses (e.g. black Princess Tiana and Middle Eastern Jasmine), the brand still epitomizes a Europeanized beauty ideal of pinched thin noses, wasp waists and butt-sweeping straight hair. Coming from the ministry of Disney, the modern woman/princess is both sexually desirable and unattainable, independent yet traditional, dependably hetero yet the shimmering object of every girl's fantasies. For women of color watching behind the scenes, the white woman and the blonde symbolize all of these contradictions. White women are "comfortable" in their skin and in their bodies because the dark Jezebel has freed them from the yoke of depravity. They are free to be sexual adventurers because they aren't marked as universal "hos."

Within Catholic traditions, the ubiquitous image of the pure as the driven snow self-sacrificing Virgin Mary is the model for femininity. But the Virgin's white purity is only validated by the fallen dark whore: The black, Asian, Latina or Native American woman whose body is "the sign of sexual experience."[16] As writer Yasmin Davidds Garrido notes, "It often seemed to me that unless I behaved just like the Virgin Mary I wouldn't be good enough to win God's approval. In order to be considered a good girl, I had to be quiet, submissive, and obedient...This is one way Catholicism coerces young girls to mute their voices."[17] Pushing back against these traditions, some Latinas have reclaimed the Virgen de Guadalupe, the indigenous version of the idealized white Virgin Mary, as a challenge to racist misogynist notions of Latina femininity. The brown Virgen de Guadalupe is a vivid, commanding presence in Latino art. She is a space of projection, alternately portrayed as pious and untouchable or sexualized, strong, and transgressive. Cisneros envisions the Virgen as the pre-Columbian "she before the Church desexed her," a symbol of unabashed sexuality, power, and independence. For Cisneros, the Virgen is not "The one of the Roman Catholic Church. The one who I bolted my door against in my teens and twenties [instead]...I have had to search for her in the rubble of history and I have found her. She is Guadalupe the Sex Goddess, a goddess who makes me feel good about my sexual power, my sexual energy." Cisneros' reflections attest to the importance of "alternative" spirituality for women of color disillusioned with organized religion yet unwilling to ditch faith entirely. The growing number of women who turn to spiritualism is part of a general national decline in participation in organized religion. Nonetheless, for many young women, the Virgin ideal coexists uneasily with the media's propaganda about the hyper-sexuality of women of color. Blogging about the cultural double standards imposed on young Latinas, twelfth-grader Brenda Briones asserts that:

> I have heard many Latino fathers brag about their promiscuous sons. I have never heard a Latino parent brag about a promiscuous daughter. ...in accordance with their Catholic or Christian beliefs... "Good daughters" are expected to stay virgins until marriage... This double standard makes boys think that young women are sexual objects that can be used to prove to the world that they are "true players." When we as a

> community, uphold these views, we tell young women that their value is rooted in their sexuality and not their talents or intellect.[18]

This is the backdrop against which women of color struggle with religious and secular belief systems. Even as the moral weight of their communities—reinforced by the dominant culture—is placed on them, many continue to seek refuge in faith and faith traditions because they provide moral guidance and a sense of purpose, direction, and meaning. Responding to a survey I conducted on high school-aged young women and faith, twelfth-grader Vanessa Linares agreed that African American and Latina women are packing the pews because many of them "believe that women of color need faith/religion to be moral."[19] Thus, popular reality shows like the *Bad Girls Club* and platinum-selling pop artists like wannabe Barbie doll Nicki Minaj show young women of color that hyper-sexuality is a quick and dirty form of "validation" for a select few. These women may appear to be flouting conventional sexual mores with "fuck you" alpha female sexuality, but they are still rigidly bound by them. They cannot own their bodies like the white women strutting around in Cisneros' locker room because the gender norms that they mine still rely on the contrast between the sexually-experienced, out-of-control dark other and the white innocent. But the goddess cult that so many women of color flock to is also a cul-de-sac. Goddesses, queens, princesses, and other icons of spiritual authority are by definition floating above the sorry rancid muck of mere mortals. As Diane Arellano comments:

> Somewhere in college, I felt the need to proactively counter the general assumption that as a Mexican woman, I must be a Catholic or Christian. This conscious shift in my identity was informed by my interests and participation in activism. When I searched for models of Latino activists, I was very disappointed to see or read about "seeking strength" from "La Virgen" or claiming their work is the work of "God." I thought about how oppression functions in communities of color and asked myself, isn't there a good argument that can be made about the Church's role in institutionalizing the oppressive gender, race, class, and sexuality paradigms that these activists are fighting so hard against?[20]

Ultimately, Cisneros' feminist model of the sexually-liberated Virgen is problematic because it, too, relies on the same hierarchies of human versus supernatural, and the lust for the divine, which brand flesh and blood bodies as other.

* * *

Diane, Brenda, Vanessa, and their peers are part of the so-called Millennial generation which spans from teenagers to those in their early thirties. Although national data indicate that Millennials are less devout than previous generations, faith is still a powerful anchor for most of the young women in my Women's Leadership Project program in South Los Angeles. The majority are Jehovah's Witnesses, Catholic, Christian Pentecostal or Black Church-affiliated. Many of the Latina students are part of the wave of Pentecostal evangelicalism that is being fueled by Latino immigrants. During the 2011-2012 school year, our WLP student cohort was especially devout. Faith rituals were a big part of the girls' home, social, and community life. Politicizing young women about the role sexism plays in their lives has been an uphill battle on our campuses. Young women of color, in particular, are trained to see race but not gender and sexuality as the primary source of oppression in their lives. Part of this stems from misogynist denigration of women but it also reflects the historical solidarity that women of color have with men of color. Coming to consciousness about the everyday sexism that they face, many young women express ambivalence about the "casual" slights, inappropriate touching, classroom marginalization, and misogynist language that they encounter on a regular basis. Writing in her book *My Sisters' Voices*, young author Iris Jacob notes that:

> Girls of color have forever been caretakers. That is what we are taught, from baby-sitting our siblings to cooking for our families. Part of being a caretaker means defending men of color—our fathers, uncles, brothers...We have been trained to stand by them...We as females of color have been told that sexism does not exist for us or is not important...Yet I cannot even begin to count all the disrespectful and derogatory things

> I have heard from the mouths of men of color…I know there are many wonderful, respectful men of color, so I have no reason to be angry. Yet still I am. Our men should be outraged…They should not tolerate having their mothers, sisters and daughters subject to such oppression.[21]

The legacy of racism within the mainstream women's movement has also affected the perceptions that women of color have about sexism. Civil rights battles are never framed in women's rights terms and youth of color are not taught to see the connections between the two. Nor are they taught about women of color activists like Ida B. Wells, Sojourner Truth, Maria Stewart, Dolores Huerta, Luisa Moreno, Shirley Chisholm, Wilma Mankiller, and Angela Davis who negotiated the intersection of race, gender and sexuality. On the everyday level, sexual harassment is a tacitly accepted part of most school cultures. Teaching a Women of Color in the U.S. class at one school, I was outraged by the students' easy acceptance of messages about violence against women. Underlying this trend is the deep devaluation of black girls' lives. Thus, when a popular teacher was accused of statutory rape some of the girls on campus rushed to his defense. Word was that he had to have been misled if not outright seduced by the teenage "ho" who pressured him into taking her home. This "blame the victim" mentality has become more and more acute with the so-called "post-feminist" mainstreaming of soft porn culture. Unrelenting exposure to reality TV, Jerry Springer-esque trash talk shows, hip hop videos, and "urban" films that portray young black and Latino women as expendable "bitches" and sex objects has fatally distorted the self-image of women of color. Girls are encouraged to commit public sexual acts and even film them on their cell phones in order to win the approval and acceptance of young men. Desperate to do "anything" to get a man, some young women will consent to giving oral sex in the belief that it is less risky than intercourse. As a result, sexually transmitted infections (STIs) like oral herpes have skyrocketed amongst African American young women in South Los Angeles.

Much of the WLP's curriculum focuses on HIV and STI contraction, intimate partner violence, and sexual assault prevention. Women of color have some of the highest sexual assault rates in the nation.[22] Yet, when the girls in our peer workshops were asked to speculate about why our communities have disproportionate rates of sexual assault they, trotted out stereotypes like "mixed race women are more likely to be raped because they are the 'prettiest'" and "black women get assaulted more because they have 'big butts.'" The association between black women's bodies and sexual violence was pervasive. It transcended the common belief that women encourage rape and sexual assault by what they wear or who they're socializing with. At the deepest level, girls have internalized slave-era representations of black women's bodies as pure sex: 21st century Venus Hottentots who invite assault because of the "way we are built"; complex notions of colorism, hair texture, and who the dominant culture considers beautiful are also a part of this view. Mixed-race women are believed to have high sexual assault rates because they are closer to the white beauty ideal; on the other hand, "unmixed" black women have high rates because they embody a lustful primitive.

But the lack of education and degraded self-worth amongst many young women of color is also due to social conservatism. As black and brown people we must always be more moral, more "blessed," and closer to God than white people. Again, lurking within this hyper-religiosity is a reaction to Western notions of the out-of-control primitive.[23] During the 2012 school year, students at our second campus, the majority of which were Pentecostal, were intensely involved in church activities. This campus has higher poverty rates and greater numbers of children in foster care than our other campus. Some girls couldn't participate in weekend activities because they had extensive church obligations. Several students were heavily involved in the church band, choir, and mentoring programs. One student had to have her pastor's approval to attend our two-day, all-female retreat.

* * *

In American Latino communities, contemporary Pentecostalism has a strong female orientation. This is paradoxical given what some have identified as its fundamentally patriarchal, conservative ethos. According to the Pew Hispanic survey, 62% of Latinos identify as Catholics, while 19% identify as Protestant.[24] Thirteen percent of Latinos specifically identify as evangelicals. Over the past decade, Pentecostalism amongst African Americans and Latinos has skyrocketed. The burgeoning numbers of Pentecostal worshipers is led by second-, third-, and fourth-generation Latinos who tend to be less tethered to Catholicism.[25]

The modern Pentecostal movement was spearheaded by an African American pastor named William Seymour, who broke away from the white leadership of a Los Angeles Pentecostal church after experiencing racial discrimination.[26] Based on Azusa Street in downtown Los Angeles, the revival movement was a multiracial effort. After the revival's launch, the local press scorned the movement just as much for its "miscegenated" mix of blacks, whites, and Latinos as for its histrionic focus on speaking in tongues and spirit possession.[27] The early inclusiveness of the movement was noteworthy given the deeply segregated era from which it emerged. Yet, as theologian Estrelda Alexander notes, "these intense early impulses, which went far beyond tolerance to involve actual embrace of peoples of diverse ethnic groups, soon capitulated to surrounding racial realities."[28] After the highly fractious decline of the Azusa Street revival in the teens and '20s, Pentecostalism splintered into largely separate white and black camps. Once consigned to historical obscurity, Seymour's founding role has been amplified by theologians critical of the racist erasure of Pentecostalism's African American roots.[29] Similarly, "The roots of Latino Pentecostalism reach back to the beginning of the Pentecostal movement itself. Several Mexicans were present at the Azusa Street Revival... By the 1930s there were active revivals in Latino communities across the United States, and missionaries fanned out from these early germinating grounds into the rest of Central and South America."[30] Early black Pentecostalism was reviled by both secular and religious critics as being "too African," too emotional, passionate, and animalistic.[31] This belief, coupled with the institutional racism of the Jim Crow era, helped solidify racial divisions within Pentecostal denominations.

Emotionalism and raw expressivity are crucial to the Pentecostal tradition which "encourages emotions not usually seen in middle-class churches, from moaning and personal storytelling to fits of laughter and speaking in tongues."[32] Speaking in tongues is an important form of witnessing because it gives people of all classes access to the "Spirit of God," rather than privileging those who have mastered the dominant language.[33] Speaking in tongues allows believers to give "testimonios," or testimonies that transcend the boundaries of scripture. Many of the unique characteristics of Pentecostal services—among them spontaneous prayer, speaking in tongues, ecstatic collapse, and long, improvised sermons—are manifestations of this belief.[34]

According to Drew University professor Otto Maduro, "(Pentecostal) churches were much more agreeable, congenial, welcoming to Hispanics than most of the other Christian churches—Roman Catholic or mainstream Protestant. They had a warmer atmosphere where people felt at home."[35] Whereas most Catholic priests and officials are not community-based, Pentecostal ministers generally come directly from the community and have the "same neighborhoods and socioeconomic backgrounds as the congregants."[36] The gendered appeal of Pentecostalism is evident in the 2008 American Religious Identification Survey. The survey concludes that "Latino religious polarization may be influenced by a gender effect, as in the general U.S. population, with men moving toward no religion and women toward more conservative religious traditions and practices. Two traditions at opposite poles of the religious spectrum exhibit the largest gender imbalance: *The None population is heavily male (61%) while the Pentecostal is heavily female (58%)* (italics added by author)."[37]

Because of its "democratic" bent, Pentecostalism appeals to working-class congregants shut out of traditional sermon-based church services that anoint a few chosen authorities to speak for God. It has also had great appeal to women practitioners and congregants, who use testimonies to mull over social conditions, interpersonal relationships, and personal tribulations, allowing them to connect more deeply with fellow congregants.[38]

For some Latinas, Pentecostalism has also been a dynamic medium for community organizing and social justice. In her article "The Ladies Are Warriors: Latina Pentecostals and Faith-Based Activism in New York," Elizabeth Rios writes that, "Latina Pentecostals have not let gender biases, fear, and other obstacles hinder them from serving others."[39] Rios focuses on a community of Puerto Rican Pentecostal women who are involved in progressive social justice organizing. They provide resources for the poor and needy through food programs, counseling, health care, homeless shelters, child care, and aid for domestic violence victims. Rios contrasts this commitment with the view that "the Pentecostal mindset has historically been defined as one that ministers to the individualistic and personal element, which makes it inner-directed and vertical," rather than geared toward social transformation.[40] The women in her study were also part of a multiracial, woman-centered ministry that mentored budding female pastors, which included a number of African American women.[41] Throughout her study Rios stresses the cross-cultural vision of progressive Latina Pentecostals, some of whom modeled their social justice activism on that of African American pastors. But female pastors' activism always bumped up against the gender hierarchies and norms of church and family. Religion scholar Gaston Espinosa explains that, "As at the Azusa Street revival itself, women's roles in the Hispanic Assemblies were somewhat paradoxical—women were exhorted to exercise their prophetic gifts in the public sphere but submit to their husband's authority in the private sphere of the home. Early Hispanic Pentecostals did not believe the point of the prophetic gifts was to erase gender distinctions, but rather to empower men and women for Christian service in the end-time drama in which they found themselves actors. This kind of paradoxical domesticity has remained the norm for many Hispanic Pentecostal women throughout the twentieth century."[42]

From Faith to Secular Activism

This recurring theme of only being "allowed" to go so far within the constraints of male-dominated power structures has resonance for Latina Pentecostals and Catholics, as well as African American women in the Black Church. As a multicultural woman of Puerto-Rican and Irish descent, freethought activist Margaret Downey grappled with many of these sexist religious prescriptions. Growing up in a devout Catholic Latino family in the 1950s and 1960s, her passion for freethought was sparked by the deep divide between a Catholic religious morality based on bowing down to good patriarchs and the bitter reality of her upbringing. Her own absentee father was a virtual stranger who never provided for his family:

> My father's abandonment of the family actually brought about some deep thinking concerning belief in a god. My father-figure could not be counted on to help in any way. My father-figure would not respond

> to any type of communication...Why would I honor such a man? *If we wanted or needed something it was up to us to make it happen.* From an early age I decided to give honor and respect to those who earned it! I was sitting in church when I realized that the people around me might as well have been praying to my father figure. *Their* "heavenly father" was not responding to their prayers and pleas either.[43]

Downey is part of a generation of freethought activists whose transition to non-belief coincided with second-wave feminism and the waning years of Jim Crow. In 1993, she founded the Freethought Society after a high-profile, anti-discrimination battle with the Boy Scouts of America over her son's rejection by a local troop.[44] The Boy Scout suit spanned nearly a decade and garnered national recognition for Downey. Nonetheless, she has not had the same kind of visibility as male leaders with doctorates and academic "cred." Struggling to get her AA degree as a seventeen-year-old single mother also made her acutely aware of the double standard for male success in the insular world of freethought/secular/atheist activism. She notes that "A lot of men were in control of the non-theist community when I first started and (they) made it hard for women to get into leadership positions such as (on the) board of directors or as officers." Although atheist activist Madalyn Murray O'Hair had long been a polarizing, high-profile, national figure, Downey's grassroots local leadership was the norm for many secular women organizers. Simply transitioning from faith to secularist activism was no guarantee that women would achieve parity in traditionally white male-dominated secular contexts. Male issues and priorities were still privileged as the "gender neutral" universal norm. National leadership and political platforms were still oriented around traditional themes of church/state separation and the creationism versus evolution divide. Coming from a multicultural family she also vowed that she would "change the (composition) of the nontheist community...to make it more diverse and inclusive."[45]

As a former teen mother, Downey's experiences were radically different from that of the average white middle-class male atheist who represents the most visible demographic within atheism. Downey describes being condemned as a sinner by the local priest at her boyfriend's church. Pregnant and scared, she recalls "being told that the priest might concede to allow us to marry…if we proved that we were worthy of his blessing." After the priest told her that both she and the baby inside her were sinners he advised her to take marriage classes with her boyfriend. When she accused the priest of hypocrisy because he'd never been married, he ordered her to leave.

Downey's encounters vividly underscore how the sexist prescriptions of Catholicism have motivated some Latinas to become non-believers. Schoolteacher and atheist Marialupe Duarte argues that most Latinos are seen as dogmatic devout Catholics, which leads to "condescending attitudes, abuse and deprivation of (our) voice in political and social environments."[46] In mainstream American media, older Latinas are seldom portrayed as anything more than rosary bead-clutching caregiver maids who shuttle from spicy tortilla factory kitchens to Catholic mass. With rare exception, older Latina film and TV characters' sole purpose is to dispense sage advice to anyone within earshot and meddle in their children's lives. The late Latina actress Lupe Ontiveros once commented that she'd played over one-hundred-and-fifty maids throughout her career in Hollywood. Clearly Ontiveros' willingness to work made her the industry's most prolific Latina actress because what contemporary white actress has been offered a maid role over one-hundred-and-fifty times? Zero. "Sexy" nannies notwithstanding, white character actresses rarely appear as maids or domestics in mainstream TV and film. While white women increasingly enjoy a wider range of roles that fall outside of the traditional mother-wife-girlfriend troika, the range of possibility for women of color is still grossly limited.[47] Ontiveros' experiences, and that of scores of Latina actresses, highlight how deeply entrenched racist sexist stereotypes and low cultural expectations impact professional opportunities. If, as Duarte believes, Latinos are seen as rosary bead-clutching religionists, then there is little in mainstream media to counter this view.

The Pew Hispanic report does not shed any light on the percentage of Latinos who identify as non-believers. Instead, it highlights the increasing number of Latinos (at 16%) who are religiously unaffiliated but cautions that "this suggests the unaffiliated are not non-religious as a group."[48] On the other hand, the 2008 American Religious Identification Survey cites 12% of Latinos as non-religious, although again there is no disaggregation of the non-religious as atheist or agnostic, as opposed to say spiritual or Deist. As Juhem Navarro-Rivera notes, "Though Latino Nones (including atheists and/or agnostics) are all around us, they are hard to find."[49] This is "Despite being the second-largest religious group among Latinos (after Catholics) and the fastest-growing religious group within the fastest-growing ethnic group in the United States." Navarro-Rivera laments the fact that mainstream media tend to ignore Latinos who don't "fit the stereotype of the poorly educated Spanish-speaking fanatic."[50] But the high rates of religious observance amongst Latinas cannot be separated from limited economic, educational, and social opportunities available to women of color. This is why the demonization of abortion is ground zero in secular women's struggle against religious authoritarianism. My WLP students frequently reflect on how many of their friends and acquaintances have gotten pregnant while in high school or even middle school. Most of their peers claim that abortion is not an option because they don't want to "kill" a baby or be condemned by God. One of the most common refrains that I hear is "while I am not personally for abortion, women should have the right to choose." Abortion, rather than pregnancy, is something that *other* girls do. Even though the dominant culture stigmatizes teen and/or single mothers of color, pregnancy is still celebrated as something a good woman submits to. And even though many girls see their teenaged peers with one, two, and sometimes three kids and no male support constantly struggling, they are still deeply ambivalent about, if not hostile to, abortion. Yet, when I talk to WLP students about forced pregnancy as slavery, and abortion as a life-saving, moral human right, their world views begin to shift.

Howard University student Georgina Capetillo contends that the right to abortion should be a leading humanist issue for Latinas breaking free from religion.[51] She cites the disproportionately young age that Latinas have children as a major barrier to their education and workforce participation. Capetillo believes that there is less sexism and misogyny in secular societies. While this is a matter of degree, what is less debatable is the fact that, in secularized societies (like Western Europe) with a more equitable balance between the private and public sphere, women enjoy greater personal freedom and professional mobility. Hence, secularism in and of itself doesn't provide greater gender parity but the benefits of a comprehensive social welfare safety net do. Secularism in a capitalist economy without unlimited access to reproductive health care, living wage jobs, transportation, housing, and education is especially untenable for women of color. In the U.S., morally-repressive attitudes about female sexuality and abortion go hand-in-hand with capitalist, market-based notions of women's bodies as private property. It's no accident then that the most Christian super-capitalist nation on the planet is the hub of a multi-billion dollar hard- and soft-core porn industry beefed up by ultra-violent, racially terroristic images of women of color. For women in the so-called post-feminist secularized U.S., liberty Americana style signifies hypersexuality and Virgin/whore morality. All of the mainstream messages that women of color receive about their sexuality revolve around these two polarizing figures. But since women of color can never be the Virgin, when compared with the white woman, they are supposed to be gloriously free of the guilt, shame, and modesty that "normal" women feel about their bodies. Clearly, sassy black vixens, spicy Latinas, earthy Native American "squaws," and slutty Asian dragon ladies can never be the sexually liberated "material girl" Madonna or the bodacious Virgin refugee strutting around in Sandra Cisneros' locker room. As a result, women of color are compelled to be more chaste, modest, and guilt-ridden about their sexuality. For some atheist women of color, rejecting these dichotomies strongly informs both their feminism and their shift to non-belief. As atheist artist and WLP program coordinator Diane Arellano explains, "I don't feel the shame or guilt that many of my religious women of color peers (feel). In my experience, my religious friends often feel the pressures of complying with 'good womanhood.' These pressures include having children at an early age that they aren't in the least economically ready for."[52]

The majority of women of color who come to this awareness do not make the daunting leap to non-belief. Gods, goddesses, spirits, and ancestors are still deeply seductive, culturally binding, and visceral in a way that the unvarnished natural world, and its sole guarantee of everlasting death, is not. Nonetheless, over the past few years more women of color have stepped up to assume leadership roles in secular, atheist, and humanist organizations. They have done so in a movement that is blithely ignorant of, if not explicitly hostile to, the lived experiences, cultural capital, community context, and social history of people of color in the U.S. In 2011, Kim Veal, president of the Black Non-Believers of Chicago, founded her group after being exasperated with participating in predominantly white groups where she was treated like she was an "enigma."[53] Echoing the sentiments of other non-believers of color who have been turned off by the vibe of white groups she says, "this was disenchanting; you don't know if they are truly interested in getting to know you or are trying to pick the brain of their new token."[54] Mandisa L. Thomas started the Black Non-Believers of Atlanta as a safe space for non-believers in the heavily evangelical South. Veal and Thomas, along with activists like Ayanna Watson of Black Atheists of America, Debbie Goddard and Jamila Bey of African Americans for Humanism, Nicome Taylor of my organization Black Skeptics Los Angeles, and Bridget Gaudette of Secular Woman, are part of a small wave of women of color leaders in the atheist movement. While national leadership amongst non-believers of color is still marginal, women of color have stepped up in greater numbers than men. Thomas attributes this to "our dominance in the community and our natural leadership roles. We're mothers and career oriented; a lot of us are very dominant and…passionate about helping non-believers. We're coming out of these sexist/misogynist roles and asserting ourselves a lot more."[55] Thomas' comment underscores the paradox of atheist organizing amongst African Americans. Black women are the most steadfastly religious group in the nation, yet it is precisely because they receive the brunt of sexualized racist stereotyping and objectification that they have become more vocal in atheist organizing. In addition, black women non-believers are continuing a long tradition (ironically fostered in the Black Church and religious civic and charitable organizations) of community organizing and outreach. And, like their religious foremothers, they are encountering some of the same sexist opposition and resistance to women's leadership. As Thomas notes:

> I believe women are at the forefront…because we're willing to stand up and take the hit. There are quite a few men out there that could stand up but they're not. I often detect some anti-feminist resentment that won't respect what I have to say. One of the gentlemen in my group will say the same thing I have to say and he will be respected and I won't. We still have the same patriarchal mindset as those in the religious community.[56]

This patriarchal mindset is not exclusive to the religious community but is embedded within the dominant culture as a whole. As I have argued elsewhere, non-believers are not magically exempt from sexism, patriarchy, and white supremacy. If black women's leadership on secular, atheist, and humanist issues is devalued it is because black men's uplift is still privileged as the linchpin of progress for African Americans. For black women, being at the intersections is simply a part of living and breathing. Writing in the groundbreaking anthology *Homegirls*, Barbara Smith captures the dialectical nature of black women's experiences:

> The concept of the simultaneity of oppression is still the crux of a Black feminist understanding of political reality and...one of the most significant ideological contributions of Black feminist thought...We saw no reason to rank oppressions, or, as many forces in the Black community would have us do, to pretend that sexism, among all the "isms," was not happening to us. Black feminists' efforts to comprehend the complexity of our situation as it was actually occurring...began to deflate some of the cherished myths about Black womanhood, for example that we are 'castrating matriarchs' or that we are more economically privileged than Black men.[57]

Smith's comment captures the crosshairs position that black women have always occupied. It's a dynamic that is reflected in Maria Stewart's speeches and Ida B. Wells' battles with sexist black male and racist white female leadership. It's embodied by the marginalization of sexual terrorism against black women in civil rights history. Wells' activism was consistently ignored and marginalized by white feminists and black male civil rights leaders. Organized opposition to the lynching of black men was viewed as the rightful focus of early 20th century black civil and human rights activism. The sexual exploitation and rape of black women was not accorded the same weight within the modern civil rights movement. And Wells was perhaps the first journalist to speak out on the racist and sexist implications of lynching. In her editorials she consistently blasted the hypocrisy of white savagery against black men accused of raping white women and exposed the long history of black female sexual exploitation by white men. Despite decades of black feminist activism, the notion that black women "have it better" than black men, and are the toweringly strong, rock-hard matriarchs ball-busting a race of cowed emasculated men, continues to be the mantra in both mainstream and black America. This falsehood makes sexism seem like a fantasy that black women have cooked up to deflect from the "real" problem of racism against black men. So it is not surprising that secular black women find themselves in much the same position as supposedly less liberated black female religionists. As journalist Jill Nelson notes, "Sometimes it seems as if everyone wants a piece of me to use for their own—usually negative—purposes. White male politicians demonize me as a welfare cheat, illegitimate baby-making machine...white feminist women ignore me, cut deals for themselves, and then invite me to the meeting, panel, or forum as an afterthought...to give their self-interested agenda the image of inclusion. Black men single me out when they need either help or an example of why they are "endangered" or hindered."[58] This is the context in which black female secular activists do their work. The concerns of our communities are not the concerns of the dominant culture, nor are they the concerns of the secular/atheist/humanist movements at large, which essentially reflect the dominant culture.

* * *

Black women can pray until Jesus comes down from the cross but they will always be among America's "original" heathens. In the American imagination, black women are the poster children for disreputable irresponsible motherhood and Latina "illegals" a close second. From birth to adolescence, every girl of color must navigate a political climate in which Ronald Reagan's racist welfare queen caricature casts long shadows. When mainstream media wants to find a face for shiftless families on the dole, this caricature is always waiting dependably in the wings. At the height of the 2012 recession, the *L.A. Times* served up red meat for welfare queen watchers with a front page article entitled "Caught in the Cycle of Poverty."[59] The article profiles 27-year-old Natalie Cole, a jobless, unmarried, unskilled, black mother with four kids. It trots out an expert from Harvard who sagely proclaims that "poverty is bad for kids." The expert offers no further analysis on how the richest, most militarized nation on the planet pimps out its children. Instead, the reader is given a titillating tour of Cole's hot mess of personal failure and pathology. We learn that Cole comes from a long line of young single mothers and that by the time she was 17 she was raising two children. We learn that she can't be bothered to do a résumé or use birth control to avoid having a fifth child. The prayer *"God in heaven, hear my prayer keep me in thy loving care"* is taped to her bedroom wall. Clearly Cole won't be getting an Oxygen, TLC or Lifetime reality show any time soon.

The tagline to the article foreshadows Cole's moral failure. In naturalist language that apes a Theodore Dreiser novel, Cole's fate is summed up by the observation that "Choices, challenges and chaos keep undermining a woman's attempt to escape the struggles her mother and grandmother faced." Cole "wants to provide a better life for her children but seems not to know how." She is the polar opposite of the hard-working Erin Brockovich white single mother strivers or undocumented immigrant Horatio Algers that power the inspirational human interest narratives of contemporary mainstream journalism. Her inability to chart a course out of grinding poverty represents the failing of an entire race, a criminal urban culture, a community that is so steeped in ghetto chaos and so far outside of normal American values as to be third world.

The *Times*' verdict on this struggling young woman was especially enraging to me because during the last semester of my Women of Color in the U.S. class I found out that one of my most inquisitive students was pregnant at sixteen. A few weeks before, I'd met with her mother to see why she'd been ditching class. Her mother told me that the Women of Color class was one of the few that she enjoyed. Still, she was frequently absent and had a failing grade. As Diane Arellano writes in her article "Next Wave Atheist Leaders and White Privilege,"[60] Boys are not generally expected to stay at home and watch their younger siblings or go with their mothers to clean houses. While boys of color face numerous challenges in K-12 education, they are not expected to be caregivers or sacrifice their life ambitions for an unplanned pregnancy. During discussions about abortion and birth control, students are quick to condemn girls who have unplanned pregnancies, often moralizing that "promiscuous" girls should simply "suffer the consequences" and have the baby. Several of my Women's Leadership Project alums, who worked their asses off to become the first in their families to go to college, speak of friends who have had children shortly after graduating from high school. As budding feminists they are overly familiar with the double-edged "validation" pregnancy supposedly provides working-class young women of color. Inundated with media propaganda that hyper-sexualizes black and Latina women and demonizes abortion, young women are damned if they do and damned if they don't.

In these South Los Angeles school-communities, only a tiny fraction of the student body goes on to four-year colleges. Small evangelical storefront churches grossly outnumber living-wage job centers. God and Jesus are touted as some of the biggest "cultural" influences. High teen pregnancy rates are a symptom of the expendability of "other people's children" (to quote education activist Lisa Delpit).[61] Thirty-five years ago, scoring a living-wage job with benefits was still a possibility for a South L.A. teenager with a high school diploma from Washington Prep High School. Though waning, the aerospace industry was still a major source of employment, job stability, and middle-class entry for African American workers. Defined benefit plans were the rule rather than the exception. The War on Drugs had not yet ravaged urban neighborhoods. The pell-mell violence of gang warfare and drive-by shootings was largely unheard of. The South L.A. of my childhood was political canvassing and selling chocolate bars alone door-to-door for the elementary school candy drive. It was sprawling across the prickly lawns of immaculately-kept, single-family homes in marathon games of tag and touch football. It was the fascination of seeing the streetlights flicker on in the summertime, when kids played in the streets well into the night. And it was the ever present fear of the male predators—on the street and behind closed doors—that populate every girl's childhood.

Back then, the misnomer "South Central" was used as a catch-all description of Los Angeles' black communities. But the term had not yet devolved into a global pop culture epithet. Typical of how South Central/South Los Angeles gets read is this racist description from a white Australian writer commenting on the Space Shuttle Endeavor's trek through the community to its final resting place at the California Science Center in October 2012: "It's the only time in my life I'm ever going to say I wish I lived in South Central L.A.—home of the riots, gangs, and many of the city's murders."[62] South L.A. is a cesspit of violence and chaos where riots, gangs, and murder dominate. No sane person would choose to live there. And there is nothing socially or culturally redeeming about the communities that lie behind the headlines of murder and mayhem. This was and is the prevailing Middle American view of black and Latino communities. Over the past two decades, this racist propaganda has been heightened by the regime of mass incarceration and the deeply-ingrained belief that violence and crime epitomize African American culture. Hyper-religiosity thrives amidst the downward spiral of the African American dream. Back in the day, it was taken as gospel that each new generation would do better than their parents' generation. Many people of color believed that the promise of unlimited upward mobility was what uniquely defined being American. Native-born Americans were suckled on the Technicolor myth that people from other cultures festered in blind envy over "our" standard of living. Even the most downtrodden American could eventually enjoy a standard of living unrivaled anywhere else in the world. Younger generations would be more prosperous and better educated than previous generations. But in post-racial exceptionalist America, black college graduates are less likely to meet much less exceed their parents' incomes. Indeed, it has been said that when America catches a cold, black America gets the flu. The titanic wealth gap between white and black America means that socioeconomic mobility for black college graduates has actually declined. Priced out of the rental market, greater numbers of young adults are camping out on their parents' sofas, squirreling up in their old bedrooms and competing for entry-level jobs that once would have only required a high school diploma. Thirty years ago, scoring a living-wage job with benefits was still a possibility for a South Los Angeles teenager with only a high school diploma. Now, having a college degree is the absolute bare minimum for getting a decent paying job and it pays not to have a first or last name that's "too Black."[63] Thirty years ago it was less common for African American families to have relatives in the prison system. Growing up in the 1970s and 1980s, I was the only one among my close friends who had relatives that had been incarcerated. Having incarcerated family members was a source of embarrassment, if not shame. Now the regime of mass incarceration touches many black families and virtually all segregated black neighborhoods. According to the Justice on Trial report, one in six black men has been incarcerated and one in three black men between the ages of 20 and 29 is incarcerated. In some instances, whites with criminal records elicit more favorable responses from employers than do black or Latino applicants with no records.[64] Mainstream media focus on the staggering unemployment rates of men of color has eclipsed attention to the economic downturn's equally devastating impact on black women. Deepening segregation, diminishing job prospects due to the gutting of public sector employment (23% of black women are employed in public sector jobs), and mental health crises have pushed more women of color into the church pews, or alternative spirituality, with a vengeance.

Closer to God: Black and Latino Communities

On a quaint corner off Manchester in South Los Angeles, the Deeper Life Bible Ministries flank a defunct TV repair shop, a liquor store, and a dry cleaners. Tacked onto a hulking security door, its tiny slapdash sign is like a decal for suspended time. There is always another storefront church waiting to be discovered on these streets. They peer spectrally from amidst the beauty shops and the boarded-up businesses that sputtered and died after a few seasons. They squeeze between the brownfields and vacant lots that bookend some thoroughfares, dueling with the makeshift 99-cent stores that pass for commercial retail development in urban communities of color. Wherever there is high poverty, a glut of vacant cheap rentals, and a tax code that toadies to faith, houses of worship will proliferate with whack-a-mole speed. Before the dawn of the storefronts it was possible to catch movies a stone's throw away from each other on Manchester—a double helping of pulp in *Blacula* and the Ray Milland gem *Frogs*; a triple threat of *The Exorcist*, *The Shining*, and *The Fog*. Built in the late 1930s, in their heyday these theatres were symbols of the galvanic influence of Hollywood on white suburbia. They embodied a time when South Los Angeles was white, Inglewood was to be the gateway to the Academy Awards, and the film industry taught everyone how to be a good, patriotic American.[65] In their waning Reagan-Bush administration years, they were B-movie havens that provided local kids, steeped in our largely black insular world, with a dependable weekend escape. For us, these single screen theatres were the last gasp of celluloid nirvana, the swan song before the blaxploitation reels were carted off from the murk of the projection booth and multiplexes began their reign. One theatre was converted to a church. The other was briefly inhabited by a church but is now boarded up and cadaverous, remnants of the phrase "Coming soon" still frozen on the marquee from when the theatre closed down in the '80s.

Now a predominantly black and Latino community, Inglewood was the scene of several Klan marches in the 1920s. As greater numbers of African Americans moved to the city during the post-war era, ferocious struggles over integration erupted. Once considered a fount of corn-fed Americana, post-white flight Inglewood was deemed to be the heart of the ghetto. The area was dismissively dubbed "Ingle-Watts," a moniker that belies a violent history of curfews for blacks and virtually lily-white schools up until the '70s. Even though most white Inglewood residents did their civic duty and fled to outlying westerly neighborhoods, 2010 census figures classify 23% of Inglewood's residents as white. This quirk is due to significant numbers of Latino residents claiming white status. Language barriers, colorism, racial discrimination in employment, "racialized" gang turf wars, and immigration continue to influence relations between blacks and browns. But provisional white status for Latinos exists in the shadow of white supremacist colonialist legacies of American terrorism in the Southwest. At the same time, skin color and caste hierarchies in Latin America shape Latino perceptions of African Americans and darker-skinned Latinos of African descent. Numerous studies have shown that skin color is an index of class mobility and social acceptance. So while darker-skinned Latinos are not able to access white privilege ala European American whites, they are still marked as immigrant others (regardless of actual generation), not black others who have "squandered" the supposed natural benefits of being born in the U.S.

On the other hand, black resentment of the growing Latino presence in formerly African American strongholds like South Los Angeles is a very real part of these schisms. Over the past decade, the shrinking black Los Angeles population and widening achievement gap in K-12 schools have elicited a push for progressive, culturally-responsive reforms that specifically target black students. While local social justice organizations like the Community Coalition and CADRE[66] have often spearheaded these efforts, they have also been joined by churches and faith-based organizations. When white secular critics of organized religion condemn churches and faith-based organizations, there is typically no recognition of the pivotal role these institutions play in segregated communities of color. Historically, secular activists like A. Philip Randolph and Black Panther Party head Huey P. Newton were well aware of the peril of attacking religious institutions in a vacuum. Despite their vociferous criticism of what Randolph dubbed "orthodox Christianity," they tailored their activism, mindful of the key role the Black Church played in every aspect of black political, cultural, and socioeconomic life. As Anthony Pinn notes, "The (Black Panther) Party softened its position when it recognized the central role the church held in Black communities. Like the Communist Party, the Panthers' recognized that recruitment would be difficult if open hostility existed with the black churches. Hence, the Panthers fostered a relationship of convenience and socio-political necessity, but without a firm commitment to its theological underpinnings."[67]

In short, activists like Randolph and the Panthers knew that their initiatives would fail if they weren't culturally responsive. However legitimate it was to slam the Black Church, non-religious organizations had to provide a viable alternative. As one of the most vociferous black critics of organized religion, activist-intellectual Hubert Harrison grasped this dilemma but was ultimately stymied by it. In his essay "The Negro, A Conservative," he blasts Christianity as the fount of black mental and physical subjugation.[68] Since "Christian America created the color line…it should seem that Negroes, of all Americans, would be found in the Freethought fold since they have suffered more than any other class from the dubious blessings of Christianity."[69] That this was not the case convinced Harrison of the backwardness of black social thought and intellectualism. Blacks were politically stunted by their blind allegiance to Christianity. Blacks reveled in being the oppressed underdog, dutifully lapping up white Christian America's moral table scraps. And the few black "Agnostics" Harrison knew of were not "openly avowed."[70] Thus, "so long as our 'leaders' are dependent on the favor of our masses for their livelihood, just so long will they express the thought of the masses." For Harrison, political radicalism, grassroots organizing, and scientific inquiry were incompatible with the black community's overwhelming investment in organized religion. Religion kept black folk shackled, unable to confront the intellectual challenges of the 20th century. Because the "church among Negroes exerts a more powerful influence than anything in the sphere of ideas," Harrison believed African Americans would remain a "servile population."[71]

As one of the first truly public 20th century intellectuals, the self-taught Harrison bucked black orthodoxy with his unwavering embrace of freethought rationalism and challenge to intra-racial black hierarchies of color caste. In a statement that has powerful resonance today, Harrison lamented that "the slang term nigger is heard more frequently among Negroes themselves than among white people; and in love, courtship, marriage, and their social life generally, lightness of color is the great desideratum."[72] Blacks' blind religious faith, colorism, and liberal use of the word "nigger" as self-description were yoked in his mind. Harrison believed that colorism was rampant in certain Northeastern black churches. In these congregations, preference for light skin over dark skin determined the social pecking order and ostracized darker-skinned blacks.[73] It was blacks' dirty little secret, the bludgeon of a self-hating mulatto elite, and further evidence of black conservatism. Harrison correctly noted that colorism had its most insidious effect on black women, who were degraded by the Eurocentric beauty standards which dominated every aspect of film, theater, and commercial advertizing.

Nearly a century later these issues are still burning in African American communities where many black women are beholden to the moral universe of the Bible and the collection plate. Colorism is still the norm in mainstream advertizing, film, and TV (embodied by a global multi-million dollar industry of skin lighteners that are popular in Asian, Latin American, and African countries), which routinely lightens actresses of color to appeal to "crossover" audiences. While the number of American "nones" (those not affiliated with organized religion) has risen, religious devoutness amongst black women has not budged. Religious devoutness and "spiritualism" have deepened against the backdrop of black women's disfiguration, in a global climate where beauty marketers have reaped millions preying on black women's self-loathing, peddling hair weaves, colored contacts lenses, and skin lighteners as the gateway to nirvana. What is the relationship between these trends and black female hyper-religiosity? The connective tissue between the obscene glut of hair shops, beauty parlors, and storefront churches that dominates the built-landscape in "inner city" black neighborhoods, the street corners littered with telephone poles sporting signs that extol the magical properties of authentic "Indian hair"? In the ravaged economy of segregated urban communities, bone-straight Rapunzel-esque hair and God-on-demand seem to be the only bankable magical commodities. For some black women, "God" is a medium for self-invention, self-reflection, and self-creativity, a redemptive space in the midst of a crushing invisibility that flowing Rapunzel-esque hair cannot remedy. If we are closer to God then there must be a reason for the unrelenting violence against black women, the epidemic of black women who are beaten, stabbed, stalked, and murdered without so much as a whimper from the community. If we are closer to God then the blight of segregation must be part of some cosmic design, some epic plan of heavenly deliverance that will punish those who lie, cheat, and steal in "his" name.

Historically, black non-believers and secularists have been aligned with radical politics. Yet the careers of both Harrison and Randolph attested to the failed promise of freethought and radical politics, specifically socialism, amongst African Americans. In many respects, Harrison's lament about black conservatism was reflected in Randolph's tireless yet frustrated efforts to yoke socialist activism with black intellectualism, trade unionism, and community organizing. As Jervis Anderson notes about Randolph, "it was his dim sense that ... getting religion was a way of escaping their social condition...and if that kind of emotion were translated into politics, it would represent 'the awakening and even the uprising of the masses.'"[74] Writing in the *Messenger*'s 1919 Thanksgiving issue, Randolph declared, "We wish to give thanks. We do not wish to thank God for anything nor do our thanks include gratitude for the things which most persons give thanks at this period. With us, we are thankful for different things and to a different Deity. Our Deity is the toiling masses of the world." Radical politics was the foundation of both Harrison and Randolph's freethought. It was a world view driven by the fervent wish that African Americans would embrace socialism as the most workable solution for their condition. Yet, the course of American social justice has favored legislative remedies that left structural inequities of race, class, gender, and sexuality untouched.

Randolph, like James Baldwin decades later, believed that misguided religious fervor could be channeled into political activism. But his view was short-sighted. As the glaring example of the U.S. illustrates, modernity and secularization are not synonymous, and secularization has rarely translated into political activism amongst people of color. Rather, faith for the "toiling masses" is not only a means of escape but of enduring, meaning-making, and community-building—especially in an economy where black wealth has virtually shriveled into non-existence, living-wage jobs are a figment of the distant past, and blight is pervasive in many black neighborhoods. Like mold in a moist environment, hyper-religiosity thrives under capitalism. It festers and entrances in gross extremes of poverty and wealth, binding the poor and indemnifying the super-rich. When asked to name an adult role model or inspiration in their lives, some of my WLP students cite their pastors as their biggest influence. The local church across the street from Washington Prep advertizes free lunch programs for youth. Scholarships for black students are pipelined through some of the city's most prominent black churches. In communities like these, where mass incarceration touches nearly every family, ex-offenders and prisoner advocates use churches as a platform to organize around voting rights, employment, and housing.

* * *

In the post-Civil and Voting Rights Acts era of so-called equal opportunity under the law, residential segregation has only intensified. King's widely caricatured vision of little black and white kids holding hands is the stuff of Hallmark cards, PC liberal arts college brochures, and smarmy GOP propaganda. American K-12 schools are distant galaxies separated by inner city (i.e., black, Latino and "deprived") or suburban (i.e., white and privileged), and "diversity" has become quick and dirty shorthand for smacking down uppity Negroes who want to talk institutional racism. It's for this reason that the social capital of black believers and non-believers is closely intertwined—why black people, the most staunchly Christian group in America, can live in a

Christian Nation and still be reviled as the heathen other. And it is for this reason that religious and secular whites are bonded by economic privilege, by homes and neighborhoods that have higher property values than that of the average person of color, and by the security of a police state that is designed to protect them. For example, discriminatory lending practices such as those employed by former mortgage giant Countrywide make residential mobility elusive for people of color. Despite the fantasy of unlimited post-racial access and mobility, a U.S. 2010 report entitled "Separate and Unequal: The Neighborhood Gap for Blacks, Hispanics, and Asians" concluded that residential segregation is even more intractable now than two decades ago. Indeed "as black-white segregation has slowly declined since 1990, blacks have become less isolated from Hispanics and Asians, but their exposure to whites has hardly changed. Affluent blacks have only marginally higher contact with whites than do poor blacks."[75] Hence, blacks and Latinos of all income levels generally live in black and Latino neighborhoods. Most tellingly, "The average affluent black or Hispanic household lives in a poorer neighborhood than the average low-income white resident."[76]

If higher-income people of color are not able to buy homes in white enclaves and escape the "ghetto," what does this say about the nature of black and Latino social capital? About the white conservative lie that Newt Gingrich's mythical poor neighborhoods are cesspits for the lazy and shiftless? Because of the mobility gap, communities of color are more likely to be economically depressed and heavily transit-dependent. Transit-dependency means isolation. It means less access to living-wage jobs, quality schools, affordable housing, and park space—resources that have been deemed privileges, not rights, in the world's greatest democracy. Small wonder then that some of our youth, like WLP twelfth-grader Victory Yates, view their churches as a lifeline. Even though her faith in God has wavered due to the hardship she's experienced as a former foster care youth, her church is one of the few safe spaces in a neighborhood where young girls are routinely accosted by would-be pimps on the street. In our conversations about faith, she expresses curiosity about agnosticism and frustration with the so-called therapeutic power of prayer. Naturally inquisitive, she's begun to make the first tentative steps toward investigating the truth claims of religion. At the intersection of two freeways, the street where Victory lives with her family is served by several bus lines and a shuttle to the Green Line train. For churches in poor and working class communities, transportation plays an important role in keeping congregants and attracting new ones. The ubiquitous church van is a permanent fixture in working-class black and Latino neighborhoods. After all, being too poor, sick or infirm shouldn't be a barrier to worship and beefing up the collection plate. This come-as-you-are approach keeps many small working-class congregations in business. As theologian Otto Maduro observes, owning a van is essential for Pentecostal pastors. For "many members new to the United States and subject to the whims of a fickle job market, shifting living conditions and unreliable public transportation—having a van is no small thing." The majority of those who use public transportation in the U.S. are women, youth and the elderly. In cities like Los Angeles that lack fully accessible affordable public transportation, having to rely exclusively on public buses and trains is a mark of second-class citizenship. As the capital of American car culture, walking or riding public transportation in L.A. is a byzantine process. The unwieldy sprawl of the city defies easy navigation for bus riders. Making bus connections can take hours; while walking to a job, school campus or health care facility is a luxury that only a lucky few have.

The dearth of integrated pedestrian culture obscures the presence of storefront Pentecostal churches. On hot nights the vitality of these churches surfaces in tiny snatches, when their doors open onto traffic and pounding testimony drifts out into the air as congregants sway in the pews, arms-raised, fresh off from work, from the 212 bus that plows from Hollywood grunge to Hawthorne doldrums. For drivers, the world of buses and trains, like that of the storefront church, is a parallel universe, an alternate city with a separate timescape, outside of the straightjacketing rush of chaotic modernity, freedom, and confinement that characterizes being dependent on a private car. Both churches and public transit straddle the divide between public and private space. Mental retreat and solitude are only possible through public immersion, loss of control, and surrender—to the will of God, the pastor, and the good of the congregation, to the immediacy of waiting, riding with scores of strangers, and abiding by the rules of being a passenger.

In the absence of community-based institutions that offer cultural reinforcement, social welfare, and fellowship, what does humanism have to offer poor and working-class communities of color? This question goes to the heart of why Latinas are leading the surge in Pentecostalism. It speaks to why national surveys on the increase of non-believers show that atheism remains a predominantly male thing. Several years ago an older white male rep from a major atheist organization suggested to me that science could rescue black people from their reliance on religion. This is a common view amongst white atheists who can't see beyond the lily white inner sanctums of atheist conferences and Sam Harris best-sellers hawking "science" as savior and moral arbiter. The arrogance of New Atheist discourse that reductively focuses on raising "science" (shorn of its historical context, cultural baggage, and discursive power) to the status of shining antidote to social injustice is especially insidious for communities of color.[77] "Science" is not nor has it ever been a neutral arbiter of moral value. Western scientific traditions in particular have always been value laden, shaped by the vagaries of historical and cultural context, and frequently used to buttress social inequality and regimes of power. For example, discussing how 19th century scientific inquiry on racial difference revolved around black bodies, science historian Evelynn Hammonds noted:

> If we just take African Americans as an example, there's not a single body part that hasn't been subjected to this kind of analysis. You'll find articles in the medical literature about the Negro ear, and the Negro nose, and the Negro leg, and the Negro heart, and the Negro eye, and the Negro foot — and it's every single body part. And they're constantly looking for some organ that might be so fundamentally different in size and character that you can say this is something specific to the Negro versus whites and other groups. Scientists are part of their social context. Their ideas about what race is are not simply scientific ones, are not simply driven by the data that they are working with. That it's also informed by the societies in which they live."[78]

The frequently-invoked New Atheist claim that Western civilization is ipso facto morally superior than that of backward, barbarous non-Western (i.e., Islamic) civilizations is undermined by the West's relentless militarism, titanic wealth gaps, and mass incarceration of people of color. In October 2012, this contradiction was underscored by the mainstream media's championing of a young Pakistani girl named Malala

Yousufsai, who was shot by the Taliban because she wanted to go to school. The Taliban's brutal religious fundamentalism has been widely condemned as an affront to human and women's rights. Although the Taliban's attack on Yousufsai was the subject of global outrage, anti-imperialist activists noted that the routine killing of thousands of Pakistani children by American drones never elicited a similar response or garnered media attention.[79] American military might (backed by the West's finest, most advanced science) has always been framed as moral. Dark others who get caught in the crossfire of U.S.' defense of "democracy" are simply expendable as collateral damage. It's okay to bomb Muslim children "back to the Stone Age"[80] because they come from a savage culture that is in violent opposition to secular and Western Judeo Christian values. In the same vein, simply relying on science to define a moral path might tell us that African Americans who commit a disproportionate number of the nation's violent crimes and pack its prisons are a deviant population in need of containment and social engineering.

At the end of the day, young women like Victory, Vanessa, and Nellie can't just trot down the street to the local center of reason and science for a healing dose of evolution when there is a crisis in their families. Over the past several years, the gutting of social services, as well as diminishing job opportunities, has only increased the burdens of caregiving on working-class women of color. For some, involvement in faith communities is an antidote to the depression, stress, anxiety, and isolation they experience being their families' 24/7 caregiver, breadwinner, counselor, and on-call maid. Certainly, the devastation of the recession has made the programs and resources (no matter how nominal) of small churches more appealing to residents of low income communities. Stable, nonprofit social welfare organizations that serve the *working poor* are few and far between. Increasingly, the class divide between middle- and working-class people of color is narrowing, while the divide between working class-whites and middle-class people of color is widening. Hence, whites generally live in white neighborhoods with greater access to social services, park space, and job centers. According to U.S. 2010, "in the 50 metros with the largest black populations, there is none where average exposure to neighborhood poverty is less than 20 percent higher than that of whites, and only two metros where **affluent** blacks live in neighborhoods that are less poor than those of the average white."[81]

These findings belie white nationalist claims that people of color are making gains at the expense of working-class white people. The neighborhood gap signifies that white working-class people have *greater* mobility than the black and Latino middle class. Thus, melting pot bromides are even more of a sham now than they were during the so-called Ozzie and Harriet/Leave it to Beaver era. Black and Latino homeowners hold onto a wisp of middle-class status in communities where spectral storefront churches are vectors of poverty and segregation, not the cultural primitivism that some New Atheists decry.

Black Macho and God's Reality Show

During a discussion on black humanism and non-belief at Zion Hill Baptist Church, one woman, who described herself as spiritual and agnostic, lamented the absence of cultural community spaces that weren't faith-based. "There are no other centers in our community besides the churches," she said, over a generous spread of refreshments that had been provided by church staff. While she decried the white supremacist orientation of Christianity she also acknowledged the ways in which churches support the community with social services, gathering space, recreational opportunities, financial literacy seminars, and counseling. Zion Hill has a gym, several meeting rooms, and two chapels. Pastor Seth Pickens is keenly aware of the need to maintain visibility in a community that already has a glut of churches. Block clubs and other civic groups hold their meetings at the church. Throughout the year it hosts neighborhood street functions that are open to all on its grounds.

Assuming a "whole community" posture is something that the best progressive churches do expertly and the malfeasant ones ape half-assed in order to exploit parishioners and keep them dependent. Of course, churches have always relied upon this interface of public and private. For African American men (and a tiny handful of women) they were some of the only avenues of unchecked wealth, glory, power, and influence. Barred from private enterprise and most government employment in the pre-Civil and Voting Rights Acts era, "the only professional jobs open to blacks were pastoring and school teaching."[82] Barred from decent schools and higher education, aspiring African Americans could eke out their own version of the American dream through the pulpit. How else could an uneducated black man become a capitalist and tax exempt "industrialist" without the fetters of white America?[83] How else could an Eddie Long (embattled pastor of New Birth Missionary Church), other than through professional sports, buy land, amass a fleet of cars, estates and planes, and become a multi-millionaire predator?

Historically, the social construction of the black body as public commodity and ultimate racial other was critical to the emergence of African American faith-based enterprise and "social capitalism." This is a nuance that twenty-something Ponzi schemer Ephren Taylor was well-versed in. In 2010, Long sponsored Taylor at his megachurch. Taylor was touted as a boy genius financial adviser who made his fortune developing video games. A few years after his appearance with Long, the boy genius was accused by the Securities and Exchange Commission of bilking millions from elderly African American parishioners. The scam "reached into churches nationwide, from Long's megachurch in Atlanta to Joel Osteen's Lakewood Church congregation in Houston." As with most Ponzi charlatans, Taylor promised his "investors" a hefty return, duping them into believing they were investing in mundane businesses like laundromats and gas stations. Introducing Taylor to his flock, Long stressed that "everything he says is based on the word of God." Taylor shrewdly crafted his pitch to appeal to his predominantly black audiences' desire to get rich quick while charitably "rebuilding" the community. His video seminars slather on the race pride. Bespectacled and baby-faced, in one talk he brags of having achieved a "black history record" as the youngest African American to own a publicly-traded company. Unlike the faith-based financial predator of yore, Taylor banked on his youth and slick Millennial generation sensibilities to reel in his victims. A website created by one of his duped investors claims that transactions took place at Long's church as well as a smaller church called Living Word Christian Center in Forest Park, Illinois. Taylor's website describes how "his socially-conscious programs revive older neighborhoods, create affordable homes for working-class families, turn tenants into buyers." Prosperity gospels are all about supernaturalist bootstrapping, and bootstrapping is all about storytelling, dishing up shop-worn themes of the American dream to the spiritually parched and flailing in the desert. Blemished heroism and the charismatic power of personal narratives of struggle, triumph, and redemption are crucial to their seductiveness. Americana is nothing without the gilded sheen of the prosperity gospel, extolling free enterprise and the supernatural might of free markets. God helps those who generously help themselves. He rewards hard work with riches, riches and more riches, and condemns sloth with poverty. He wants faithful hardnosed bootstrappers like Long to enjoy all the fruits of their labor and to provide less fortunate less talented souls with guidance for enjoying theirs. Tithing, unswerving devotion, sexual favors, ass licking, and whoring are only a small price to pay for access to the Midas touch of a Long, Osteen, Dollar, Price, or Jakes.

The gospel of social capitalism was unpacked with salacious brio in writer-director Russ Parr's 2012 film *The Undershepherd.* Set in Los Angeles under luminous blue skies, the film provides a window onto the cesspit of thug religiosity. In the opening scene two "junior pastors," Roland and L.C., from First Baptist church, chafe at the leadership of a cabal of older pastors led by veteran actors Louis Gossett Jr. and Bill Cobbs. When the head pastor is exposed in an embezzlement scandal, the young pastors embark upon separate ministerial paths. In typical Cain and Abel form, the story focuses on the opposite arcs of virtuous Roland, who branches out to start his own storefront church, and best friend turned rival, corrupt messiah complex preacher L.C. Roland skews toward Billy Graham; L.C. toward Jim Bakker. L.C. assumes leadership of First Baptist and spirals down into a cesspit of sex, lies, and depravity, Roland and his good woman/first lady minister to the poor and struggle over the light bill. Played by the expertly diabolical Isaiah Washington, L.C. is a caricature of swaggering preacherly sleaze and machismo. He dips generously into the church till, abuses his wife, impregnates a senior pastor's daughter, and pins the rap on one of his minions, then orders him to take the woman to get an abortion (which, like most female characters on the big screen, she's adamantly opposed to). Parr pulls his punches at the beginning of the film by having a commentator provide a "this doesn't reflect all of the Black Church" disclaimer. Moreover, gender roles are rigidly prescribed; the black female characters fit neatly into the Jezebel/temptress or loyal, God-fearing/caregiver mode. For the females, being God-fearing is signified by prairie dresses with "tastefully" revealing necklines. The men are locked in a duel for power, but the women's clichéd backbone-of-the-church status bear out Jill Nelson's caveat about the nexus of religious power and gender: "If black women boycotted religious institutions for a week, they'd cease to function. Instead we continue to worship faithfully, tithe, answer the phone, and cook the minister's lunch."[84] Nonetheless, the film ably spotlights predatory religious masculinity. L.C. liberally uses scripture to justify his debauchery. The church elders are portrayed as inept, overbearing and incapable of leading their way out of a paper bag. Meetings devolve into bickering and incoherence. The pecking order for who gives a sermon turns on ego and dominance. L.C. repeatedly attempts to upstage one of the elders with overwrought "can I get a witness" whooping and hollering. Church funds are secretly used to buy a condo hideaway in the Bahamas. The coup de grace comes when L.C. tells a church deaconess who accuses him of being a fraud that *he* is God, kisses the microphone he's holding, then proceeds to poke her breast with it.

Throughout the film, Parr contrasts L.C.'s lust for stardom and celebrity with Roland's humble struggle just to keep a roof over his storefront congregation's head. L.C. brings in the cameras and turns his services into a reality show. He browbeats parishioners and even publicly chastises a shiftless father with a new girlfriend on his arm for deserting his kids. L.C.'s gross hubris becomes a metaphor and cautionary tale for the pitfalls of prosperity gospel demagoguery. It's implied that Roland is closer to the Christ model and L.C. to the Pharissee. True Christians don't act this way, or so the party line goes. The L.C. types pervert the true spirit and letter of the Bible and betray its overriding message of tolerance, charity, love, and humanity. Thus, L.C. and his real life counterpart Creflo Dollar give Christianity a bad name. In 2012, Dollar was arrested for hitting and choking his teenage daughter after she defied him about attending a party. He was soundly trounced in the media for hypocrisy, abusiveness, and sullying "true" Christian values, even as his flock predictably rallied around him with "he's a true Man of God" declarations. So what would Jesus, protector of the meek and defenseless, do? He would cast out the false prophet Dollars of the world and protect the lambs from their predations. Why hasn't this happened? Why do the prosperity gospel predators continue to rake in tax-exempt billions decade after decade with no divine oversight or intervention? The standard Christian rationalization is that they will pay in hell. But instead of punishment one can see collusion, deftly skewered by Harlem Renaissance author Nella Larsen in her book *Quicksand*: "How the white man's god must laugh at the great joke he had played on them! Bound them to slavery, then to poverty and insult and made them bear it." Indeed, there is no evidence that Jesus was simply a kinder gentler Michael Jackson milquetoast lover-not-a-fighter vision of tolerance and forgiveness. In the New Testament he slams Jews, smacks down non-believers and wants to kill the babies of adulterers (John, 3:18, 15:6). But the propagandists for a sanitized Christ always want to have it both ways. They want to cherry pick scripture to amplify Jesus' essential benevolence while keeping critics from cherry picking the bad "out-of-context" stuff. As Dan Barker of the Freedom From Religion Foundation notes, "Believers often accuse skeptics of ignoring the good while picking out only the bad parts of the bible. Believers ask why we don't join them in emphasizing that which is good and beautiful in the bible. This might appear to be a fair question until it is turned around and we ask them why they don't join us in denouncing the ugly parts. Then, they don't see the questions as being quite so fair."[85]

It's precisely this kind of hyper-masculine license that allows the cult of the charismatic preacher to dominate the landscape of black America. Because the Bible is filled with so much rot, hatred, and anti-human rights vitriol, Christian propaganda about its moral righteousness is a schizoid enterprise. Although Larsen's caveat about the gullibility of African Americans within the context of religious debasement rings true, the white man's God has long since morphed into the God of black bootstraps opportunity. The legacies of slavery and racial apartheid have made the church one of the easiest venues for black entrepreneurialism. Drive down any urban street and the explosion of small ministries, makeshift spiritual centers, inner-city temples (one right around the corner from me is headed by a man who calls himself "Prophet"), and other low-rent vehicles of worship attest to the enduring power of this entrepreneurial hucksterism.

Prayer on the Frontlines

The fair at prosperity gospel preacher Fred Price's Faith Dome in South Los Angeles has drawn a smattering of recruiters and thousands of weary job seekers. Some have been out of work a few days, some months, some years on end. Job fairs at churches are not uncommon here. In a community where unemployment is a whopping 24%, churches are the most visible form of private enterprise. But American bootstraps lore that free enterprise via the private sector will redeem poverty and unemployment is as phony as a nine dollar bill. According to Chris Tilly of the UCLA Institute for Research on Labor and Employment, "The nature of private-sector investors is to look where the payoff is. If you've got large swaths of the city where there are bad schools, poor people and crime, that's not where private investment will go."[86] In fact, the current jobs' climate in South Los Angeles is bleaker than in 1992 when the region started to reel from the decline of the aerospace industry. In the ensuing years after the '92 civil unrest, private sector employers like Toyota and IBM came and went, resulting in little long term job creation

The deserted shell of a Toyota training center sits on Crenshaw Boulevard, sandwiched in between a funeral home and a strip mall. A stone's throw away on Crenshaw and Rodeo, prayer warriors have descended on a Ralph's supermarket parking lot. The first sentry, a skinny man in athletic shorts, weaves through the parked cars on an old Schwinn. He flags down the driver of a T-Bird. They exchange quick greetings then bow their heads and join hands, oblivious, for the moment, to the crash of street traffic, the manic dance for parking spots, the rustle of grocery bags and runaway shopping carts. On this hallowed plot of blacktop time is suspended and God vibrates through the chassis of each parked car as the men bond in the simple bliss of scripture.

I caught the parking lot prayer warriors a week before I was scheduled to speak at the Texas Freethought Convention, an annual October gathering of non-believers in Houston. It was an ironic send-off for my pending trip, a reminder of the visceral hold of Jesus and the unique challenges of black secularism. Five years ago, two men holding hands in this particular lot might have elicited homophobic double takes or a beat down. But now, the public performance of prayer, street preaching, and proselytizing in urban communities of color is back with a revivalist vengeance borne of the vicious arc of recession. The license plates tell the tale: God's favorite child, blessed 4 life, Diva4God, etc. On Sundays at the edge of historic Leimert Park elderly men wave banners at traffic that proclaim "Jesus loves gangsters too."

Long before Occupy Wall Street's critique of capitalism made it fashionable to lament the demise of the American dream, joblessness, foreclosure, and homelessness were a fact of life for many in South Los Angeles. At 8.7% of L.A. County's population, African Americans are 50% of its homeless and 40% of its prison population. Lines at ministry-based food assistance programs swell with first-timers. In this era of endless recession, the prayer warriors have become both a bellwether and a vector of social malaise. Prayer is intimately woven into the landscape of public life, a quick and dirty lingua franca that has morphed into a social movement exemplified by the 24/7 International House of Prayer (IHOP) in Kansas City, Missouri. IHOP is at the epicenter of what the *New York Times* characterizes as "one of the fastest-growing segments of Christianity, attracting millions."[87]

For African Americans and Latinos, prayer is an important means of establishing sanctuary, solidarity, in-group status, and out-group stigma. Death, tragedy, misfortune, ambiguity—all can be managed through the soothing bromide of prayer and unlimited God petitioning, in private, public or somewhere in between. Although Christian NFL football player Tim Tebow has become a pop culture sensation (and verb tense) with his maudlin, YouTube-ready displays of Astroturf prayer, public prayer circles before community events have long been a staple in communities of color. Education conferences, community meetings, block club association confabs, K-12 sporting events, and school assemblies—none escape the intrusion of God's imprimatur when the urge strikes his earthly surrogates. As evangelicalism has become more mainstream prayer has become a public fixture. To have good fortune (even in a secular context) is to be blessed. To show empathy and caring is to put someone on your prayer list for the day. If someone, somewhere is not praying for you then a dark ontological cloud hangs over your head. In segregated communities of color, prayer has become the last sham gasp of agency, dynamism, and "control" under capitalist neoliberalism. It provides the illusion of action with no commitment to struggle or evidence. It illustrates Mikhail Bakunin's caveat that "The idea of God implies the abdication of human reason and justice; it is the most decisive negation of human liberty, and necessarily ends in the enslavement of mankind, both in theory and practice…he who desires to worship God must harbor no childish illusions about the matter but bravely renounce his liberty and humanity."[88]

The mainstreaming of prayer also exemplifies Pentecostalism's rise as a global and domestic force. Pentecostalism's baptism in the Spirit worship rituals involve collective oral prayer, the laying on of hands, and the raising of hands in call and response rapture. As I mentioned earlier in the chapter, Latino Pentecostals are fast eclipsing the dwindling white evangelical population. If Pentecostalism provides ethnic solidarity, a sense of belonging, kinship, and a bridge to social services for multigenerational families, it may also provide affirmation of moral standing in a national context that has become more violently hostile, racist, and xenophobic towards people of color.

Against this complex backdrop of marathon devoutness, xenophobia, and white nationalism, it wasn't difficult to see why there were few people of color "feeling" Texas Freethought. Although more grassroots black non-theist groups have emerged over the past few years, "freethought" in Texas looked pretty much like the usual white suspects (Richard Dawkins, Christopher Hitchens, Michael Shermer, et al) speaking to rapt audiences that mirror the deep racial divide of segregated America. As the sole person of color scheduled for a general session, my talk focused squarely on the national context and politics of this divide. I addressed the prevailing climate of racial and gender inequality vis-à-vis the white-dominated secular movement's complicity in the myth of "Kumbaya" colorblindness, highlighting the anti-racist, anti-sexist and anti-imperialist foundations of black freethought. If mainstream freethought and humanism continue to reflect the narrow cultural interests of white elites who have disposable income to go to conferences, then the secular movement is destined to remain marginal and insular.

During a panel I participated on entitled "Expanding Our Movement," the facilitator asked how the secular movement could attract freethinkers (presumably from racially and culturally diverse backgrounds) who weren't at the convention. Panelists Sunsara Taylor of Revolution Newspaper, Jason Torpy of the Military Association of Atheists & Freethinkers, and Rich Rodriguez of the Rational Response Squad unpacked the challenges of broadening a movement that has a straight, white middle-class face. Taylor, a young white activist who has been an outspoken radical voice on anti-racism and social justice, called on whites to confront white privilege and the belief that racism can be reduced to explicit in-your-face prejudice rather than being reflected in institutions like the prison complex and segregated schools.

But white privilege means never having to be in an environment in which whites are the racial others, and secularism means more than freedom from religion. It means never having to be conscious that the black and brown hotel "help" outnumber the paying participants of color at plush academic conferences. It also means never being discomfited by the backslapping culture of good old boys at nice Southern hotels. There was much discussion amongst the African American freethinkers that I spoke to about the implications of the abysmally low turnout for black investment in the secular movement. Activist Donald Wright of the Houston Humanists Discussion Group was involved in the early planning stages of the convention. Wright, author of the book *The Only Prayer I'll ever Pray*, a gripping analysis of his journey from church deacon to non-believer, expressed frustration with the shoe-horning of "diversity" into one brief panel. Washington Area Secular Humanist board member and writer Naima Cabelle Washington spoke of the need to frame secularism from a radical social justice lens from the outset, rather than append diversity as an afterthought. Both agreed that if there is no emphasis on intersectionality within the broader movement, non-theists of color will have little long-term interest in the tiresome work of dragging resistant white secularists along.

Case in point is the organization American Atheists (AA). In 2012, the predominantly white group with a largely white leadership slapped up a billboard in a Harrisburg, Pennsylvania neighborhood featuring a picture of a shackled naked black slave and a bible quote that said "slaves obey your masters." The ad was intended to protest Pennsylvania's boneheaded declaration of 2012 as the so-called "Year of the Bible." Much to the "astonishment" of AA reps, the billboard was reviled, defaced, and labeled a hate crime by some in the African American community. After the billboard appeared, a complaint was filed with the Pennsylvania Human Relations Commission. According to the Patriot-News, Harrisburg resident Aaron Selvey said, "If this had been Detroit, there would have been a riot."[89] Apparently offended black folk just weren't intelligent enough to grasp the sage lesson that American Atheists, prominent champion of anti-racist social justice, was trying to teach them. Instead, some "misconstrued" the message as racist, concluding that, in a country where white nationalists have issued a clarion call to take back the nation from the Negro savage/illegal alien in the White House, "slaves obey your masters" probably still means them.

Responding to the billboard controversy, Naima Washington wrote:

> I happen to view the biblical directive for 'slaves to obey their masters' in a couple of ways. First...we are probably all in agreement that the passage wasn't written by a slave but by a slave master. While many say that the passage is used to *justify* slavery, in some ways I think that's irrelevant. The willingness to rob a person of the fruits of their labor by forcing them to work for free against their will; the ability to wield ruthless and unchecked power and control over other human beings; the ability to see other people as property who can be bought and sold; the right to steal, buy, and sell the children of slaves; the right to commit sodomy, rape, and incest; the right to hold the power of life and death over others, and the ability to accumulate unearned wealth all represent *reasons* for perpetuating slavery. The bible may have provided its justification, but in a society where slavery is legalized, sanctioned, and protected, why would a slave master ever have to justify owning slaves? Even if we throw in the nonsense about (blacks as having) the curse of Ham, it was *racism* which eventually made slavery synonymous with African people.[90]

Washington deftly outlines the economic implications of racial slavery; a reality which continues to define American society. But the complex legacy of slavery and its impact on African Americans wasn't the point of American Atheists' quick and dirty history lesson. As atheist blogger Raina Rhoades argues, "Talking about why blacks were enslaved and continue to deal with discrimination and economic and political disenfranchisement means having a long uncomfortable conversation about white supremacy, privilege, power, etc. That is just the reality of the situation. One cannot boil down slavery to the bible."[91] American Atheists' ahistorical paternalistic ignorance is one of the reasons why the face of New Atheism is still white and racially segregated. Organized religion is dominant in communities of color because urban retail and commercial development is moribund, green space is at a minimum, and many schools have been turned into fortresses. But most secular organizations don't give a damn about the realities of urban communities of color in the U.S. White folks from all walks of life have the luxury of not really seeing the segregated black neighborhoods they bypass on the expressway. White atheist elites are not steeped in regimes of mass incarceration, educational apartheid, and residential segregation. They don't have to be aware that these regimes give them the freedom to get tenured STEM jobs, publish books, and travel the world proselytizing about secularism. They don't have to be on the frontlines pushing for universal pre-school or college prep as a civil secular right. Their children don't have to go to the "hellhole" inner city schools depicted in charter school propaganda horror films like "Waiting for Superman".[92] They don't have to view economic justice as anything other than a buzz phrase, as they diddle around trying to "check" inconvenient critical Negroes like myself.[93]

In his article "Atheism and the Class Problem," David Hoelscher addresses the absence of New Atheist critique of economic inequality:

> It is too often overlooked that economics is inextricably mixed up with religion. David Eller, an atheist and anthropologist, helpfully reminds us that the realistic view on this point is the holistic perspective. It sees religion as a component of culture, and as such "integrated" with and "interdependent" on all the other "aspect[s] of culture—its economic system, its kinship practices, its politics, its language, its gender roles, and so on." It was not for nothing that Max Weber insisted that, in the words of Joel Schalit, "the economic order is a reflection of the religious order." It is no accident, then, that in the face of massive public debt and a wretchedly inadequate social safety net, various levels of ostensibly secular government in the U.S. grant 71 billion dollars in subsidies annually to religious organizations.[94]

Hoelscher cites Noam Chomsky's criticism of the New Atheism: "The New Atheist message...is old hat, and irrelevant, at least for those whose religious affiliations are a way of finding some sort of community and mutual support in an atomized society lacking social bonds... if it is to be even minimally serious...the 'new atheism' should focus its concerns on the virulent secular religions of state worship' [such as capitalism, imperialism and militarism]."[95]

Hoelscher rightly faults atheist writers and secular intellectuals for essentially protecting their class interests. Yet the article nonetheless sidesteps the primary reason economic justice has not been a focus in New Atheism. As I've argued previously, racial politics and American apartheid implicitly shape "New Atheist" rhetoric. Unlike socialist/communist movements of the early twentieth century, in which atheism was an element but not a driving cause, contemporary atheist movement activism is far from radical. Flying the atheist flag for church/state separation and Big Science poses no inherent challenge to existing class power structures. This partly explains why atheism has achieved mainstream popular appeal amongst a cross-section of American whites. And it stands to reason that class analysis is marginalized, not only because of the myth of a classless America, but because you can't talk class without talking race and racism in a nation obsessed with the myth of the savage ghetto cesspit.

* * *

In 2010, Donald Wright founded the national "Day of Solidarity for Black Non-believers". The annual event is designed to promote greater visibility for African American atheists negotiating black religiosity and white-dominated atheism. Predictably, some in the atheist community labeled it "segregation," apparently uncomfortable with the notion that black people could claim territory of their own without white folks' approval.[96] In 2012, Wright and former pastor Mike Aus founded Houston Oasis, a humanist center for fellowship and community. Wright had long wanted to develop a safe place for non-believers in the otherwise conservative city of Houston. He envisioned the Oasis as a long term effort to build initiatives that emulate the solidarity and social foundation that the best religious organizations offer, minus the dogma and proselytizing. However, as a progressive African American, Wright acknowledges the inherent difficulty of joining historically-marginalized black non-believers with older middle class white non-believers who have the luxury to be disengaged from social justice issues. He notes that "there has been some push back on this. This (predominantly white) group is not very activist at all and it is going to be a hard sell. I don't know if this is indicative of this group specifically or humanists in general."[97] Wright's dilemma points to the central problem with "diversity" and secular organizing. There are few out black non-believers in Houston with whom he can make common cause. But religious African Americans are bonded by centuries of tradition that grew directly out of anti-racist struggle. Churches are segregated because of the reality of American race and class hierarchies. Thus, in the absence of anti-racist redress there will always be a deep divide between an overwhelmingly white secular movement with social power and economic privilege and people of color who must navigate racial segregation daily in white America.

For non-believers of color, the argument about whether or not secular organizations should address social justice is a privilege that only white people have. American Humanist Association (AHA) development director Maggie Ardiente challenges humanist organizations to address social inequality directly. She contends that just as faith-based organizations are designed to meet their communities' social welfare, education, and political needs, so humanist organizations should be. Despite being a native-born Filipina-American, she has gotten the question "where are you (originally) from?" throughout much of her life, echoing the experiences of many Asian and Latino Americans who are automatically assumed to be foreign-born. In the eyes of mainstream America and much of the world, American citizenship is still defined as white. Racial others with non-European names—and even "homegrown" dark-skinned people with European names—are non-citizens until they can produce papers to prove otherwise.

One of the primary reasons people of color do not enjoy full rights of citizenship is deepening educational apartheid. A humanist/secularist movement that does not address this social atrocity is bankrupt. In 2013, Black Skeptics Los Angeles spearheaded a "First in the Family" scholarship fund for undocumented, LGBTQ, homeless, and foster care youth. These students are some of the most under-served and underrepresented in the four-year college-going population. They must deal with mental health trauma, teacher discrimination, absent caregivers, homophobia, sexual abuse, and the threat of deportation. These are challenges that they face *in addition* to "simply" getting the required college prep courses, financial aid, and other academic resources they need to go to college.

Diane Arellano of the Women's Leadership Project speaks forcefully about these issues in "Next Wave Atheist Leaders and White Privilege":

> Over the past several years, we've worked at schools where students who aren't considered gifted or "college material" aren't encouraged to prepare for college. For example, African American students are disproportionately shut out of college prep Advanced Placement and Honors classes. And undocumented students are often told straight up by racist teachers that "my taxes shouldn't pay for you to go to college." Black and Latino students are searched, profiled, and basically considered guilty until proven innocent. Girls of color are ritually silenced when it comes to speaking out about basic rights like freedom from sexual harassment or access to birth control... For our girls, abortion is freedom and reproductive justice is life, period. So, no, trying to get Ten Commandments displays taken down or challenging prayer in school are not our priorities as atheists and freethinkers of color teaching in urban schools.[98]

Arellano's comments expanded on an incisive piece written by DePaul University student activist Andrew Tripp, who criticized mainstream atheist organizations' narrow focus on young, virtually all white church/state separation activists.[99] Responding to Arellano's article, one reader wrote that "it's just not true that being white is a salient feature of any atheist's identity (being an atheist in a very religious country pretty much crowds everything else out)." This mentality that whiteness is an unraced identity and that religion is the fount of all evil reflects white entitlement in a nation where the wealth of people of color has declined to "third world" levels.[100] Atheist, Christian, Satanist, Wiccan—if you're a person of color in the Christian U.S., you're subjected to a racist educational system that dehumanizes you as a non-achieving, violent, potential dropout, a racist criminal justice system that automatically criminalizes you as a dysfunctional crack-snorting, gang banging scourge, and a white supremacist media that promotes white beauty ideals, white heroism, white leadership, and white humanity as the universal norm.

Over a century after Emancipation, the paradox of worshipping the "white man's god" remains. But for many people of color, religion provides cultural validation and political leverage denied them in an increasingly polarized nation. Interviewed by the *Los Angeles Times* about the 2012 presidential campaign, an elderly African American woman named Ruth Skinner-Poteat quipped, "I say I sleep with three men. God the father. God the son. And Barack Obama."[101] Skinner-Poteat's faith in this "trinity" is perhaps the ultimate challenge to freethought in communities where storefront churches and prayer warriors run deep.

CHAPTER SIX

Seeing Things

Taught the same economics, history, philosophy, literature and religion which have established the present code of morals, the Negro's mind has been brought under the control of his oppressor. The problem of holding the Negro down, therefore, is easily solved. When you control a man's thinking you do not have to worry about his actions. You do not have to tell him not to stand here or go yonder. He will find his "proper place" and will stay in it. You do not need to send him to the back door. He will go without being told. In fact, if there is no back door, he will cut one for his special benefit.

--Carter G. Woodson, *The Miseducation of the Negro* [1]

The two young men of color walk through the gallery transfixed. There is so much to see and so little time to see it in; no docents handy to provide a frame, no earphones to squawk on about context and artist's intent. The trip from their South L.A. school to the L.A. County

Museum of Art (LACMA) in the Miracle Mile section of Wilshire Boulevard is figuratively a world away. As the first car-euphoric corridor in Los Angeles, Miracle Mile still retains its sheen. The museum's multi-million dollar exhibits and au courant architecture showcase the pinnacle of Western culture—from classic to modern to contemporary avant-garde. The wing that the students walk through is the brain child of billionaire philanthropist Eli Broad, an ethereally-lit sanctuary that brings them face-to-face with artist Glenn Ligon's anatomy of black otherness. Ligon's exhibit beckons with written evaluations from his elementary school teachers. Their comments range from praise to quizzical disappointment. One implies that he is squandering his potential. Another pronounces that he has insufficient "black consciousness." As records of one student's arc they are unremarkable, inviting a voyeurism that only piques interest in the context of the artist's success. However, as grade school primers of the genealogy of Ligon's marked body and, implicitly, that of all black students, they are deeply moving.

In the art gallery, time is suspended. It is crafted as a hermetic space, a rebuke to the outside world where quiet contemplation is a rare commodity, fast becoming the province of the super rich. At this particular exhibit, guards of color stand silently at the ready. There is a black presence stationed in every room, a reminder of the invisibility of people of color in the high flying corporate art scene. With their stiff uniforms and stoic expressions, the guards both comment on and perform the authority of the museum. They are there and not there, breaking from the tedium of their posts to remind students to put away their cell phones and refrain from taking pictures. They protect the secular sanctity of the gallery space through the veneer of enforcement, adding another layer of seeing and surveillance.

What do the students see in a culture in which they are trained to view art and aesthetics as the province of white geniuses? How do they navigate seeing in a culture in which the vision of white geniuses defines universal standards of beauty, value, goodness, and human worth? How do they learn, as Carter G. Woodson says, to breathe, swallow, and regurgitate the template of white universal subject-hood as sacred creed and covenant? How do they learn—how did they learn—to become blind to themselves, to see themselves as the Other?

The politics of seeing are part of what drives God lust. God provides a blank canvas for all fears, anxieties, hopes, ambitions and dreams. He/she/it becomes the tabula rasa for the dreamer, the universal fail-safe for the fucked up, the crushed, the abject and the abandoned. In an intensely capitalistic, racially-segregated culture, God-dreaming is a kind of art-making. God is closely tied to self-making and invention. It's a realm that offers both the illusion of agency or control and the conceit of subjection.

Ligon's show includes a re-examination of the infamous Robert Mapplethorpe Black Book exhibit from the 1990s. Photo after photo of naked black men sprawl next to quotes from commentators, critical theorists, and art mavens. The quotes weigh in on the public blasphemy of eroticized black male bodies, musing about whether Mapplethorpe's images were exploitative. The comments run the gamut from appreciation to outrage, many of them conceding the ambiguity of representation and desire. Interspersed with the provocative poses of the mostly taut, virile young men, Ligon's arrangement of the quotes underscores the ways in which the black body has always existed as contested space, as politicized. In an era in which mass incarceration and criminalization have become the predominant mediums for black embodiment, Mapplethorpe's photographs are even more difficult to view within the lens of aesthetic pleasure. Mapplethorpe's identity as a prominent white gay male photographer cannot be separated from the photos' reception. Nor can his identity, power, and privilege be distanced from the tragic downward spiral of his black gay subjects, many of whom died of AIDS. It's nearly impossible to imagine a black gay photographer gaining intimate access to the lives of white men for a similar photo essay. Heady pronouncements of colorblind equality are even more farcical in the context of the segregated art world, where artists of color are routinely ghettoized into "ethnic" shows. But art-making has an especially critical relationship to knowledge construction and human value. Who has the authority to make art, whose art will be considered as "great," canonical or universal is deeply connected to the standards of what is worth being seen.

In the twelve-plus years since Ligon's original Mapplethorpe exhibit, and fifteen-plus since the book's publication, the art world template for the white genius as all-seeing and all-powerful has not changed. What has changed during this period is that HIV/AIDS has become a leading cause of death for young African Americans and mass incarceration has been deemed the "New Jim Crow."[2] Against this backdrop, god-lust amongst African Americans has morphed into a more fevered, strategically public practice. It's not uncommon for young blacks to retort that some wayward person should get "right with God." It's rare to go to a black public event that isn't kicked-off or concluded with a prayer from a local pastor. On TV shows like CNN's *Black in America: Silicon Valley*, scenes of black folk bowing their heads and joining hands in prayer before a stressful event are pro forma. Black NFL players like Kurt Warner and coaches like Tony Dungee routinely attribute their success on the field and in life to God's co-piloting. Over the past several years some Black churches have even declared Halloween a new "Satanic" ritual, offering their own kid-friendly, fall-themed festivals as suitably God-fearing alternatives. T-shirts and paraphernalia with scripture and religious references flood the streets in predominantly black communities, where disposable income is an oxymoron for most.

Embracing, invoking, and bowing down to God have become shorthand for achieving upward mobility. In *Essence* magazine, Tasha Smith, a popular actress and fixture in Tyler Perry films, reflects on her journey to success. This particular actress is habitually cast as the kind of ball-busting Sapphire alpha men love to hate and white women love to fetishize. Smith's specialty is channeling the hand on hip tell-it-like-it-is keepin' it real "bitch" who is never afraid to slice and dice her man in a high-octane public throwdown. Consequently, the reader is "shocked" to learn that she was once an atheist—frustrated, adrift, and emotionally scarred by a traumatic childhood.[3] It's implied that her lack of faith was a kind of spiritual albatross. As told to *Essence*, her subsequent transition to a God-fearing woman of faith hastens her rise to fame, wealth, love, and redemption via that rarefied cultural vehicle—the Tyler Perry film. The profile on the actress assures us that giving one's life/fate over to God is an authentic rite of passage, a naked reclamation of self in the midst of a cold spiritual wilderness. God enables vision, and, ultimately, upward mobility. Godlessness signifies rudderlessness and absence of self-control, a potentially fatal flaw for a black woman trying to bootstrap to a moral life. Being a good black woman is defined by masochism. It is only through the crucible of self-sacrifice, by extending one's faith until it hurts, that redemption can be achieved.

Witness: an acquaintance experiencing extreme economic hardship pledges to lay her life down to God after an email solicitation yields a gift of $50. The "ask and ye shall receive" regime of the prosperity gospel has become the cult of true blackness. On the surface it's a rebuke to black invisibility, a bird flip to a dominant culture that revels in the myth of black downward mobility driven by lazy blacks shuffling from government handout to government handout.

If God is Black America's co-pilot then what does that say about the landscape of 21st century United States, where black wealth is virtually nonexistent? What does it betray about a country where residential segregation of African Americans and Latinos has become more prevalent now than during the 1980s? It's tempting for some religious skeptics of color to dismiss these displays as indicative of backward thinking from uneducated black folk. But, as the faith-based pandering of President Obama and other politicians demonstrate, education and religiosity are not mutually exclusive. Just as there is no shortage of storefront churches in poor black communities, there is no shortage of mid-sized to megachurches in middle-to-upper-middle-class black neighborhoods. Faith and religiosity don't exist in a political, social or economic vacuum. Nor are they static. One female interviewee from the 2010 gospel documentary *Rejoice and Shout* acknowledged that Christianity was originally the "white man's" religion but dismissed the claim that blacks were brainwashed or indoctrinated. The gender pageantry of the Black Church is on vivid display in the grainy archival footage from this fascinating documentary (and document) of black life in the early 20th century. Black women getting the Holy Ghost crowd the church aisles, writhing, gesticulating, and testifying to the Lord's transfixion. Every now and then the camera captures a swooning male congregant, but, for the most part, the men sit upright and respectable in the pews as the reverends hold sway in the pulpit. It's implied that performance and possession—the raw abandon of getting the Holy Ghost—are a woman's medium, a manifestation of their natural sexual otherness, their closer relationship with the body, and, thus, their irrationality. Here, religious performance, the collision between sacred and secular, becomes a kind of artistry. Ecstatic religious expression is portrayed as a powerful device in a social context that does not afford poor black women agency, creativity or visibility.

For black women, religious performance becomes a means of both re-claiming and transcending the body. The Bible tells you that you are unclean, impure and promiscuous, the source of Original Sin. Being a good woman, a keeper of the faith, requires masochistic devotion to a creed based on the degradation of the female body. In her book *Women in the Church of God in Christ,* Anthea Butler discusses how "church mothers" sought sanctification as a form of social agency within sexist Black Church hierarchies.[4] An alternative to ordination, sanctification allowed black women to "negotiate for and obtain power both within the denomination and without it…Church members pursued sanctification through…fasting, prayer, scripture study, and other disciplines, creating moral and spiritual authority."[5] In short, church mothers in the Church of God in Christ, or COGIC, created meaningful spaces to compensate for their exclusion from official channels of power and authority. Nevertheless, Butler's emphasis on the importance of sanctification to black women in COGIC begs the question as to why they had to engage in these practices to achieve value, worth, and visibility in the church in the first place. Butler's analysis speaks to the age-old issue of how oppressed peoples develop a sense of personhood under disenfranchising conditions. It's no revelation that religion has been a primary medium for allowing oppressed peoples an outlet. The moral stakes are high for black women because they have always been marked as fallen, as other, as savage, as hyper-sexual—in contrast to the pure, innocent white ideal of authentic European femininity. In American pop culture, white female performers like Madonna have parlayed this legacy into lucrative global careers that supposedly challenge conventional norms of female sexuality. Critiquing the Madonna phenomenon in her 1992 book *Black Looks*, bell hooks argues, "We have always known that the socially constructed image of innocent white womanhood relies on the continued production of the racist/sexist sexual myth that black women are not innocent and never can be. Since we are coded always as 'fallen' women in the racist cultural iconography we can never, as can Madonna, publicly 'work' the image of ourselves as innocent female daring to be bad. Mainstream culture always reads the black female body as sign of sexual experience."[6]

Late 19th-early 20th century activist writer and publisher Ida B. Wells campaigned tirelessly against the terroristic control of black women via lynching, sexual assault, and rape. Catapulted into the 21st century, she might not be surprised at the power that this legacy has had on contemporary media images of black femininity. Yet, to watch these scenes from a 21st century vantage point is to grasp the perilous state 20th century black women existed in. Sexual terrorism was widespread, and the first wave feminist movement was itself stubbornly racist, classist, and heterosexist. These regimes of sexualized power and control put the lie to a post-feminism that is speciously framed as either the right to be hypersexual or the right to be Suzy Homemaker. Institutional racism and economic inequality ensure that this is an especially false dichotomy for black women, who are frequently trotted out as the bad slut or sage caregiver to white women's beleaguered mother/career woman/virginal little girl. Bad slut sage caregivers are symptomatic of the severe health disparities black women face. For example, the HIV/AIDS epidemic in Black America exemplifies the intersection of heterosexism, sexism, and institutional racism. Epidemic HIV contraction rates amongst black women stem from inequitable health care access, patriarchal gender roles, and heterosexist/sexist intimate partner relationships that undermine women's self-determination. Why do African Americans have the highest HIV contraction rates in the so-called first world and why are these rates skyrocketing in the era of the first black president? Rising poverty rates and the normalization of pornography have led to an increase in sex trafficking and prostitution amongst young black women. Images of post-feminist equality and hypersexuality have ensnared some in abusive intimate-partner relationships. The schizoid nature of American "democracy" is disorienting. Perhaps the reality of deepening racial and gender equality explains the ferocity of black women's 21st century devoutness.

Christianity was one of the primary means by which African Americans learned the lexicon of becoming subjects through otherness. This is a uniquely American dialectic, borne of the soul-killing terrorism of slave ships, and, later, the plantation, a gulag awash in the new republic's corrupt gospel of individual liberty. When my students traveled to the California African American museum last year, they had a chance to see and imagine the terror of these spaces. They walked through galleries with floor-to-ceiling inscriptions chronicling the birth dates, family lineages, appearances, habits, and idiosyncracies of slaves. They marveled at the relevance and medievalism of the notorious Willie Lynch manifesto. Their blood ran cold at the military assemblage of black bodies in the slavers' hull. They stood mesmerized, contemplating the sheer number, weight, and scope of intertwined bodies, twinned in the endless sea voyage, hour after murderous hour. Enraged, many of them wondered how these obliterated ancestors made it out alive. How they resisted the gnashing white turbine of the sea and the urge to rise up against their savage captors.

> Often did I think many of the inhabitants of the deep much more happy than myself. I envied them the freedom they enjoyed, and as often wished I could change my condition for theirs.
>
> *Olaudah Equiano, 1789*

Later, in the classroom, we read Alice Walker on the spirituality of art-making. She wonders about the enslaved "genius" great-grandmothers denied the right to their own bodies. The space of the trascendent artist is that of the white male, the universal subject, the hero, the kingmaker, the muse chasing romantic. Their art hangs timelessly on museum walls funded by billionaires and corporations. Their art demands time, self-presence, self-possession, insularity, a privileged distance from the relentlessness of everyday life and the oppressive inconvenience of the body. The caricature of the masturbatory white male artist is one of the crazy booze swilling, dick swinging, T&A besotted libertine whose creativity is powered by testosterone and angst. Within the Western artistic canon, the woman exists to provide sex, inspiration, and succor, to be a pious sacrifice at the altar of male genius. As John Berger remarks in his book *Ways of Seeing*:

> To be born a woman is to be born into an allotted and confined space, into the keeping of men. The social presence of women has developed as a result of their ingenuity in living under such tutelage within a limited space. But this has been at the cost of a woman's self being split in two. A woman must continually watch herself. She is almost continually followed by her own image of herself.[7]

In this sense, women watch themselves being watched and looked at. The woman as the ultimate visual object of desire is the predominant theme in advertising, film, TV, video, and the Internet. Women's bodies sell billions and every new generation of American women and girls are socialized to view their bodies as public terrain, as there for the taking. Of course, Western art traditions have had a major influence on cultural perceptions of femininity. Christianity has played a seminal role in artistic representations of the female form. Berger identifies how early European nude portraiture revolved around depictions of Adam and Eve in the Book of Genesis. The "primal" scene of Adam and Eve's expulsion from Eden was popular with Medieval and Renaissance era artists. The central message of Genesis is that "The woman is blamed and punished by being made subservient to the man. In relation to the woman, the man is the agent of God."[8] Hence, the shameful dirty body of the female is the source of original sin. Women are cursed with menstruation, with childbirth, with being ruled by men. As "agents of God" men have authorial power as agents of the gaze. The male gaze is based on the dichotomy between the hyper-visible sexualized female body and the unseen male body. As Berger notes, "When the tradition of painting became more secular, other themes also offered the opportunity of painting nudes. But in them all there remains the implication that the subject (a woman) is aware of being seen by a spectator."[9]

Western art-making, as a proxy for godliness, supposedly embodies universal objective standards of beauty and truth. Within this context, femininity is constructed as an eminently visual space that secures male "objectivity." From the time they are kindergartners to the time they are college students, students of color are told that Western art-making traditions reflect a universal aesthetic and cultural standard against which all other traditions are measured. They are trained not to see that white men dominate Western art history and education. They are socialized to believe that Western traditions reflect universal objective standards of beauty and truth. These standards tell them what the deep complexities of authentically human experience are, rather than that of their own cultures and communities. Before we went to LACMA, none of my students could name a visual artist that looked like them. The reason why they couldn't is because mainstream public education tells them that there is no cultural space for the female genius of color who is also connected to her community. Creating visual art is a luxury, a privilege, the province of an insular leisure class they may only see in textbooks or in the media. So these everyday "genius" artists have been "lost" to the fields, the kitchens, the church pews, the crushing demands of families they may not have wanted. There is a secret space of mourning for their loss. Alice Walker captures it brilliantly, and powerfully evokes this regime in her essay *In Search of Our Mother's Gardens*, which contemplates the contradictions of black female creativity and "genius" within the holocaust conditions of slavery. She asks:

> What did it mean for a black woman to be an artist in our grandmothers' time? In our great-grandmothers' day? It is a question cruel enough to stop the blood. Did you have a genius of a great-great grandmother who died under some ignorant and depraved white overseer's lash? Or was she required to bake biscuits for some lazy backwater tramp…or was her body broken and forced to bear children (who were more often than not sold away from her)—eight, ten, fifteen, twenty children. When her one joy was the thought of modeling heroic figures of rebellion, in stone and clay?[10]

Walker cites the example of her mother, who channeled her creative passion into gardening. She also references Phillis Wheatley, the enslaved 18th century poet who was the first black woman to be published in the United States. In her poem *On Being Brought from Africa to America,* Wheatley extolled the glories of Christian redemption.[11] She acknowledges that white supremacist culture views blacks as barbarous but insists that Christians "remember that Negroes may be refin'd and join the angelic train." In an era in which the Bible was used to validate the dehumanization of black slaves, Wheatley's literary talent was a counterweight. Wheatley was the exceptional genius black woman who garnered acclaim from white society; Walker's mother was the "faceless" black woman whose creativity was beholden to the "unremarkable" circumstances of her everyday life. Walker, herself deemed an exceptional black woman, seeks to redeem her mother's unacknowledged artistry through her own writing. Like countless nameless faceless radical freedom fighters, the accomplishments of these genius foremothers will only be brought to light through activist writing and scholarship. Yet, in mainstream K-12 public education, the most recognized historical figures of color are Martin Luther King, Rosa Parks, and Cesar Chavez. Many of my students don't know who Walker is. But as they read her words they are quiet as death, and, perhaps, newly enflamed. As students of female sacrifice, they know the savage politics behind her canvas. They are intimately aware of the blood price women of color must pay to be free in this so-called post-feminist society, in which white male politicians trivialize sexual assault with dangerous tautologies like "forcible rape."

In Wheatley's era, black women having the right to their own bodies was an oxymoron. Black women's bodies were commodities, both for white supremacist capitalist patriarchy as well as for black patriarchy. White women may have been burdened with the legacy of Eve's betrayal but they still wielded considerable power over the bodies of black slaves in their homes and communities. White skin, flowing hair, and pure, "untainted" bloodlines with no Negroes lurking in the dynastic woodpile commanded a high price in plantation society. Among other things, it provided the luxury of knowing your children would never be forcibly sold away from you versus knowing they could be sold off as chattel to anyone at any time. It was the difference between knowing that you could be raped by anyone without the barest hint of legal protection (and that even the term "rape" was a deemed a contradiction) versus knowing that you at least had some legal status as a person worthy of protection and defense. As historian Deborah Gray White notes, "From emancipation to more than two-thirds of the twentieth century, no Southern white male was ever convicted of raping or attempting to rape a black woman."[12] Rape of black women and theft of savage heathen children were all crimes that were promoted in a Christian universe. In her book *Medical Apartheid*, Harriet Washington documents how the field of gynecology developed through experimentation on black female slaves. Black women were used for gruesome experiments that often left them maimed and/or infertile. In 1852, a white physician named Marion Sims was credited with pioneering the groundbreaking vesicovaginal fistula procedure. Sims' research, which involved fashioning silver sutures to stabilize the vagina, had been pioneered on the bodies of captive black women.[13] Washington notes that the condition is now most prevalent amongst poor women in sub-Saharan Africa. Thus, "the beneficiaries of the surgery today are many, but the same sort of women who made the surgery possible (are) excluded."[14] In contrast to today, medical protocols for procuring informed consent from patients participating in medical experiments had not yet been standardized. However, even if these protocols had existed they would not have extended to black slaves.

Did faith become black women's canvas against this backdrop, a spiritual constant and aesthetic anchor in a world in which black women's bodies were not their own? The 18th century Great Awakening taught the so-called Giddy Multitude that faith was the great equalizer, a public medium for personal reckoning and reclamation. If powerful white religious leaders like Cotton Mather said that slaves could get religion and go to heaven with the right dose of subservience and humility, then anything was possible. Wheatley's old-time religion domesticated the African savage/heathen and provided European Americans with a moral and ethical rationale for white supremacy. But white supremacy rested on white purity and Christian piety. It was legitimized by the establishment of a hierarchy of women that placed black women on the bottom rung. Regardless of their literary or artistic accomplishments, Wheatley's descendants were both sexual predators/wenches and sexual prey. Unlike white women, black women watch themselves being watched by *all* whites and men of color. In this regard, white women are not just passive subjects of the gaze but active agents of the Western gaze. The Western gaze is based on the presumption of white female sexual purity as a symbol of cultural morality. Although the notion of whiteness as the pinnacle of human morality was enshrined in the Bible, it gained special resonance in the American colonies. As Richard Dyer notes in his book *White*:

> The earliest example given by the *Oxford English Dictionary* of the word "white" being used to refer to a race of people was in 1604, and both (Winthrop) Jordan and (Martin) Bernal locate the emergence of the term in the American colonies. Yet grafting morality through the hue on to the skin of the person was already in place in painting and literature by then even where no developed notion of race was explicitly in play. It is in the Christian tradition.[15]

Again, cultural associations between whiteness and moral superiority became more widespread during the Renaissance era. Paintings of biblical scenes and icons were pervasive. Indeed, portrayals of the Virgin Mary are the "supreme exemplar(s) of whiteness. Her fair hair and complexion, often in white robes and association with lilies and doves all constitute her undisputed virtue in terms of white hue and skin. Mary is an image of motherhood without intercourse. She is never seen pregnant. She goes even further than the most refined white lady; she reproduces without sex."

By contrast, the over-sexed black Jezebel was neither a virtuous woman nor a sufficiently self-sacrificing mother. Accounts from the Middle Passage note the frequency with which black women were impregnated during the voyage. And compulsory pregnancy and childbirth were the recurring theme in black women's lives. As breeders, black women's sexual availability was "reinforced" by their pornographic display on the auction block, where every inch of their naked bodies was surveyed and inspected with leering relish by white buyers who also queued up to purchase livestock. In these marketplaces of human flesh, the stark difference between genteel modest white ladies and dark wenches was writ large. Swathed in bonnets and petticoats, genteel modest *Christian* white ladies, or Miss Anns, were the antidote to hot-blooded half-naked raggedy scarf-wearing black women. Miss Ann was the demonic object of desire watching contemptuously over the shoulder of the black cook. She was the effortlessly evil icon—vividly personified by actress Sandy Duncan in the 1977 debut of the *Roots* miniseries—that black girls across the nation wanted to reach into the TV and snatch up. She was the ultimate betrayer—part Virgin Mary, part Eve—a symbol that "sisterhood" was not inherently global. In *Roots*, Miss Ann allows Kizzy, the slave she has grown up and bonded with, to be sold away to an even more brutal future after she is caught teaching other slaves to read. The two cross paths years later as elderly women. When Miss Ann, oblivious to Kizzy's identity, asks her to fetch her some water, Kizzy spits in her cup behind her back.

Watching in the comfort of our post-Jim Crow living rooms, we cheered this small act of resistance and rage. Cinematically, the Kizzy-Miss Ann encounter was a rare instance of naked exposure. It laid bare the intimate contours of white female complicity, amplifying Charles Dickens' caveat about the "grinning skull beneath" the ideal of (white) female beauty. Even the white kids at my elementary school talked about Kunta Kinte, captivated by the novelty of this global media event. Bussed into our predominantly black neighborhood through a dwindling school integration program, the intertwined genealogy of blacks and whites was a foreign concept to the white kids. Before *Roots*, their sole connection to black lives was through the zip coon sitcoms of the '70s—mainstream shows like *The Jeffersons* and *Good Times*. These portrayals were not far removed from the caricatures of the plantation. But my white classmates could open any art book in our small school library and see their ancestry validated as the pinnacle of civilization. And on Fridays, flush with anticipation of the weekend, meditating on the bus back to their mostly white neighborhoods, they may have shuddered at the vividly rendered atrocities of *Roots*, then settled back into their seats, "safe," knowing that those evil back-in-the-day whites weren't them. After all, *our* ancestors didn't own slaves, they thought, surfing the otherworldly divide between now and then.

But it's not difficult to draw a line from the pornographic display of black women's bodies under the plantation regime to the degradation of black women in contemporary film, TV, and video. As art object of desire, the black body has played a profound role in legitimating American nationhood.

What separates these phantom classrooms of memory from the hyper-segregated ones of today? It is a limp Monday morning, and a slo-mo Southern California dreariness settles over the class as I write the phrase "all great art was created by white men" on the board. It is meant to provoke, to unsettle, to jar my students out of the snarl of resistance and complacency they bring to the first school day of the week. A week after their trip to LACMA they vehemently disagree. But what in this post-racial colorblind culture will allow them to continue to see otherwise? What will enable them to think critically about the annihilating images that they've been programmed to identify with and acquiesce to, drowning in a sea of narratives about the march of Western progress and American greatness? And what will drive them to a blinding rage as descendants of slaves and immigrant freedom fighters sitting in classrooms where there is still no history between the covers of high school textbooks that they can claim as their own?

CHAPTER SEVEN

Ungrateful Dead

The black is permitted to beseech the same God as whites, but not to pray to him at the same altar. He has his own priests and churches. One does not close the doors of Heaven to him; yet inequality hardly stops at the boundary of the other world. When the Negro is no longer, his bones are cast to one side, and the difference of conditions is still found even in the equality of death.

--Alexis de Tocqueville, On America [1]

They are the last and they are insane. They suffer from a mass delusion. They all believe that they are…eternal, that they are immortal. And they didn't get the idea from me.

--Martin Amis, "The Immortals" [2]

Many small stones are in remembrance of infants or children who died at an early age, often three or four in the same family…What I noticed most though…was that time had utterly taken away the histories and attachments and emotions that had once closely wrapped around these dead, leaving nothing but their families and names and dates. It was almost as if they were waiting to be born.

--Roger Angell, "Over the Wall"[3]

The Inglewood cemetery in South Los Angeles is a marvel of frozen angels and frozen time. Here, tiny babies dead for over a century mingle with the ancient; grizzled World War I veterans with teenage gangstas; the Americana pride of deepest Iowa with the promise and innocence of South L.A. It is a testament to time's paradoxes; to how the cultural geography of a community shifts in the face of social upheaval, migration, and white flight. On the eastern side of the cemetery, the newer plots ripple nakedly in the sun, while the older ones sprout gothic gilt and marble headstones, winged guardians with arms outstretched, ready to ferry their charges to the other side. Like city streets, American cemeteries are monuments to and markers of segregation. Historically, slave era and Jim Crow burial traditions denied African Americans the right to proper burial and placement. Black burials were also segregated in cities where Jim Crow laws were not in force.[4] In the palace of the cemetery, death was a strictly apartheid affair. Even amidst the fraternity of rotting corpses, the purity of whiteness had to be maintained.

Angels are perfect Americana symbols of purity, innocence, and transcendence. They are death's rock stars, objects of endless childhood fascination, the safe space of Hallmark cards and infant eulogies. Asexual, bush league immortals, they soothe the living with the fantasy of innocuous death. But what happens when a culture ceases to memorialize dead children as angels? Rips the veil of eternal prospects away from the short lives of innocents? A minister once told me that he admired atheists because of their brave outlook on death. This particular man of the cloth was a fierce fundamentalist, an ardent believer in the righteousness of the GOP culture war against abortion, gay marriage, and evolution. He had presided over countless funerals, dropping words of wisdom, comfort, and condolence to umpteen families mourning children who'd died suddenly. Nonetheless, like many pastors gnashing through scripture until their eyes bled, he was secretly intrigued by atheists. With no illusions about an afterlife, non-belief was both liberating and scary, the glimmer of a dark illicit path not taken. Pastors are so deeply ensconced in the wretched business of rationalizing the irrationality of death that the temptation to cut loose in one drunken salvo of there-is-no-fucking-purpose-to-it-all must be irresistible.

On any given day, men of the cloth work the cemetery like strippers clawing for another pole. Cramming in one last salvo over the freshly dug graves they flash a pithy Matthew here, a lick of Jesus and the Lord's Prayer there, twirling eleventh hour petitions for the fence sitters and the godless grateful damned like silk stockings. Some of the newer headstones have pictures of slain young black men, faces brimming with intelligence. The mystique of the young dead is a commodity that every culture craves. But, of course, the death industry has special resonance in communities where death at an early age is an unrelenting presence; it is both bleak reality and cliché. Blackness and death are linked in the mainstream imagination. Americans are accustomed to seeing the dead body of the Other arrayed row after row, National Geographic-style, in "primitive" third world countries from plagues, natural disasters, and genocidal warfare. They are accustomed to flipping past news reports (when they fleetingly appear) of murdered young black men in so-called urban ghettoes. After the Jonestown massacre of People's Temple members in 1978, front page pictures of hundreds of dead black people captured the global imagination. The People's Temple was a multiracial Pentecostal congregation founded by the Reverend Jim Jones in the 1960s. Fearing government persecution, Jones' followers relocated to Guyana on his instructions. In what has been dubbed the largest murder-suicide in world history, they were widely believed to have been forced to drink a lethal cyanide cocktail made with Koolaide. The term "drink the Koolaide" became shorthand for the gullibility of Jones' mostly African American followers and a synonym for brainwashed cultists.[5]

The horrific Jonestown photos of sprawling dead bodies was not only a visual metaphor for the insidiousness of cults but a cautionary tale for poverty-inspired groupthink. Before it was revealed that the majority of those who died were forced to drink poison (or be injected with it), the world wondered how those "crazy people" could have allowed their children to perish with the rest of the flock. But since these were just crazy *black people* (who were naturally prone to emotionalism and irrationality anyway) the media wasn't that probing. The branding of the Jonestown massacre as the architecture of cult-hood has been challenged by some black religious scholars. They note the degree to which African American members of the People's Temple were attracted to its dynamic ethos of multiracial solidarity, social justice, and communalism. As Anthony Pinn points out, "Much of what has been said about People's Temple has entailed a response to negative constructions masked by an offensive grammar of "cults" and "sects"...This new conversation... often results in limited attention to the presence of African Americans in the temple and the significance of African Americans with respect to religious aesthetics, history, and cultural sensibilities."[6] Thus, it wasn't just that large numbers of black people blindly followed a charismatic white preacher to their death. Most black People's Temple followers were deeply invested in the "utopic" wish of racial equality and the revolutionary promise of grassroots organizing.

One of the central critiques of religious belief from secular and atheist thinkers is that religion robs human beings of agency. People live in fear and doubt, crippled by the inscrutable judgments of gods, grasping at the promise of an afterlife. Belief in the supernatural becomes a way to control the terms of death. When death is pervasive, unrelenting, and undiscriminating, the afterlife is a rich balm. When social and economic justice is elusive, religion and its marquee item—"The Afterlife"—provide a tolerable bridge between life and death. Heaven becomes life's spiritual money shot. The slaughter of innocents is given meaning, purpose, and cosmic heft. In his critique of religion, Marx argues that heaven and religious adherence are a function of human suffering. He argues that material conditions of economic and social injustice compel "man" to erect this alternate reality as a panacea:

> Man, who has found in the fantastic reality of heaven, where he sought a supernatural being, only his own reflection, will no longer be tempted to find only a semblance of himself—a non-human being—where he seeks and must seek his true reality. The basis of irreligious criticism is: *Man makes religion*, religion does not make man...*Religious* suffering is, at one and the same time, the *expression* of real suffering and a *protest* against real suffering. Religion is the sigh of the oppressed creature, the

heart of a heartless world, and the soul of soulless conditions. It is the *opium* of the people.[7]

In essence, religion has a dialectical relationship with the so-called human condition. To say "religious suffering is (both) the expression of real suffering and a protest against real suffering" is to acknowledge that religion springs from and thrives within a broader social context of oppression. Contrary to what some atheists believe, the need for religion will not simply evaporate when the masses get a steady diet of reason, science, and logic. Religious belief will not recede by lecturing people of color or working class whites about how ignorant they are to believe. Unless structural inequality is radically redressed, religious belief amongst disenfranchised peoples, both globally and within the U.S., will continue to thrive. The tragic allure of People's Temple speaks to this reality. The dominance of storefront churches in urban neighborhoods from Los Angeles to New York epitomizes it. Drive the length of any thoroughfare in urban America and the storefront church and its cousins—the abandoned building, the vacant lot, the brownfield—are signposts of American racial apartheid.

Marx identified the poverty of "reality" as a symptom of unequal material relations. Acquiescence to crushing inequality compels human beings to cling to the God concept and redemption in the afterlife. Yet, there is a fundamental disconnect between the fantastic reality of heaven and believers' lack of desire to actually go to heaven right now. In the face of good deeds and model citizenry, why must heaven wait? If heaven is such a paradise, a land of milk, honey, and godly blessings, why defer the everlasting? Why mourn the loss of innocents to the other side? Hundreds of People's Temple members did not commit revolutionary suicide in the jungles of Guyana on Jim Jones' orders. They resisted his paranoid edict that they sacrifice their lives and children for heaven. They begged for another chance at life and became mass murder victims. Mass murder was their reward after years of living simply "like Jesus"—doing hard labor while enduring physical and emotional abuse by Jones. It was God's ironic promise after giving up their jobs, savings, property, and independent will to a faith healer whose most sensational sideshow trick was flinging the Bible on the ground in front of stunned parishioners. In the aftermath of the massacre, religionists branded Jones a psychopath false prophet who duped his followers into believing he was god. But Jones and his "cultist" ilk are just the most flaming examples in recent history. Scratch the majesty of Gods—be they ten thousand years or ten days old—and you get man's reflection, leering back from the funhouse mirror.

Jonestown was also a metaphor for global perceptions about black death. The victims were assumed to either be complicit in their own deaths or ignorant of the depth of Jones' megalomania. Their desire to emigrate in order to escape conditions of racial apartheid in the U.S. was largely dismissed as crazy and baseless by the American public. But the Jonestown dead silently remind us about public reckoning with the scores of black murder victims ritually erased from the headlines. Young black men are more likely to suffer or die from gunshot wounds than any other group in the U.S. Yet, unlike the deaths of suburban white children in the 2012 Sandy Hook elementary school massacre in Newtown, Connecticut, the deaths of black children have never compelled a wholesale shift in public perception about gun laws or the gun lobby.

Even though mass murder is virtually non-existent in so-called inner city schools of color, it is doubtful that an attack on a predominantly African American or Latino facility would have inspired national outrage and soul searching about America's love affair with guns. White religious leaders would not have scrambled to explain why God forsook innocent American children of color in the "greatest" country on earth. Due to the relentless devaluation of black and brown lives in mainstream America, religious and spiritual explanations for life and death are often more immediate for people of color. Religious coping with death is about ritual, custom, and public celebration of the lives of the dead, in explicit recognition that "God" has beckoned and heaven awaits. Local stories about the murder of yet another African American child are always replete with soothing references to "going home to God." Because homicide is a leading killer of young black men and women, the threat of sudden death is ever present in many communities of color. According to the Violence Policy Center, African Americans comprise only 13% of the population yet account for 49% of all homicides in the U.S.[8] When a young person is cut down by a random shooting or police violence, the personal grief and mourning of the family becomes that of the entire community. At an early age, youth of color are shown that they are not unique, that senseless violence can occur anywhere and to anyone, and that the innocent are often caught in the crossfire. A few months after the Newtown murders, Shirley Chambers, an African American mother of four from Chicago whose children had all been killed in shootings, was featured on page fifteen of the L.A. Times.[9] Chambers' first son Carlos was shot in 1995. Her daughter LaToya and son Jerome were killed within months of each other in 2000. Her youngest son Ronnie was murdered thirteen years later in the same neighborhood. Before his murder, she'd "prayed hard" that he would be spared.

It is taken as gospel amongst youth of color that their deaths seldom elicit national coverage in the mainstream press. Black victims only rise to headline and name recognition status after a groundswell of community outrage, á la the Trayvon Martin case or that of Chicago teen Hadiya Pendleton.[10] In 2002, when I founded the Women's Leadership Project (WLP) as a pilot program at two South Los Angeles middle schools, one of my students' main concerns was the lack of media coverage of murders in their own communities. After the shooting death of 14 year-old Clive Jackson, one of their former classmates at Audubon Middle School, WLP students wrote letters to the local press challenging the imbalance in representation. Teaching students to become critically conscious about the way corporate media devalues the lives of people of color is a crucial part of the program. Yet, underneath it all is the persistent experience of death in the lives of youth who are barely teenagers, but are nonetheless forced to cope with trauma like adults.

Part of the innocence of white childhood is the slim likelihood that it will be marred by the police's murder of a friend, relative or classmate. In 1979, I attended a political protest with my father, after a woman named Eulia Love was gunned down by two Los Angeles Police Department (LAPD) officers in South Central. She had allegedly threatened the officers with a butcher knife. The killing elicited a firestorm in a community still reeling from the aftermath of the 1965 Watts Rebellion. What stood out for me as a child was the fact that this was a black woman victim, a mother, killed in cold blood at her own house. Home was supposed to be a safe space and a private sanctuary. It was what every proper, moral girl supposedly aspired to keep. In the white popular imagination, home was the maternal blur of Ozzie and

Harriet reruns, the dayglo of the uber-blond Brady Bunch, the toasty smell of Donna Reed's oven. Home, according to the white ideal, was supposed to be immune to outside forces. It was supposed to be a retreat guarded by the "good guys" who were sworn to "protect and serve" (the motto emblazoned on the side of LAPD squad cars). Yet, good guys from L.A.'s finest pumped several rounds into Love's body as she lay on the ground.

Love was killed during the reign of infamous LAPD chief Darryl Gates, the Bull Connor of the Wild Wild West. Gates used battering rams to ransack poor neighborhoods and once stated that blacks didn't respond to chokeholds like "normal people." Normal people meant white people, the gold standard for human biology, culture, and civilization. "Guilty until proven innocent", black people weren't normal because they didn't have homes, families or children worth protecting.

Because of this legacy, it is virtually impossible to escape the corporate media drumbeat that real victims are white and (mostly) female. Commenting on the devaluation of black life, Marsha Houston of Tulane University argues that "the killing of a white person is always treated as a significant loss." Certainly, the killing of *every* white person is not treated this way. However, by contrast, the killing of a black person is typically dismissed with an "assumption that that person was involved in the drug scene" and was expendable anyway.[11] Because African Americans are reflexively associated with crime, dysfunction, and violence, black death and victimhood is perceived as routine, customary, and hence less than noteworthy.[12] In their 2001 book *The Black Image in the White Mind*, Robert Entman and Andrew Rojecki maintained that "Television news portrays blacks in urban communities with a limited palate that paints a world out of control and replete with danger. Here, victimizers are more often black, and victims more often white. Racial coding also applies to lawbreakers: white victimizers often appear as personalized named individuals while black victimizers are often depersonalized nameless threats depicted in mug shots."[13] Over a decade later the trend continues. As Nadra Kareem Little notes:

> In December 1995, *American Journalism Review* wrote about a year-old Chicago study documenting that white victims of crime received more television news time than their minority counterparts. Recent research indicates that the trend continues in mainstream media. White victims

> in the United States frequently become household names. Decades after being raped and stabbed in 1964 within earshot of more than three dozen neighbors in the New York borough of Queens, Catherine "Kitty" Genovese remains one of the most memorable murder victims in the nation's history. In ensuing years, many other whites achieved notoriety as crime victims. These included Sharon Tate in 1969, Patty Hearst in 1974, Adam Walsh in 1981, JonBenet Ramsay in 1996, Laci Peterson in 2002 and Caylee Anthony in 2008 [and the list goes on and on]. Although blacks, Latinos and other persons of color also suffer from violent and random crimes, they typically do not garner major media attention.[14]

Thus, rounding out the overrepresentation of whites as victims is the overrepresentation of both blacks and Latinos as "lawbreakers." As Entman and Gross argue, "these patterns are more disturbing when one considers that blacks and Latinos may not appear as frequently as whites outside the crime-news context. Because of the value that defines the newsworthy, blacks in criminal roles tend to outnumber blacks in socially positive roles in newscasts and daily newspapers."[15]

It is small wonder then that religious memorials have outsize significance in communities of color. These rituals are a way of amplifying the value of lives that are deemed less valuable and not "newsworthy". They provide a counter-narrative to the dominant culture's historical erasure of black lives and black bodies. As Beverly Wallace and Paul Rosenblatt point out in their book *African American Grief*:

> For grieving African Americans, narrative is often about the larger societal context for the loss and the grieving. For people that have been denied a voice in the larger society, denied their own voice, and denied the voices of other African Americans in similar circumstances…there is a sense that grief is not only about the specific loss but about slavery and other forms of oppression that followed slavery and that, in many cases, continued up to the present.[16]

Within the context of religious memorials, the hopes, dreams, aspirations, and uniqueness of the dead (be they murder victim or natural death) become art. Prayer rituals, religious funerals, testimonials, and roadside memorials (if the death occurred in public) are part of the narrative process of assimilating pervasive death for communities of color under siege.[17]

Writing in 1903 about the death of his two year-old son Burghardt, W.E.B. DuBois expresses his ambivalence about the child's passing given the reality of racial terrorism and dehumanization. In his flowery elegy "Of the Passing of the First Born," he says:

> Nay, blame me not if I see the world thus darkly through the Veil—and my soul whispers ever to me, saying, 'Not dead, not dead, but escaped; not bond, but free.' No bitter meanness now shall sicken his baby heart till it die a living death, no taunt shall madden his happy boyhood. Fool that I was to think or wish that this little soul should grow choked and deformed within the Veil! I might have known that yonder deep unworldly look that ever and anon floated past his eyes was peering far beyond this narrow Now. In the poise of his little curl-crowned head did there not sit all that wild pride of being which his father had hardly crushed in his own heart? For what, forsooth, shall a Negro want with pride amid the studied humiliations of fifty million fellows? Well sped, my boy, before the world had dubbed your ambition insolence, had held your ideals unattainable, and taught you to cringe and bow. Better far this nameless void that stops my life than a sea of sorrow for you.[18]

DuBois laments the life of third class citizenship his son might have lived under the Veil of racism. Better that he be dead, delivered from the soul-killing muck of apartheid, from the scraping, bowing, and crushed ambition that gutted black self-determination. Biographer David Levering Lewis recounts that DuBois and his wife Nina were called "nigger" by whites on the street as they walked behind the carriage with Burghardt's coffin.[19] Death was painful solace, his son's fleeting time on earth a mixed blessing, the "nameless void" cold redemption for a boy who could never have submitted to being a mere "nigger."

DuBois, the skeptic, stops short of willing his son to a better place. Though inconsolable, he refrains from giving him wings, a bugle, and a passport to eternity. This, after all, was the one time apostate who, upon returning from the Soviet Union, dismissed religious belief as fairy tales and "moral disaster." But the narrative of homecoming, or joining God in heaven as a prophecy and life cycle fulfilled, looms large in many African American grief rituals. Here, Afrocentric notions of death often mingle with and complement traditional Christian perspectives on homecoming. In *African American Grief*, Wallace and Rosenblatt observe that "Afrocentric views on grief include death not being an end but a progression to something else…i.e., death is God's will, death is not to be feared, and life on earth is a preparation for life beyond death."[20] These traditions are directly related to Africa and the diaspora. Indeed, "evidence of similarities between Africans on the continent and their descendents dispersed across the Atlantic can still be seen when modern visitors frequent slave cemeteries…enslaved people, like their African predecessors often customarily interred personal items with the deceased."[21] Funeral parlors also play a large role in the pageantry of death, reflection, and the narrative of stolen or lost youth. For generations, funeral home chains have been a thriving business in African American communities. Like churches, they were some of the only business enterprises that were open to African Americans under Jim Crow segregation.[22] Like churches, they are a prominent part of the built landscape in communities of color, both because of the higher frequency of death amongst people of color and the legacy of racial segregation.[23]

In South Los Angeles' Crenshaw District, there are three funeral homes within a one mile radius of each other. On bright sunny days young people pour out from the mortuary doors after viewing hours, lingering on the steps reminiscing, sporting t-shirts with pictures and art work commemorating the dead. In a freeway bound culture steeped in car worship, vehicles are often rolling R.I.P. memorials of the dearly departed, the tragedy of stolen youth ornately inscribed on rear windows for the world to see. When death is intimately woven into the experience of being a child, nostalgic Americana notions of childhood as a carefree idyllic time are disrupted. In working class communities of color, part of the normal context of death and grieving is the trauma of sexual abuse, domestic violence, transience due to unemployment, incarceration, and social invisibility. Sudden and untimely death often compels youth to question the iron cultural grip of blind faith. In the juvenile justice journal *The Beat Within*, an incarcerated youth in northern California asks:

> How can I live?
> How can I breathe?
> How can I praise God while he watches me bleed?
> How do I know?

How do I find?
How do I find love when my friends are dead and family left behind?
How can I live this life knowing there is only two ways it's going to end?[24]

For this young person, the constant threat of mortality forces a crisis of faith. Pushing aside the dead to live, the uncertainty of God's omnipotence is like a noose. Writing in the early 1900s when lynch mob justice was pervasive and race riots ripped through Northern ghettoes, W.E.B. DuBois noted: "Among Negroes especially today it is most natural for preachers to sneer at the man who is 'merely' good and emphasize the transcendental value of the person who is too dumb to question any fairy-tale forced upon his belief. Yet the young person who questions, who refuses to accept as truth all that he is told, is the salt of the earth and the hope of the future."[25] And still, scores of incarcerated youth are exhorted to "just pray". God will listen and give a sign. And, if he doesn't deliver you from the evil of racist sentencing and imprisonment laws it is not because he is less omnipotent, loving and all-seeing. Like an ideal, absentee lover, he just moves in mysterious ways. As one of the most eloquent critics of American militarism, materialism, and racism, Martin Luther King identified God as the ultimate arbiter of moral justice. In his 1967 speech condemning the Vietnam War, King criticized U.S. materialism and its emphasis on a culture of things. Materialism was a secular evil promoted by a world that had lost its spiritual compass in the divine. Secularism, as distinguished from the spiritual, is caricatured as the fount of moral decay. But decades after King's assassination, African American wealth has shriveled. On God's watch, the American dream has devolved into a brutal sham, and the gargantuan disparities between the capitalist elite and working people has made economic justice more elusive now than during the Jim Crow era. But still, young people are exhorted to pray…to have faith. While "God" watches them bleed in the streets, prisons, and homeless shelters of the wealthiest most religious nation on the planet.

The Immortals

The white men lie in wait outside the abortion clinic. They are separated by nearly a decade of political bloodletting and fifty crazy quilt states, but they are still kin under the skin, brothers in arms, God's anonymous foot soldiers for the unborn. When I had my first abortion in Los Angeles in 1990 one brother was there, traffic at his back, posters of smashed fetuses swinging crisply in the breeze. When I had another abortion in Connecticut in 1997, the second brother had morphed into a limp biscuit for Armageddon, rasping canned slogans about slaughtered innocents through nicotine breath. The Planned Parenthood clinic was staffed with the kind of caring, unsung professionals whose lives and dignity have been ransacked by three generations of Christian fundamentalist propaganda and terrorist violence. The next morning after the procedure I went running, my body returned to me, the specter of the brotherhood beaten back out of sheer geographic and historical luck.

Since then, the white nationalist terrorist movement to "save" the unborn has claimed the lives of several activist doctors and clinic workers. By demonizing these frontline providers the movement has jeopardized the lives and families of scores of women from the South to the Midwest. It has ginned up the narrative of black and brown women as dangerous irresponsible breeders and revitalized the shorthand of the American plantation when empire began and ended with black women's bodies.

In the eighties and nineties, Operation Rescue, a radical right evangelical Christian anti-abortion organization, was the storm trooper of the movement. Through violent paramilitary street theatre it succeeded in erasing the bodies of pregnant women "from the image (allowing) the fetal form to become a token in a discourse of and about men."[26] This fixation on the fetus and the unborn, magically divorced from the body of the mother, has fueled a new generation of anti-abortion legislation. Personhood amendments and fetal homicide laws have entered into the mainstream of public policy. And in an era in which Catholic Ireland is the only other Western nation to have more extreme anti-abortion laws, criminalizing bad mothers and reclaiming reproduction has become a centerpiece of the U.S.' radical right nationalist revolution.

Speaking for "God," the storm troopers for the unborn lay waste to science and terrorize all women with the threat of subordination to the "civil rights" of fertilized eggs. Women who betray the insurgent citizens lurking in their uteruses betray their allegiance to god, the state, and patriarchy—merchants who seek omnipotent control over life and death. Religious narratives promoting the falsehood about fetuses' silently screaming in pain have long mired abortion rights in an insidiously anti-woman debate about when life begins. But one of the most unsettlingly simple yet profound questions I've heard from a child is, "where was I before I was born?" Was I dead? In their roles as little scientists, children grasp that before birth is a kind of death. They know intuitively that there is a connection between the infinite and unfathomable period of time before birth and the forevermore of death.

What would it mean to bottle this genius, the skeptic sense that, despite the grand tortured egocentric blip-on-the-screen wishes of human beings, there is no dance with the infinite, no immortality beyond the residue of our inventions, memories, artifacts, no cosmic solace beyond the dust we're ground into inside a pig's shit-stained snout? Whole industries devoted to fetishizing eternity would be decimated. The American death industry pimps eternity hard, squeals about redemption, then tasks the faithful with collecting the bloody dividends. For the believer, the death of an atheist or agnostic loved one is a theological crap shoot. This event invariably inspires fantasy, creative license, and outright betrayal of the deceased's principles.

Such was the case with Alfee Enciso, a family friend and middle school administrator who collapsed during a basketball game at his school, went into a coma, and never regained consciousness. One afternoon when I went to visit him in the hospital I stumbled right into the middle of a raging prayer circle. Heads bowed, hands joined, voices hushed, three friends and family were deep in the throes of spiritual reconnaissance over Alfee's bed.

Thanks, but no thanks, he would have said. At 54, Alfee was a hardcore skeptic, an agnostic-atheist who never took anything on faith and made it his business to slash sacred cows of all stripes. An esteemed educator, he ruled his classrooms like a prize fighter, inspiring all who entered to think critically about institutional racism, classism, sexism, and sociopolitical conditions in communities of color. As one of my mother Yvonne's first teacher mentees he put her ethos on teaching as radical humanist art into practice. His lessons drew on everyone from Bob Dylan to Toni Morrison to Tupac to Shakespeare to Sandra Cisneros. He used these authors' explorations of social justice, morality, and life's paradoxes to inspire black and Latino students who'd had it drilled into them that they weren't cut out to be intellectuals or scholars. Having learned from my mother's rigorous example, Alfee's approach was to bring it on—lavishing his students with both multicultural and canonical "Great White Men" literature, schooling them in how institutional racism was at play from everything to the fast food that they ate, the crappy, chronically-late public buses they had to ride, and the draconian prison system that ensnared their friends and family at an early age.

But none of his passion for freethought was captured in the marathon orgy of Catholicism that was his memorial. During the ceremony, Alfee's ashes were paraded down the church aisle in a little urn while the pastor declared to the faithful that "our brother has been called home." It was a spectacle that he would have certainly parodied—he, the Chicano blasphemer who once wrote (in response to one of my pieces on death and religion) that "this rips the covers off the hypocrisy and the monarchical role that religion plays in our society. It (religion) swears out its conformity and power to the downtrodden it shackles every day. Let's examine the nexus between corporate obscenity and the hand-holding of their gospel spewing brethren in the tax free halls of America. Neither pay taxes, both exploit and we the benighted beg at their altars for alms, or forgiveness, or both."

When my twin infant son Jay died ten days after his birth I was spared the prayer circles but got sprayed by the angel talk and the Jesus juice. Jay was going to be a Black angel with white wings hurtling up to take his place with the Lord. He was going to be one of the elite gold card cherubs that "God" had watched suffer and die. In a candid moment he would get to ask God, "Why did you fuck me?" And be told "Membership has its privileges."

In death, faith is the easiest breeziest coziest bromide fondue. Snatch it away and there is savagery. The savagery of outliving one's young child. The savagery of a "Christian" nation that lets communities like mine bury its children week in and week out while spending billions on immoral imperialist wars. The savagery of the good dying young and the evil wanking into dotage. The savagery of organized religion that only makes the death of a child assimilable through fraud deities that, as Epicurus sagely protested, have neither the power nor the will to give or spare life in the first place:

> *Is God willing to prevent evil, but not able? Then he is not omnipotent. Is he able, but not willing? Then he is malevolent. Is he both able and*

willing? Then whence cometh evil? Is he neither able nor willing? Then why call him God?

In her *Free Inquiry* article "Grief Beyond Belief," atheist writer Rebecca Hensler talks about the difficulty of dealing with God talk after the death of her son. Seeking solace in other bereaved parents she says, "I found myself alienated by (their) constant talk of being reunited with their children someday. I had no patience with credulous stories of signs from beloved sons and daughters."[27] The experience motivated her to start a Grief Beyond Belief Facebook page for those who need secular spaces to mourn. Secular grieving and its rituals are still a nascent enterprise. In communities of color where hyper-religiosity and "spiritualism" become the default categories to memorialize death, secular spaces are virtually non-existent.

But Hensler recognized that the experience of untimely, sudden, and/or violent death was especially acute for grieving loved ones, often prompting them to question belief in God, heaven, and eternity: "If anything, (the need for secular grief resources) was even more raw in those who had been believers until the death of a loved one…for those new non-believers, especially those surrounded by religious friends and family members, the support of other grieving nonbelievers might ease the transition."[28]

When the doctors took my son off of life support, my husband Stephen and I decided we could not bear to witness it. The thought of seeing the inevitable, of watching the life leave his small body, was agony. The shadow of his short life reverberates with the absence of friends, lovers, and experiences that will never be.

Non-believers refuse to waste time and energy on an afterlife but the abyss still stings, as Bob Dylan once sang, "like a corkscrew to the heart". All of the rituals of religious redemption have been stripped, delivered up to the cold light of day as a Disneyland front for the bloody, ugly, untamable, Sisyphean TKO of the right-here-right-now, where the dead are "immortal" in the living, and the living slouch each second toward the dead.

Endnotes

INTRODUCTION

[1] Thomas Shapiro, et al. "The Roots of the Widening Racial Wealth Gap: Explaining the Black-White Divide," Institute on Assets and Social Policy, Brandeis University, Institute on Assets and Social Policy, February 2013.

[2] Sarah Huisenga, "Newt Gingrich: 'Poor Kids Don't Work Unless it's Illegal,'" *CBS News*, December 1, 2011, (http://www.cbsnews.com/8301-503544_162-57335118-503544/newt-gingrich-poor-kids-dont-work-unless-its-illegal/). (Accessed March 2, 2013).

[3] The Obama administration introduced Race to the Top in 2009 to promote greater "accountability and competitiveness" across school districts. Principally, the initiative lavishes funding on districts that tie teacher performance/assessment to high stakes testing and encourage charter school creation.

[4] Walmart's Walton Family Foundation alone has poured over 84 million into the Los Angeles school system, promoting charters, backing charter-friendly candidates, and political action committees. As Peter Dreier notes, "we must ask why are the Waltons, a largely out-of-state family with no ties to Los Angeles' children and little background in education, intent on turning our communities' educational choices into a junior version of the cutthroat, profiteering corporate world?" Dreier, "Why Are Walmart's Billionaires Bankrolling Phony School Reform in L.A.?" *L.A. Progressive*, February 28, 2013. (http://www.laprogressive.com/walmart-bankrolling-school-reform/?utm_source=LA%20Progressive). (Accessed March 2, 2013).

[5] Education Trust-West, "At a Crossroads: A Comprehensive Picture of How African American Youth Fare in Los Angeles County Schools," *Education Trust-West*, February 2013.

[6] Sikivu Hutchinson, "Feminist Pedagogy and Youth Advocacy in South Los Angeles," *International Journal of Learning,* Volume 11, 2004, p. 646.

[7] The first Africans were believed to have come in the 1500s, one-hundred years before the Mayflower and the Jamestown, Virginia settlers. Juan Garrido was the first documented black person to arrive in what is now known as Florida.

[8] When Hurston began to study world religions she saw that they shared the common theme of divine deliverance from earthly suffering. She then concluded that faith merely allowed the masses to deal with their "fear of life and its consequences." See Zora Neale Hurston, "Religion," from *Dust Tracks on a Road* (New York: J.B. Lippincott, 1942), pp. 215-226.

CHAPTER ONE

[1] James Ledbetter, "What is American Exceptionalism," *Reuters*, January 23, 2012 (http://blogs.reuters.com/great-debate/2012/01/23/what-is-american-exceptionalism/). Ledbetter notes that during the presidential race GOP candidates Mitt Romney and Newt Gingrich consistently questioned Obama's commitment to exceptionalism: "Although they spend a lot of time these days at one another's throat, appeared on the night of the South Carolina primary to agree on at least one thing: Each believes in "American exceptionalism," and, they say, Barack Obama does not… Gingrich even devoted an entire book to the subject." Gingrich has portrayed exceptionalism as a manifestation of God-bestowed greatness stemming from the U.S.' advancement of democracy and individual liberty; rather than exemplifying a uniquely republican heritage based on secular freedoms.

[2] Newt Gingrich, *A Nation Like No Other: Why American Exceptionalism Matters* (New York: Regnery Publishing, 2011), pp. 7 & 18.

[3] In reviewing the papers from the American Presidency Project, Robert Schlesinger reports that Obama has used the term exceptionalism to describe the U.S. more than any other modern president, including right-wing icons Ronald Reagan and George W. Bush. See Robert Schlesinger, "Obama Has Mentioned American Exceptionalism More Than Bush," *U.S. News and World Report*, January 31, 2011 (http://www.usnews.com/opinion/blogs/robert-schlesinger/2011/01/31/obama-has-mentioned-american-exceptionalism-more-than-bush).

[4] Gingrich, p 21. "The Declaration's writers understood there was a force in the universe greater than themselves, and they incorporated this humbling recognition

into their work…If our rights are given by a divine Creator, then there is a divine plan for humanity."

[5] David Cheesbrough, *Frederick Douglass: Oratory from Slavery* (Greenwood, CT: Westport Publishing, 1998), p. 116.

[6] Mignon Moore, *Invisible Families* (Berkeley: UC Press, 2011), pp. 182, 206-207.

[7] Ibid., p. 207.

[8] David M. Barnes and Ilan H. Meyer, "Religious Affiliation, Internalized Homophobia, and Mental Health in Lesbians, Gay Men, and Bisexuals," *American Journal of Orthopsychiatry* (Volume 82, Issue 4), October 2012, pp. 505-515. The study was conducted exclusively from 2004-2005 to New York city. Though the study was not exhaustive, the "results supported the general hypothesis that non-affirming religion was associated with higher internalized homophobia."

[9] Derrick McMahon, "Boys and Baby Dolls," *Our Weekly*, June 16, 2010, p. 8.

[10] (http://www.witnessfortheworld.org/founder.html). (Accessed December 3, 2012).

[11] Ibid.

[12] Dan Avery, "California Governor Brown Signs Bill Banning Reparative Therapy," *Queerty*, September 30, 2012 (http://www.queerty.com/breaking-ca-governor-browns-signs-bill-banning-reparative-therapy-into-law-20120930/).

[13] Kapya John Kaoma, "Colonizing African Values: How the U.S. Christian Right is Transforming Politics in Africa," Political Research Associates, 2012, p. 4.

[14] In youth culture the letter "Q" stands for questioning.

[15] See the American Humanist Association, LGBT Humanist Councils (http://www.lgbthumanists.org/). (Accessed December 12, 2012).

[16] It's estimated that one in seven foster care youth become homeless. See "Hopes and Hurdles: California Foster Care Youth and College Financial Aid," Report by *The Institute for College Access and Success*, 2009, p. 5.

[17] "No Way Home: Understanding the Needs and Experiences of Homeless Youth in Hollywood," Report from Children's Hospital Los Angeles, 2010, pp. 18-19. The overrepresentation of African Americans is also reflected in the broader Los Angeles County homeless population.

[18] Nicholas Ray, "Lesbian, Gay, Bisexual and Transgender Youth: An Epidemic of Homelessness," National Gay and Lesbian Task Force Policy Institute and the National Coalition for the Homeless, 2006, pp. 4-6. The report questions the granting of service provision funding to religious organizations that have historically viewed homosexuality and gay people as sinful. Under former president George W. Bush, faith-based initiative subsidies were indiscriminately doled out to religious organizations with no accountability. Under the faith based initiative policy religious organizations can discriminate in hiring and service provision. Covenant House is a recipient of faith based funding and has only recently begun to adopt culturally-responsive policies that allow trans youth to be considered as the gender they identified with, rather than their biological sex, and live in non-segregated quarters.

[19] Covenant House Texas was accused by LGBT activists of "identifying its transgender clients according to the gender shown on birth certificates and…ignoring complaints of bullying and discrimination." Josef Molnar, "Covenant House Opens up to Transgender Youth," *Out Smart*, June 16, 2011 (http://outsmartmagazine.com/2011/06/covenant-house-opens-up-to-transgender-youth-gender-preference-now-recognized-by-center).

[20] Ibid.; See also, Ray, pp. 4-6.

[21] Ibid.

[22] Tom Gallagher, "Helping Kids, One Bold Kindness at a Time," *National Catholic Reporter*, October 13, 2012 (http://ncronline.org/news/people/helping-kids-one-bold-kindness-time).

[23] Jerome Hunt and Aisha Moodie Mills, "The Unfair Criminalization of Gay and Transgender Youth: An Overview of the Experiences of LGBT Youth in the Juvenile Justice System," Center for American Progress, June 29, 2012, p. 1.

[24] *The Institute for College Access and Success*, p. 2.

[25] The bullying-related suicides of Phoebe Prince and Tyler Clementi elicited national coverage; prompting condemnation from president Obama and the creation of the "It Gets Better" anti-bullying campaign.

[26] As with the dominant culture, many of my students believe that open displays of bisexual or even lesbian desire is more acceptable amongst girls who are "feminine" and gender-conforming than for non-gender conforming girls or more "masculine" girls.

[27] Langston Hughes, *The Collected Poems of Langston Hughes* (New York: Random House, 1995), pp. 166-167. In this volume, editor Arnold Rampersad writes that "Goodbye Christ" and other radical poetry, "would haunt Hughes' career for the rest of his life, with conservative political and religious groups citing them as evidence of his alleged communist beliefs and associations. Under such pressure, Hughes repudiated 'Goodbye Christ' and in general suppressed the bulk of his radical poetry," p. 4.

[28] Ibid.

[29] In addition to decrying his personal attack on her in the poem, Mcpherson slammed Hughes' Communist sympathies as anti-American. See Matthew Avery Sutton, *Aimee Semple Mcpherson and the Resurrection of Christian America* (Cambridge: Harvard University Press, 2007) pp. 244-246.

[30] Ibid., p. 246.

[31] As the *Los Angeles Times* reports, "Even though public opposition to same-sex marriage and gay rights is rapidly eroding, the locker rooms and clubhouses of the country's four major sports leagues remain among the last bastions of homophobia in the U.S." The article states that there have been no active professional sports players in the NFL, NHL or NBA that have come out during their careers. See Kevin Baxter, "In Pro Sports, Gay Athletes Still Feel Unwelcome," *Los Angeles Times,* December 29, 2012 (http://www.latimes.com/sports/la-sp-sports-homophobia-20121230,0,5283191.story).

[32] Among the charges were that LGBT students were being disciplined more harshly and bigoted religious condemnations were made toward out students and faculty.

[33] See, for example, Francine Ramsey, Marjorie Hill, et al, "Black Lesbians Matter: An Examination of the Unique Experiences, Perspectives and Priorities of the Black Lesbian Community," *The Zuna Institute,* July 2010, pp. 5-6; Sabrina Tavernise, "Parenting By Gays More Common in the South, Census Shows," *New York Times,* January 18, 2011, (http://www.nytimes.com/2011/01/19/us/19gays.html). According to this article, childrearing in the South is more prevalent than in any region of the country and the majority of gay Southern parents are people of color. Black and Latino couples are "twice as likely as whites to be raising children."

[34] Aisha C. Moodie-Mills and Karen Miller, "Black Churches May Be More Friend than Foe to Gay Congregants," Center for American Progress, October 30, 2012 (http://www.americanprogress.org/issues/lgbt/news/2012/10/30/43299/black-churches-may-be-more-friend-than-foe-to-gay-congregants/).

[35] Ibid.

[36] Ibid.

[37] Irene Monroe, "Will Obama's Support of Marriage Equality Keep Some Blacks Home on Election Day?" *The Huffington Post*, September 25, 2012 (http://www.huffingtonpost.com/irene-monroe/will-obamas-support-of-marriage-equality-keep-some-blacks-home-on-election-day_b_1895246.html).

[38] Tavernise, A1.

[39] Though widely attributed to Niebuhr, there is controversy about the origins of the prayer. See Laurie Goodstein, "Serenity Prayer Stirs Up Doubt: Who Wrote It?" *New York Times*, July 11, 2008 (http://www.nytimes.com/2008/07/11/us/11prayer.html?_r=0).

CHAPTER TWO

[1] Kenneth Jackson, *Crabgrass Frontier: The Suburbanization of the United States* (New York: Oxford University Press, 1985), p. 172.

[2] Ibid., p. 174.

[3] In 2011, Microsoft introduced a cell phone app designed to allow users to "avoid neighborhoods with unsafe conditions…or harsh temperatures." Because it relied on crime stats to identify so-called bad neighborhoods it was dubbed the "avoid ghetto" app within the industry.

[4] Jane Mayer, "Bully Pulpit," *The New Yorker*, June 18, 2012, p. 57.

[5] Ibid., p. 61. So says Bryan Fischer.

[6] Ibid.

[7] Mary Kane, "Suit Alleges Trusted Blacks Drew Minorities to High-Rate Loans," *Washington Times*, September 17, 2009.

[8] Tara Siegel Bernard, "Blacks Face Bias in Bankruptcy, Study Suggests," *New York Times,* January 20, 2012 (http://www.nytimes.com/2012/01/21/business/blacks-face-bias-in-bankruptcy-study-suggests.html). According to a 2011 study published in the *Journal of Legal Empirical Studies*,African Americans are twice as likely as whites to be steered to Chapter 13 bankruptcy: "The disparity persisted even when the researchers adjusted for income, homeownership, assets, and education. The evidence

suggested that lawyers were disproportionately steering blacks into a process that was not as good for them financially, in part because of biases, whether conscious or unconscious."

[9] The federal Dream Act would provide a path to citizenship for undocumented young people. Over the past several years it has been the subject of fierce Republican opposition in Congress.

[10] According to the 2010 U.S. Census, over 30% of Latinos identify as white. The Pew Hispanic Research Center has found that 36% of Latinos identify as white. See Taylor, Hugo Lopez, et al. "When Labels Don't Fit: Hispanics and Their Views of Identity."

[11] Joseph Graves, *The Race Myth: Why We Pretend Race Exists in America* (New York: Plume, 2004), p. 17.

[12] Earl Smith, "Gatekeeping in the Halls of Science: The Continuing Significance of Race (Part I)," Racism Review, August 25, 2011 (http://www.racismreview.com/blog/2011/08/25/gate-keeping-in-the-halls-of-science-the-continuing-significance-of-race-part-1/). See also, Donna Ginther, et al. "Race, Ethnicity and NIH Research Awards," *Science* 19, August 11, 2011, pp. 1015-1019.

[13] Frank Douglas, "Discrimination in Academia," *The Scientist*, July 31, 2007 (http://classic.the-scientist.com/news/display/53451/).

[14] Passed in 1996, Proposition 209 prohibited government institutions from considering race, sex or ethnicity in public sector employment, education and contracting. It has severely reduced admissions of African American and Latino students to UC campuses.

[15] Jill Nelson, *Volunteer Slavery: My Authentic Negro Experience* (Chicago: The Noble Press, 1993), pp. 90-91.

[16] Alom Shaha, "The Accidental Exclusion of Non-White Atheists," *The Guardian*, November 17, 2010 (http://www.guardian.co.uk/commentisfree/belief/2010/nov/17/non-white-atheists-exclusion).

[17] Interview with Ian Cromwell, September 19, 2012.

[18] Ian Cromwell, "No, This is How We Get More Black People Involved in the Movement," *Racialicious*, September, 9, 2011 (http://www.racialicious.com/2011/09/07/no-this-is-how-we-get-more-black-people-involved-in-the-atheist-movement/).

[19] Ophelia Benson, "Nontheism and Feminism: Why the Disconnect?" *Free Inquiry*, Vol. 33, No. 1, December 2012/January 2013, p. 32.

[20] Michael Shermer, "Feminism Disconnected: A Response to Ophelia Benson and a Caution on Tribalism in Secularism," eSkeptic Blog, December 12, 2012 (http://www.skeptic.com/eskeptic/12-12-12/#feature).

[21] PZ Myers, "That's not a response, Michael, it's a denial," *Pharyngula Blog,* December 12, 2012 (http://freethoughtblogs.com/pharyngula/2012/12/12/thats-not-a-response-michael-its-a-denial/).

[22] Several studies have connected experiences and perceptions of racism to higher rates of depression amongst people of color. See for example, Fernando Sunam, "Racism as a Cause of Depression," *International Journal of Social Psychiatry,* March 1984, 30:1, pp. 41-49: Rodney Clark, et al., "Racism as a Stressor for African Americans," *American Psychologist,* October 1999, 54:10, pp. 805-816: Sharon Lambert, Keith Herman, et al. "Perceptions of Racism and Depressive Symptoms in African American Adolescents: The Role of Perceived Academic and Social Control," *J Youth Adolescence,* April 2009, 38:4, pp. 519-531.

[23] Ahmed Zewail, "How curiosity begat Curiosity," *Los Angeles Times,* August 19, 2012, Section 1, p. A22

[24] Donald Bogle, *Toms, Coons, Mulattoes, Mammies and Bucks: An Interpretive History of Blacks in American Films* (New York: Continuum International Publishing, 2001), p. 131.

[25] Daniel H. Wilson and Anna Long, *The Mad Scientist Hall of Fame* (New York: Citadel Press Books, 2008), p. ix.

[26] See Caitlin Wolfinger, Steve Mattox, et al. "Representation of Gender and Race of Scientists in Children's Earth Science Textbooks," MSTA Journal, Fall 2011, pp. 19-22.

[27] Zewail, p. A22.

[28] Sandra L. Hanson, *Swimming Against the Tide: African American Girls and Science Education* (Philadelphia: Temple University Press, 2009), p. 46.

[29] Ibid., p. 14: See also Diann Jordan, *Sisters in Science: Conversations with Black Women Scientists on Race, Gender and Their Passion for Science* (Oklahoma: Purdue University Press, 2006), pp. ix-xii. Jordan comments that girls express high interest in math and science but their interest in science declines during the middle school years.

[30] Hanson, p. 16.

[31] Ibid., pp. 50-51.

[32] Ibid., pp. 75-83.

[33] Stephen Ceasar, "Summer Means Science for These Minority Students," *L.A. Times*, August 5, 2012 (http://www.latimes.com/news/local/la-me-teen-science-20120805,0,1677437.story).

[34] Ibid., pp. 10-12, 19. Disparities are especially egregious in regions like Washington D.C. With African Americans comprising over 90% of its student body, D.C. is only at 33% equity, while Latino students (at 17%) have achieved 100% equity. High schools that had exemplary AP preparation and enrollment programs for African American students were in Texas, Maryland, Florida and Illinois.

[35] Advanced Placement courses enable college-bound students to gain college credit. Students have the opportunity to take special AP tests that provide them with credit based on the score they receive. According to the College Board, "Earning a three or higher out of a possible five on an AP exam is one of the best predictors of college performance, with AP students earning better grades in college and graduating from college at higher rates than their peers in controlled groups." See Michelle J. Nealy, "In Some States AP Course Access and Scores Improve for Hispanics But Not For Blacks," *Diverse Education,* February 14, 2008 (http://diverseeducation.com/article/10659c2/in-some-states-ap-course-access-and-scores-improve-for-hispanics-but-not-blacks.html).

[36] College Board, *AP Report to the Nation*, February 9, 2011, p. 3.

[37] See for example, "Teacher Quality and Student Achievement Research Review," The Center for Public Education, 2005 (http://www.centerforpubliceducation.org/Main-Menu/Staffingstudents/Teacher-quality-and-student-achievement-At-a-glance/Teacher-quality-and-student-achievement-Research-review.html).

[38] Geneva Gay, *Culturally Responsive Teaching: Theory, Research, and Practice* (New York: Teacher's College Press, 2000), p. 46.

[39] See for example, Gail Thompson, *Through Ebony Eyes: What Teachers Need to Know But Are Afraid to Ask About African American Students* (San Francisco, CA: Jossey Bass, 2004), pp. 1-37: Gay, pp. 1-46.

[40] Jamaal Abdul-Alim, "AP Courses Not Available for Black Students," *Diverse Issues in Higher Education*, February 9, 2012 (http://diverseeducation.com/article/16822/).

[41] There is voluminous research to support this claim. See, for example, The Justice Center, "The School Discipline Consensus Project," The Council of State Governments, July, 2011; Daniel J. Loesen and Russell J. Skiba, "Suspended Education, Urban Middle Schools in Crisis," Southern Poverty Law Center, September 2010; Russell J. Skiba, Robert S. Michael, et al. "The Color of Discipline: Sources of Racial and Gender Disproportionality in School Punishment," Indiana Education Policy Center, June 2000.

[42] See Loesen and Skiba, 2010; "Test, Punish, and Push-Out: How Zero Tolerance and High Stakes Testing Fuel the School to Prison Pipeline," The Advancement Project, March 2010; Peter Balfanz, "Putting Middle Grades Students on the Graduation Path," Johns Hopkins University, Everyone Graduates Center, June 2009.

[43] Academic Institutions of Minority Faculty with Science, Engineering and Health Doctorates, NSF, October 2011 (http://www.nsf.gov/statistics/infbrief/nsf11320/).

[44] Donna Nelson, "Barriers for Black Scientists," *Nova*, February 6, 2007 (http://www.pbs.org/wgbh/nova/physics/barriers-black-scientists.html).

[45] Interview with Devin Waller, August, 2012.

[46] In my experience nursing is the number one profession of interest for high school girls of color; rather than expressing interest in being doctors and/or scientists many of my female students aspire to be nurses. When girls do express interest in being doctors they invariably cite becoming a pediatrician as their number one preference.

[47] Nichols wanted to quit after the first year because the Uhura part was marginal. However, after a young black fan told her that her presence on the show inspired her to do better in school she decided to stay.

[48] Thomas L. Good and Jere E. Brophy, *Looking in Classrooms* (New York: Harper Collins, 1991), p. 30.

[49] Harriet Washington, *Medical Apartheid: The Dark History of Medical Experimentation on Black Americans from Colonial Times to the Present* (New York: Anchor Books, 2006), p. 21.

[50] Ibid., pp. 9 & 25.

CHAPTER THREE

[1] Jeffrey Perry, *Hubert Harrison: The Voice of Harlem Radicalism, 1883-1918* (New York: Columbia University Press, 2009), p. 233.

[2] Chris Hedges, " The Rise of Christian Fascism and Its Threat to American Democracy," *Alternet*, February 7, 2007, (http://www.alternet.org/story/47679/the_rise_of_christian_fascism_and_its_threat_to_american_democracy). (Accessed January 27, 2013).

[3] Earl Ofari Hutchinson, *Betrayed: A History of Presidential Failure to Protect Black Lives* (Boulder: Westview Press, 1996), p. 2.

[4] Paula Giddings, *Ida B. Wells and the Campaign Against Lynching* (New York: Harper Collins, 2008), p. 226-7.

[5] Scott Malcomson, *One Drop of Blood: The American Misadventure of Race* (New York: Farrar, Strauss, Giroux, 2000), p. 352.

[6] Carla Kaplan, *Zora Neale Hurston: A Life in Letters* (New York: Anchor Books, 2003), p. 728.

[7] Dom Apollon, "Don't Call Them 'Post-Racial': Millennials Say Race Matters to Them," *Colorlines* Magazine, June 2011 (http://colorlines.com/archives/2011/06/youth_and_race_focus_group_main.html). (Accessed June 3, 2012).

[8] Peter Berger, Grace Davie and Effie Fokas, *Religious America, Secular Europe? A Theme and Variation* (Burlington, VT: Ashgate Publishing, 2008), p. 17.

[9] Steven Mintz, *African American Voices: A Documentary Reader,* 1619-1877 (Oxford: Wiley-Blackwell, 2009), p. 16.

[10] Seventeenth Century Virginia Law stated that, "Whereas some doubts have arisen whether children got by any Englishman upon a Negro woman should be slave or free, be it therefore enacted and declared by this present Grand Assembly, that all children born in this country shall be held bond or free only according to the condition of the mother; and that if any Christian shall commit fornication with a Negro man or woman, he or she so offending shall pay double the fines imposed by the former act." See Ania Loomba and Jonathon Burton, *Race in Early Modern England* (New York: Palgrave McMillan, 2007), p. 229.

[11] Ibid.

[12] F. James Davis, *Who is Black? One Nation's Definition* (Philadelphia: Pennsylvania State University, 1991), p. 13.

[13] One-Drop Rule Persists," *Harvard Gazette*, 12/2010 (http://news.harvard.edu/gazette/story/2010/12/%E2%80%98one-drop-rule%E2%80%99-persists). (Accessed July 9, 2012).

[14] Davis, p. 17.

[15] Jill Lepore, "The Politics of Planned Parenthood and Women's Rights," *The New Yorker*, November 14, 2011.

[16] Under Title X, clinics cannot receive funding for abortions but can provide "non-directive counseling" to pregnant women, which includes information on "pregnancy termination." See Cynthia Dallard, "Challenges Facing Family Planning Clinics and Title X," *The Guttmacher Report on Public Policy*, April 2001 (http://www.guttmacher.org/pubs/tgr/04/2/gr040208.pdf). (Accessed June 2012).

[17] Ibid.

[18] Berkeley described the insurgents as a "Rabble Crew…there being hardly two amongst them that we have heard of who have Estates or are persons of Reputation and indeed very few who can either read or write." Ronald Takaki, *A Different Mirror: A History of Multicultural America* (Boston: Little Brown Company, 1993), p. 64.

[19] Ibid., pp. 60-68.

[20] Theodore Allen documents the shockwaves that Bacon's Rebellion sent through the colonies. At every turn, from the late 17th to the early 18th century, underclass whites were granted more and more rights and privileges: "The white-skin privileges of the poor free whites were simply reflexes of the disabilities imposed on the Negro slave: to move about freely without a pass; to marry without any upper-class consent; to change employment; to vote in elections in accordance with the laws on qualifications; to acquire property; and last, but not least, in this partial list, the right of self-defense." See Allen," '…They Would Have Destroyed Me': Slavery and the Origins of Racism," *Radical America*, Volume 9, no. 3 (May-June, 1975), p. 15 (http://www.sojournertruth.net/destroyedme). (Accessed January 27, 2013).

[21] Howard Zinn, *A People's History of the United States* (New York: Harper Collins, 2003), p. 37.

[22] Ira Berlin, "Race the Power of an Illusion: Interview" (http://www.pbs.org/race/000_About/002_04-background-02-08.htm). (Accessed June 6, 2012).

[23] Allen, p. 13.

[24] Richard Fausset, "In Alabama, a Church Sees its Latino Brethren Vanish," *L.A. Times*, December 30, 2011 (http://www.latimes.com/news/nationworld/nation/la-na-alabama-church-20111230-html,0,2812319.htmlstory).

[25] Ibid.

CHAPTER FOUR

[1] Harriet Jacobs, *Incidents in the Life of a Slave Girl* (Rockville, MD: Manor Arc, 2008), p. 74.

[2] Alex Lubin, *Romance and Rights: The Politics of Interracial Intimacy*, 1945-1954 (Mississippi: The University Press of Mississippi, 2009), pp. 151-152.

[3] The Family or the Fellowship is a Christian evangelical "ministry" comprised of politically well-connected members and power brokers. See Jeff Sharlet, *The Family: The Secret Fundamentalism at the Heart of American Power* (New York: Harper Perennial, 2008).

[4] Phone interview with Monica Hudgens, March 1, 2013. "Wrassling" is a common Southern pronunciation of "wrestling."

[5] Essie Mae Washington-Williams and William Stadiem, *Dear Senator: A Memoir by the Daughter of Strom Thurmond* (New York: Harper Collins, 2005), pp. 36-41. In her first meeting with Thurmond, which occurred in his law office, Williams oscillates between reverie and scorn, wondering why this "handsome, charming, and rich white lawyer" was not married to her mother. According to Monica Hudgens, Ms. Williams distanced herself from the memoir after its publication, dissatisfied with what she perceived as misinformation from Mr. Stadiem.

[6] "I Saw the Sign but Did We Really Need a Sign?" Crunk Feminist Collective, October 6, 2011, http://crunkfeministcollective.wordpress.com/2011/10/06/i-saw-the-sign-but-did-we-really-need-a-sign-slutwalk-and-racism/ (Accessed January 5, 2012).

[7] Ibid.

[8] Dorothy Roberts, *Killing the Black Body: Race, Reproduction, and the Meaning of Liberty* (New York: First Vintage Books, 1997), p. 31.

[9] Danielle McGuire, *At the Dark End of the Street: Black Women, Rape, and Resistance—a New History of the Civil Rights Movement from Rosa Parks to the Rise of Black Power* (New York: Vintage Books, 2010), p. 198.

[10] Ibid.

[11] Ibid., p. 206.

[12] This belief reverberates throughout the book. See Williams, p. 37.

[13] Ibid., p. 203.

[14] Ibid.

[15] Williams, p. 176.

[16] Edward Gilbreath, *Reconciliation Blues: A Black Evangelicals Inside Look at White Christianity* (Illinois: InterVarsity Press, 2006), p. 25.

[17] Matthew Richer, "Busing's Boston Massacre," The Hoover Institution, Policy Review 98, November 1 1998, (http://www.hoover.org/publications/policy-review/article/7768).

[18] Ibid.

[19] "Racism and Busing in Boston: An Editorial Statement," (Radical America, November-December 1974, Volume 8, No. 6), pp. 27-29.

[20] Ibid.

[21] Toni Morrison, *The Bluest Eye* (New York: Plume Books, 1970).

[22] Dolores Hayden, *Redesigning the American Dream: The Future of Housing, Work, and Family Life* (New York: WW. Norton and Company, 2002), p. 64.

[23] Alex Lubin, *Romance and Rights: The Politics of Interracial Intimacy, I1945-1954* (Mississippi: The University Press of Mississippi, 2009), p. 152.

[24] Susan Jacoby, *Freethinkers: A History of American Secularism* (New York: Henry Holt and Company, 2004), pp. 302-3.

[25] Ibid., p. 303.

[26] Emily Schulteis, "Rick Santorum Wins Over Conservative Women," Politico.com, March 28, 2011 (http://www.politico.com/news/stories/0312/74612.html).

[27] Emma Gray, "Lego Friends Petition: Parents, Women and Girls Ask Toy Companies to Stop Gender-Based Marketing," Huffington Post, January 15, 2012 (http://www.huffingtonpost.com/2012/01/15/lego-friends-girls-gender-toy-marketing_n_1206293.html).

[28] Writing for the Poynter Institute Roy Peter Clark notes, "Professional vigilante and mawkish sentimentalist, Nancy is full of something, but it's not grace. While accusing other lawyers of avarice and opportunism, she makes her own fortune by angry denunciations of defense efforts, almost always accompanied by lachrymose attention to the plight of the victim, especially if she is white, female, pretty — and missing." "How Nancy Grace has Reinvented Journalism's Sob Sister," Poynter.Org, July 11, 2011 (http://www.poynter.org/how-tos/newsgathering-storytelling/writing-tools/138056/how-nancy-grace-has-reinvented-journalisms-sob-sister/).

[29] National Advocates for Pregnant Women, "South Carolina: First in the Nation for Arresting Pregnant Black Women," Briefing Paper to Democratic Congressional Candidates, 2003 (http://www.advocatesforpregnantwomen.org/issues/race_and_class/).

[30] Ibid.

[31] Colorism, or preferential treatment based upon skin hue, has been found to impact the socioeconomic opportunities and achievement of African Americans within a variety of sectors. See Jill Viglione, Lance Hanon, et al, "The Impact of Light Skin on Prison Time for Female Offenders," *Social Science Journal* (2011), 48:1, pp. 250-258. The authors studied the records of thousands of women in the North Carolina prison system from 1995-2009 and concluded that, "Black women deemed to have a lighter skin tone received more lenient prison sentences and served less time behind bars."; Kwabena Gyimah-Brempong and Gregory N. Price, "Crime and Punishment: And Skin Hue Too?" *American Economic Review*, (2006), 96; 2, pp. 246-250. Based upon their study of African American men in Mississippi the authors concluded that having a darker skin tone resulted in longer prison sentences.

[32] Roberts, p. 152.

[33] Ibid., p. 154.

[34] Ibid., p. 39.

[35] Ibid., p. 37.

[36] Mickey McElya, *Clinging to Mammy: The Faithful Slave in Twentieth-Century America* (Cambridge: Harvard University Press, 2007), p. 13.

[37] Kathryn Stockett, *The Help* (New York: Penguin Books, 2009).

[38] See Jeff Martin and Jeri Clausing, "Police Handcuff Georgia Kindergartner for Tantrum, *Huffington Post,* April 17, 2012, (http://www.huffingtonpost.com/2012/04/17/police-handcuff-ga-kinder_n_1430749.html). (Accessed January 31, 2013).

[39] See Daniel J. Losen and Russell J. Skiba, "Suspended Education: Urban Middle Schools in Crisis," Southern Poverty Law Center, 2010, p. 8. "If we assume that Black and Hispanic poverty rates are similar in these districts (as they are nationally) and if we assume that Black males and females have similar exposure to poverty it becomes difficult to explain why suspension rates are so much higher for Black males than for both Hispanic males and Black females." Losen and Skiba cite previous research that has not identified a link between socioeconomic background or poverty and high rates of suspension (e.g., Skiba, 2002, Wallace 2009, APA 2008).

[40] Ibid.

[41] Ibid. pp. 3-6. Losen and Skiba report that there has been a 9 point increase in black suspensions from 1973 to the present, such that "Blacks are now more than three times more likely to be suspended than whites." Based on data from 18 districts nationwide they also concluded that white females were the least likely to be suspended and black males the most likely out of all racial and ethnic groups. See also, Russell J. Skiba, et al. "The Color of Discipline: Sources of Racial and Gender Disproportionality in School Punishment," *Indiana Education Policy Center*, Policy Research Report: SR1, June 2000, pp. 1-26.

[42] See also Losen and Skiba, p. 10.

[43] Tony Fabelo et al, "The School Discipline Project: Supporting Schools to Improve Students' Engagement and Juvenile Justice Outcomes," Justice Center, Public Policy Research Institute, July 2011, p. x.

[44] Ibid., pp. 6-8. Suspension and expulsion rates were also strong predictors of juvenile incarceration. Incarcerated youth on average missed 58% of school due to discipline penalties.

[45] Robert Balfanz, "Putting Middle Grades Students on the Graduation Path," National Middle School Association, Johns Hopkins University, June 2009. According

to The Council of State Governments' website: "A student's discretionary suspension or expulsion nearly tripled (2.85 times) the likelihood of his or her juvenile justice contact within the subsequent academic year. The multivariate model controlling for all campus and student variables except disciplinary history demonstrated that a student with no prior school discipline involvement had a 5.5 percent chance of ultimately coming into contact with the juvenile justice system, while a student disciplined 11 or more times had a 17.3 percent chance." See "Juvenile Justice Resources", The Council of State Governments (http://justicecenter.csg.org/resources/juveniles/report#faq). (Accessed February 21, 2013).

[46] At Drew Middle School (16% black) and Foshay Learning Center (18% black) African Americans represented nearly half of those suspended. Latino students, who represented 83% and 80% of each respective school's population, were grossly underrepresented in suspensions. At Mann Middle School African Americans and Latinos were equal in number yet blacks represented 71% of those suspended and a majority OT-ed (opportunity transferred). At John Muir Middle School blacks were 23% of the population and 49% of those suspended. At Peary Middle School in Gardena they were 28% of the population and 59% of those suspended.

[47] Ellen Barkan, "Got Dough? How Billionaires Run Our Schools," Dissent Magazine, March 2011, (http://www.dissentmagazine.org/article/?article=3781). (Accessed July, 2012).

[48] Erica Frankenberg, Genevieve Siegel-Hawley and Jia Wang, "Charter School Segregation and the Need for Civil Rights Standards," Los Angeles, CA: The Civil Rights Project, January 2010, p. 3.

[49] Ibid., p. 2. "A worrisome pattern in the Southwest…and elsewhere such as North Carolina is the overrepresentation of whites in charter schools…It would be very damaging to invest public money in schools that finance "white flight" from regular public schools and take with the departing white students state and federal funding badly needed for the students left behind in even more segregated regular public schools."

[50] There are numerous studies that document the deficits of charter schools. See for example, Martin Carnoy, Rebecca Johnson et al, *The Charter School Dust-up: Examining the Evidence on Enrollment and Achievement* (New York: Economic Policy Institute, 2005); Diane Ravitch, "Why States Should say 'no thanks' to Charter Schools," *Washington Post*, February 13, 2012 (http://www.washingtonpost.

com/blogs/answer-sheet/post/ravitch-why-states-should-say-no-thanks-to-charter-schools/2012/02/12/gIQAdA3b9Q_blog.html). (Accessed January 2013).

CHAPTER FIVE

[1] Alice Walker, *In Search of Our Mother's Gardens* (New York: Harcourt Brace &Company, 1983), p. 238.

[2] Jacoby, p. 71.

[3] Louise Michele Newman, *White Women's Rights: The Racial Origins of Feminism in the United States* (London: Oxford University Press, 1999), p 5.

[4] See Valerie Cooper, *Word, Like Fire: Maria Stewart, the Bible, and the Rights of African Americans* (Richmond: University of Virginia Press, 2011), p. 117. Cooper cites the example of Celia, a slave who was habitually raped and eventually impregnated by her master. Celia was convicted and executed for murdering him, despite the defense's claim that ownership did not extend to rape.

[5] Although white feminists did protest the sexual assault of black women under slavery, their arguments did not extend to attacking white supremacy and the racialized hierarchy of women that placed white women on a pedestal. Sexual assault of women of color by white men was viewed as morally debasing of black women. See Jacoby and Newman.

[6] Cooper, p. 1.; Paula Giddings, *When and Where I Enter: The Impact of Black Women on Race and Sex in America* (New York: Bantam Books, 1984), p. 50.

[7] Cooper, p. 112

[8] Ibid., p. 9.

[9] Ibid., p. 113.

[10] Giddings, p. 53.

[11] See, for example, Jacqueline Jones, *Labor of Love, Labor of Sorrow: Black Women, Work and the Family From Slavery to the Present* (New York: Basic Books, 2010), pp. 273-276.

[12] Newman, p. 60.

[13] Ibid., p. 64.

[14] Ibid., p. 7.

[15] Sandra Cisneros, "Guadalupe the Sex Goddess," from *Diosa de las Americas* by Ana Castillos (New York: Riverhead Books, 1996), p. 46.

[16] Bell Hooks, *Black Looks: Race and Representation* (South End Press, 1992), p. 160.

[17] Yasmin Davidds-Garrido, *Empowering Latinas: Breaking Boundaries, Freeing Lives* (Granite Bay, California: Penmarin Books, 2001) p. 64.

[18] Brenda Briones, "Reproductive Justice Could Save Lives in My Community," *Women's Leadership Project*, June 1, 2012 (http://www.womenleadershipproject.blogspot.com/2012/06/reproductive-justice-could-save-lives.html).

[19] Survey response, Vanessa Linares, June 2012.

[20] Diane Arellano, Telephone interview with author, April 15, 2012.

[21] Iris Jacobs, *My Sisters' Voices: Teenage Girls of Color Speak Out* (New York: Holt, 2002), p. 35.

[22] See Rape, Abuse and Incest National Network (RAINN), Native American lead with 34%, African American women 18.8%, "mixed race" women 24.4%, white women 17.7% and Asian women 6.8% (http://www.rainn.org/get-information/statistics/sexual-assault-victims). (Accessed February 13, 2013).

[23] As hooks comments on the early Madonna phenomenon, "In part, many black women who are disgusted by Madonna's flaunting of sexual experience are enraged because the very image of sexual agency that she is able to project and affirm with material gain has been the stick this society has used to justify its continued beating and assault on the black female body. The vast majority of black women in the United States, more concerned with projecting images of respectability than with the idea of female sexual agency and transgression, do not often feel we have the 'freedom' to act in rebellious ways in regards to sexuality without being punished." *Black Looks*, p. 160.

[24] Paul Taylor, Mark Hugo Lopez, Jessica Martinez, et al. "When Labels Don't Fit: Hispanics and Their Views of Identity," Pew Hispanic Research Survey, April 4, 2012, p. 35.

[25] Ibid.

[26] See Estrelda Alexander, *Black Fire: One Hundred Years of Black Pentecostalism* (Illinois: Intervarsity Press, 2011), pp. 29, 115, 139. Among other things, Seymour's mentor Charles Parham believed that blacks and other people of color were heathens who were probably beyond God's redemption. Alexander notes that Parham may also have "been taken aback by the apparent success Seymour was having at propagating the doctrine he had formulated…Parham had probably envisioned Seymour as being the emissary of his theology to the black race…To Parham blacks were designed to take a supportive role, not to lead whites."

[27] Ibid., p. 29.

[28] Ibid., p. 20.

[29] Ibid, pp. 132-135.

[30] Bruce Wallace, "The Latino Pentecostals," Drew University, Fall 2008 (http://www.drewmagazine.com/2008/09/the-latino-pentecostals/).

[31] Alexander, p. 22. Even affluent blacks in mainline denominations dismissed Pentecostalism as lower class.

[32] Ibid.

[33] "For the Hispanic who is made to feel inferior because he could not master the language of the dominant culture, speaking in tongues debunks the supremacy of English by making all believers equal in language before God." Havidad Rodriguez et al., *Latinas/os in the United States: Changing the Face of America* (New York: Springer Science, 2008), p. 228.

[34] Ibid.

[35] Ibid.

[36] Ibid.

[37] Juhem Navarro-Rivera, Barry Kosmin, et al. "U.S. Latino Religious Identification 1990-2008: Growth, Diversity, and Transformation," (Trinity College, Hartford, 2010), p. 3. The report also concludes that "women are 5% less likely than men to identify with the Nones category (agnostic, atheist, humanist, none or secular)." p. 10.

[38] Andrea Hollingworth, "Spirit and Voice: Toward a Latina Pentecostal Pneumatology," *Pneuma*, Volume 29, Issue 2 (November 1, 2007), pp. 189-213.

[39] Elizabeth Rios, "The Ladies Are Warriors: Latina Pentecostalism and Faith Based Activism in New York City," from *Latino Religions and Civic Activism in the United States,* ed., Gaston Espinoza, et al. (Oxford: Oxford University Press, 2005), p. 197.

[40] Ibid., p. 199.

[41] Ibid., p. 210.

[42] Gaston Espinosa, "Liberated and Empowered: The Uphill History of Hispanic Assemblies of God Women in Ministry, 1915-1950, Assemblies of God Heritage," 2008 (http://womeninministry.ag.org/history/liberated_empowered.cfm#_edn9).

[43] Margaret Downey, "Journey Presentation," March 12, 2012, unpublished speech.

[44] According to Downey, "the BSA discovered that we used the word "Good" instead of "God" and when they discovered that we were a "nontheist" family, they ousted us." Email correspondence from Margaret Downey, November 12, 2012.

[45] According to Downey, "When I took my half-sister to a nontheist conference and she said, 'Nobody here looks like me.' I vowed that, 'I must change the overview of the nontheist community. We need to outreach to Hispanics/Latinos and blacks more often.'" Correspondence with Margaret Downey, February 20, 2013.

[46] Marialupe Duarte, Survey questionnaire, April 20, 2012.

[47] In the 2011-2012 box office season alone mainstream media trumpeted the rise of "strong" heroines in films such as *The Hunger Games*, *Bridesmaids*, *The Girl Who Kicked the Hornet's Nest* and even the animated film *Brave*. All of these films starred white female protagonists.

[48] Taylor, et al., p. 37.

[49] Juhem Navarro-Rivera, "Media Stereotypes and the Invisible Latino 'Nones'" *Free Inquiry*, December 2010/January 2011 (http://secularhumanism.org/index.php?section=fi&page=latino_nones).

[50] Ibid.

[51] Georgina Capetillo, Survey questionnaire, May 10, 2012.

[52] Sikivu Hutchinson, "Debunking La Buena Mujer: Interview with Latina Atheist Diane Arellano," Black Skeptics Blog, May 4, 2012 (http://freethoughtblogs.com/blackskeptics/2012/05/04/debunking-la-buena-mujer-latina-atheist-diane-arellano/).

[53] Kimberly Veal, telephone interview, July 20, 2012.

[54] Ibid.

[55] Mandisa Thomas, telephone Interview, July 20, 2012.

[56] Veal, July 2012.

[57] Barbara Smith, *Home Girls: A Black Feminist Anthology* (New Brunswick: Kitchen Table Press, 1983), p. xxxiv.

[58] Jill Nelson, *Straight, No Chaser: How I Became a Grown-up Black Woman* (New York: Penguin Books, 1997), p. 3.

[59] Anna Gorman, "Caught in the Cycle of Poverty," Los Angeles Times, May 24, 2012, http://articles.latimes.com/2012/may/24/local/la-me-natalie-20120524.

[60] Diane Arellano, "Next Wave Atheist Leaders and White Privilege," Black Skeptics Blog, October 10, 2012 (http://freethoughtblogs.com/blackskeptics/2012/10/10/next-wave-atheist-leaders-and-white-privilege/).

[61] Lisa Delpit, *Other People's Children: Cultural Conflict in the Classroom* (New York: The New Press, 2006).

[62] Tom Schildberger, "South Central L.A.: final frontier for Space Shuttle Endeavor," Canberra Times, October 14, 2012 (http://www.canberratimes.com.au/opinion/south-central-la-final-frontier-for-space-shuttle-endeavour-20121013-27jm7.html#ixzz29O2M5a2I).

[63] See, for example, Marianne Bertrand and Mullainathan Sendhill, "Are Emily and Greg More Employable than Lakisha and Jamal? A Field Experiment on Labor Market Discrimination," *The American Economic Review* 94(4), 2004, pp. 991-1013. The authors responded to over 1,500 job ads using "African American" names versus more "white" sounding names. "Job applicants with white names needed to send about 10 resumes to get one callback; those with African-American names needed to send around 15 resumes to get one callback."

[64] Devah Pager and Bruce Western, Paper presented at "Race at Work: Realities of Race and Criminal Record in the New York Job Market," Schomburg Center for Research in Black Culture, 2005. Using white, Latino and black job applicant testers, the study concluded that white men with criminal felony convictions got more job callbacks and offers than did black men with no criminal records. In essence, "these

results suggest that employers view minority applicants as essentially equivalent to whites out of prison."

[65] Built in 1939, the eponymously titled Academy Theatre on Manchester was intended as the original site for the Academy Awards ceremony.

[66] Community Asset Development Re-Defining Education.

[67] Anthony Pinn, *African American Humanist Principles: Living and Thinking Like the Children of Nimrod* (New York: Palgrave MacMillan, 2004), p. 32.

[68] Jeffrey Perry, pp. 232-235.

[69] Anthony Pinn, *By These Hands: A Documentary History of African American Humanism* (New York: New York University, 2001), p. 165.

[70] Ibid., p. 168.

[71] Ibid., p. 167.

[72] Perry, p. 254.

[73] Ibid., pp. 254-255.

[74] Jervis Anderson, A. *Philip Randolph: A Biographical Portrait,* (Berkeley: UC Press, 1973), p. 41.

[75] John R. Logan, "Separate and Unequal: The Neighborhood Gap for Blacks, Hispanics and Asians in Metropolitan America," US 2010 Project, *Brown University,* 2011, p 1.

[76] Ibid., Introduction.

[77] Jackson Lears incisively unpacks Harris' thesis that science is the "source" of morality in his article "Same Old New Atheism," *The Nation*, March 16, 2011 (http://www.thenation.com/article/160236/same-old-new-atheism-sam-harris?page=0,1). "Stupefied by cultural relativism, we refuse to recognize that some ways of being in the world—our own especially—are superior to others. As a consequence, we are at the mercy of fanatics who will stop at nothing until they 'refashion the societies of Europe into a new Caliphate.' They are natural-born killers, and we are decadent couch potatoes. Our only defense, Harris insists, is the rejection of both religion and cultural relativism, and the embrace of science as the true source of moral value… To define science as the source of absolute truth Harris must first ignore the messy realities of power in the world of Big Science. In his books there is no discussion of the involvement of scientists in the military-industrial complex or in the pharmacological

pursuit of profit. Nor is any attention paid to the ways that chance, careerism and intellectual fashion can shape research: how they can skew data, promote the publication of some results and consign others to obscurity, channel financial support or choke it off. Rather than provide a thorough evaluation of evidence, Harris is given to sweeping, unsupported generalizations. His idea of an argument about religious fanaticism is to string together random citations from the Koran or the Bible. His books display a stunning ignorance of history, including the history of science."

[78] Transcript of Interview with Evelyn Hammonds, *Race, The Power of an Illusion*, Public Broadcasting System, 2002 (http://www.pbs.org/race/000_About/002_04-background-01-05.htm).

[79] A letter submitted by Jehanzeb to the Editorial collective of the online journal *The Feminist Wire* insightfully encapsulated this sentiment: "For the past four years, Pakistani anti-war activists and allies have been constantly and tirelessly speaking out against Obama's drone attacks, troop surge in Afghanistan, and his failure in holding Israel accountable for its atrocities against the Palestinians…Obama, has been killing young girls who look like Malala Yousufsai, yet this point was never addressed or brought up in the post. Those young girls, and their brothers, mothers, and fathers, wanted an education, too. They had dreams and aspirations. We don't hear about their stories because they were killed by Obama — a man that liberal America, and some radical folks, somehow sees as less violent, even though he has been continuing Bush's imperialist policies." Letter to the Editorial Collective of *The Feminist Wire*, November 3, 2012. See also, Margaret Kimberley, "Malala the Worthy Victim," *Black Agenda Report*, October 17, 2012 (http://blackagendareport.com/content/freedom-rider-malala-worthy-victim).

[80] This threat was allegedly uttered by Bush administration assistant secretary of state Richard Armitrage to Pakistani General Perves Musharraf in 2006. Suzanne Goldenberg, "Bush Threatened to Bomb Pakistan, says Musharraf." *The Guardian,* September 21, 2006 (http://www.guardian.co.uk/world/2006/sep/22/pakistan.usa).

[81] Ibid., p. 2.

[82] Philip Hoose, *Claudette Colvin: Twice Toward Justice* (New York: Farrar Strauss and Giroux, 2009), p. 4.

[83] Anthropologist Kamela Heyward-Rotimi notes that this phenomenon "depends on the denomination and time period. Post slavery is probably when you would find uneducated pastors in newly established denominations that became leading ones in

the early and mid-20th century. Otherwise, denominations like Methodist, African Methodist Episcopal etc. required seminary training. For example, my great grandfather in SC started a church in the black Methodist denomination and was required to go to seminary school. My granddad in Florida was required to attend seminary school to become an elder in the AME church and to found a church. Probably the congregations Harrison was speaking about. Yes, they did allow a few dark brown folks entrance to the decision making table." Phone interview with Kamela Heyward-Rotimi, January 2013.

[84] Nelson, p. 183.

[85] Dan Barker, *Godless: How an Evangelical Preacher Became One of America's Leading Atheists* (Berkeley: Ulysses Press, 2008), 165.

[86] Ricardo Lopez, "Blacks in South L.A. Have a Bleaker Job Picture than in 1992," *Los Angeles Times*, April 28, 2012, p. B-5.

[87] Erick Eckholm, "Where Worship Never Pauses," *New York Times*, July 9, 2011 (http://www.nytimes.com/2011/07/10/us/10prayer.html?_r=0).

[88] Mikhail Bakunin, *God and the State* (New York: Kessinger Publishing, 2010), p. 13.

[89] Diana Fishlock, "Atheist Group's Slavery Billboard Down, But Anger, Hurt, Remain for Many," *The Patriot News*, March 8, 2012 (http://www.pennlive.com/midstate/index.ssf/2012/03/atheist_groups_slavery_billboa.html). (Accessed March 20, 2012).

[90] Naima Washington, "Outrage!" Unpublished paper, April 2012.

[91] Raina Rhoades, "Billboard Brouhaha," *Rhoades to Reality*, March 7, 2012 (http://rhoadestoreality.wordpress.com/2012/03/07/billboard-brouhaha/). (Accessed February 19, 2013).

[92] *Waiting for Superman* is a 2010 film which depicts the decline of the American public school system. It fawningly portrays charter schools as the panacea for all that ails public education.

[93] PZ Myers, "Atheism Should Be Science and Social Justice, Not Science versus Social Justice," *Pharyngula*, June 7, 2012 (http://freethoughtblogs.com/pharyngula/2012/06/07/atheism-should-be-science-and-social-justice-not-science-vs-social-justice/). (Accessed February 19, 2013). Myers writes, "I have received a couple of complaints about Sikivu Hutchinson, complaints that were also cc'ed to a number of big names in the atheist movement, which is *weird*. Why complain to me?

Apparently my correspondent wants me to write a rebuttal to some remarks she made in the May issue of International Humanist News." My comments focused on the science fetishism of white atheist leaders, their investment in white supremacy and privileged detachment from issues of social and racial justice. Evidently the "correspondents" were unaware that trying to "check" a woman of color atheist within the anonymous comfort of the old boys' club network perpetuates the same racist sexist hierarchy that they so assiduously deny the existence of. See also, *Moral Combat: Black Atheists, Gender Politics, and the Values Wars*, pp.

[94] David Hoelscher, "Atheism and the Class Problem," *Counterpunch,* November 7, 2012 (http://www.counterpunch.org/2012/11/07/atheism-and-the-class-problem/). (Accessed February 18, 2013).

[95] Ibid.

[96] Naima Washington, "We Only Do Diversity When We Want To: Atheist Silence and the Day of Solidarity for Black Non-Believers," *Freethought Blogs*, February 20, 2013 (http://freethoughtblogs.com/blackskeptics/2013/02/20/we-only-do-diversity-when-we-want-to-atheist-silence-the-day-of-solidarity-for-black-non-believers/). (Accessed February 24, 2013).

[97] Donald Wright, telephone interview, November 5, 2012.

[98] Arellano, "Next Wave Atheist Leaders and White Privilege."

[99] Tripp, co-founder of the DePaul Alliance for Freethought, decried the lack of intersectionality in the atheist movement as one of the primary reasons it has remained white-dominated and willfully ignorant of the social justice struggles of communities of color. See Andrew Tripp, "No More Bandaids: A Call to the Freedom from Religion Foundation and other Mainstream Organizations," *Considered Exclamations*, September 18, 2012 (http://consideredexclamations.wordpress.com/2012/09/18/no-more-bandaids/). (Accessed February 25, 2013).

[100] According to the 2010 U.S. Census, black net worth declined to $4,955 per household compared to $110,729 for white households. The average white household had 22 times the wealth of the average black household.

[101] Maria La Ganga, "Where Obama Pride Abides," *Los Angeles Times*, November 8, 2012, p. AA5.

CHAPTER SIX

[1] Carter G. Woodson, *The Miseducation of the Negro* (Radford, VA: Wilder Press, 2008), pp. 7-8.

[2] Michelle Alexander popularized this term in her groundbreaking book *The New Jim Crow: Mass Incarceration in the Age of Colorblindness* (New York: The New Press, 2010).

[3] "Diary of a Happy Black Woman," *Essence Magazine*, December, 2011 (http://www.essence.com/2011/11/02/tasha-smith-looks-fab-on-essences-december-cover/). (Accessed February 1, 2013).

[4] Anthea Butler, *Women in the Church of God and Christ: Making a Sanctified World* (Chapel Hill: University of North Carolina Press, 2007), pp. 3, 4.

[5] Ibid.

[6] hooks, *Black Looks: Race and Representation*, pp. 159-160.

[7] John Berger, *Ways of Seeing*, from *The Feminism and Visual Culture Reader*, ed. Amelia Jones (London: Routledge, 2003), p. 37.

[8] Ibid., 38.

[9] Ibid., 39.

[10] Walker, *In Search of Our Mother's Gardens*, p. 233.

[11] Rafia Zafar, *We Wear the Mask: African Americans Write American Literature, 1780-1860* (New York: Columbia University, 1997), pp. 16-18. Zafar argues that Wheatley's reflections on Christianity and colonization were a "masked" analysis of the dehumanization of the Western gaze.

[12] Deborah Gray White, *Ar'n't I a Woman: Female Slaves in the Plantation South* (New York: Norton, 1999), p. 188.

[13] Washington, *Medical Apartheid*, p. 66.

[14] Ibid., p. 70.

[15] Richard Dyer, *White* (London: Routledge, 1997), p. 66.

CHAPTER SEVEN

[1] Alexis de Tocqueville, quoted by Doris Kearns Goodwin in *Team of Rivals: The Political Genius of Abraham Lincoln*(New York: Simon and Schuster, 2005), p. 206.

[2] Martin Amis, "The Immortals," from *Einstein's Monsters*, New York: Vintage Books, 1987, p 55.

[3] Roger Angell, "Over the Wall," The New Yorker, November 19, 2012, p. 48.

[4] Vicky M. MacClean and Joyce E. Williams, "Disposing of the Dead: Elysium as Real Estate," from *Handbook of Death and Dying*, ed. Clifton D. Bryant, (Thousand Oaks, CA: Sage Publications, 2003), p. 750.

[5] "About 75% of the members (of People's Temple) were African American, 20% were white and 5% were Asian, Latino and Native American." Steven Glazier, ed. *The Encyclopedia of African and African American Religions* (New York: Routledge, 2001), p. 241.

[6] Anthony Pinn, "People's Temple as Black Religion: Reimagining the Contours of Black Religious Studies," from *People's Temple and Black Religion in America*, eds. Rebecca Moore, Anthony Pinn, et al. (Bloomington, IN: Indiana University Press, 2004), p. 3.

[7] Karl Marx, *On Society and Social Change* (Chicago: University of Chicago Press, 1973), p. 13.

[8] Violence Policy Center, "Black Homicide Victimization in the United States," Report by the Violence Policy Center, Rhode Island, January 30, 2013, pp 1-3.

[9] Dawn Turner Trice, "Chicago Mother Has Lost all Four of her Children to Gun Violence," *Los Angeles Times*, February 3, 2013, p. A15.

[10] Pendleton was an African American teen who was gunned down in Chicago a week after she'd returned home from performing at President Obama's 2013 inauguration ceremony.

[11] Peter Downs, "Paying More Attention to White Crime Victims," *American Journalism Review*, December 1995, (http://www.ajr.org/article.asp?id=2016). (Accessed January 31, 2013).

[12] As Robert Entman and Andrew Rojecki note on the nexus of race and class, "Sadly a black murder victim in a Harlem tenement conforms to expectation so is less

newsworthy than a white corpse in a midtown penthouse. The resulting emphases profoundly imply that white life is more valued than black." See Robert Entman and Andrew Rojecki, *The Black Image in the White Mind: Media and Race in America* (Chicago: University of Chicago Press, 2001), p. 81.

[13] Ibid., p. 8.

[14] Nadra Kareem Little, "White Crime Victims Favored in Mainstream Media Reports," *Maynard Media Center on Structural Inequity*, October 18, 2012 (http://mije.org/mmcsi/criminal-justice/white-crime-victims-favored-mainstream-media-reports). (Accessed January 21, 2013).

[15] Robert Entman and Kimberly Gross, "Race to Judgment: Stereotyping Media and Criminal Defendants," *Law and Contemporary* Problems, Volume 71:93, Duke University Law School Journal, 2008, p. 99. According to a study on Orlando news coverage by Ted Chiricos and Sarah Escholz Latinos were even more likely to be portrayed as criminals vis-à-vis both whites and blacks. See Chiricos and Escholz, "The Racial and Ethnic Typification of Crime and Criminal Typification of Race and Ethnicity in Local Television News, *Journal of Residential Crime and Delinquency* 39, 2002, p. 400.

[16] Paul C. Rosenblatt and Beverly R. Wallace, *African American Grief* (New York: Taylor and Francis, 2005), p. xx.

[17] Ibid., pp. xiii-xiv.

[18] W.E.B. DuBois, *The Souls of Black Folk* (Rockville, MD: Manor Books, 2008), pp. 135-139.

[19] David Levering Lewis, *W.E.B. DuBois: A Biography, 1868-1963* (New York: Henry Holt, 2009), p. 165.

[20] DuBois., pp. xiv-xv.

[21] Anthony Pinn, *African American Religious Cultures* (Santa Barbara, CA: ABC-CLIO, 2009), p. 668.

[22] Post emancipation, black morticians and undertakers were often some of the highest status and highest paid professions in the African American community. These positions emerged from African American benevolent society or mutual aid associations that were designed to provide blacks with burial services and other resources unavailable to them in white society. See Pinn, p. 669.

[23] Black life expectancy is lower than that of whites. However, the life expectancy gap between blacks and whites has shrunk over the past several years: "From 2003 to 2008 the difference in life expectancy between black and white men shrank from 6.5 to 5.4 years, with blacks expected to live 70.8 years, compared to 76.2 years for non-Hispanic men. For white and black women, the gap slimmed from a nearly five-year difference to a 3.7 year difference." See Anahad O'Connor, "Racial Gap in Life Expectancy at All-Time Low," *New York Times*, June 7, 2012, (http://well.blogs.nytimes.com/2012/06/07/racial-gap-in-life-expectancy-at-all-time-low/). (Accessed February 2, 2013).

[24] Anonymous, "How Can I?" *The Beat Within: A Weekly Publication of Writing and Art from the Inside*, Pacific News Service, Volume A/B: 17:49, January 2013, p. 20.

[25] W.E.B. DuBois, "The Negro Church," *Crisis*, V4:1, May 1912, pp. 24-25.

[26] Peggy Phelan, *Unmarked: The Politics of Performance* (New York: Routledge, 1993), p. 133.

[27] Rebecca Hensler, "Grief Beyond Belief," *Free Inquiry*, August-September 2012, p. 31.

[28] Ibid.

Selected Bibliography

Alexander, Estrelda. *Black Fire: One Hundred Years of Black Pentecostalism* (Illinois: Intervarsity Press, 2011).

Alexander, Michele. *The New Jim Crow: Mass Incarceration in the Age of Colorblindness* (New York: The New Press, 2010).

Allen, Theodore. *The Invention of the White Race: Racial Oppression and Social Control* (London: Verso, 2012).

Amis, Martin. *Einstein's Monsters*, New York: Vintage Books, 1987.

Anderson, Jervis. *A. Philip Randolph: A Biographical Portrait* (Berkeley: UC Press, 1973).

Bakunin, Mikhail. *God and the State* (New York: Kessinger Publishing, 2010).

Barker, Dan. *Godless: How an Evangelical Preacher Became One of America's Leading Atheists* (Berkeley: Ulysses Press, 2008).

Berger, Peter and Davie, Grace et al. *Religious America, Secular Europe? A Theme and Variation* (Burlington, VT: Ashgate Publishing, 2008).

Bogle, Donald. *Toms, Coons, Mulattoes, Mammies and Bucks: An Interpretive History of Blacks in*

American Films (New York: Continuum International Publishing, 2001).

Butler, Anthea. *Women in the Church of God and Christ: Making a Sanctified World* (Chapel Hill: University of North Carolina Press, 2007).

Carnoy, Martin and Johnson, Rebecca et al. *The Charter School Dust-up: Examining the Evidence on Enrollment and Achievement* (New York: Economic Policy Institute, 2005).

Castillos, Ana. *Diosa de las Americas* (New York: Riverhead Books, 1996).

Cheesbrough, David. *Frederick Douglass: Oratory from Slavery* (Greenwood, CT: Westport Publishing, 1998).

Cooper, Valerie. *Word, Like Fire: Maria Stewart, the Bible, and the Rights of African Americans* (Richmond: University of Virginia Press, 2011).

Davidds-Garrido, Yasmin. *Empowering Latinas: Breaking Boundaries, Freeing Lives* (Granite Bay, California: Penmarin Books, 2001).

Davis, James. *Who is Black? One Nation's Definition* (Philadelphia: Pennsylvania State University, 1991).

Delpit, Lisa. *Other People's Children: Cultural Conflict in the Classroom* (New York: The New Press, 2006).

DuBois, W.E.B. *The Souls of Black Folk* (Rockville, MD: Manor Books, 2008).

Dyer, Richard. *White* (London: Routledge, 1997).

Entman, Robert and Rojecki, Andrew. *The Black Image in the White Mind: Media and Race in America* (Chicago: University of Chicago Press, 2001).

Espinoza, Gaston, et al. *Latino Religions and Civic Activism in the United States,* (Oxford: Oxford University Press, 2005).

Gay, Geneva. *Culturally Responsive Teaching: Theory, Research, and Practice* (New York: Teacher's College Press, 2000).

Giddings, Paula. *Ida B. Wells and the Campaign Against Lynching* (New York: Harper Collins, 2008).

-------------------.*When and Where I Enter: The Impact of Black Women on Race and Sex in America* (New York: Bantam Books, 1984).

Gilbreath, Edward. *Reconciliation Blues: A Black Evangelicals Inside Look at White Christianity* (Illinois: InterVarsity Press, 2006).

Gingrich, Newt. *A Nation Like No Other: Why American Exceptionalism Matters* (New York: Regnery Publishing, 2011).

Good, Thomas L. and Brophy, Jere E. *Looking in Classrooms* (New York: Harper Collins, 1991).

Goodwin, Doris Kearns. *Team of Rivals: The Political Genius of Abraham Lincoln* (New York: Simon and Schuster, 2005).

Graves, Joseph. *The Race Myth: Why We Pretend Race Exists in America* (New York: Plume, 2004).

Hanson, Sandra L. *Swimming Against the Tide: African American Girls and Science Education* (Philadelphia: Temple University Press, 2009).

Hayden, Dolores. *Redesigning the American Dream: The Future of Housing, Work, and Family Life* (New York: WW. Norton and Company, 2002.

Hensler, Rebecca. "Grief Beyond Belief," *Free Inquiry*, August/ September 2012, pp. 30-32. hooks, bell. *Black Looks: Race and Representation* (South End Press, 1992).

Hoose, Philip. *Claudette Colvin: Twice Toward Justice* (New York: Farrar Strauss and Giroux, 2009).

Hughes, Langston. *The Collected Poems of Langston Hughes* (New York: Random House, 1995).

Hurston, Zora Neale. *Dust Tracks on a Road* (New York: J.B. Lippincott, 1942).

--------------------------. *Their Eyes Were Watching God* (New York: J.B. Lipincott, 1937).

Hutchinson, Earl Ofari. *Betrayed: A History of Presidential Failure to Protect Black Lives* (Boulder: Westview Press, 1996).

Hutchinson, Sikivu. *Moral Combat: Black Atheists, Gender Politics, and the Values Wars* (Los Angeles: Infidel Books, 2011).

-------------------------. *Imagining Transit: Race, Gender, and Transportation Politics in Los Angeles* (New York: Peter Lang Publishing, 2003).

Jackson, Kenneth T. *Crabgrass Frontier: The Suburbanization of the United States* (New York: Oxford

University Press, 1985).

Jacobs, Harriet. *Incidents in the Life of a Slave Girl* (Rockville, MD: Manor Arc, 2008).

Jacobs, Iris. *My Sisters' Voices: Teenage Girls of Color Speak Out* (New York: Holt, 2002).

Jacoby, Susan. *Freethinkers: A History of American Secularism* (New York: Henry Holt and Company, 2004).

Jones, Jacqueline. *Labor of Love, Labor of Sorrow: Black Women, Work and the Family From Slavery to the Present* (New York: Basic Books, 2010).

Jordan, Diann. *Sisters in Science: Conversations with Black Women Scientists on Race, Gender and Their Passion for Science* (Oklahoma: Purdue University Press, 2006).

Kaplan, Carla. *Zora Neale Hurston: A Life in Letters* (New York: Anchor Books, 2003).

Levering Lewis, David. *W.E.B. DuBois: A Biography, 1868-1963* (New York: Henry Holt, 2009).

Lindsey, Randall, et al. *Cultural Proficiency: A Manual for School Leaders* (Thousand Oaks, CA: Sage Publications, 2009).

Loomba, Ania and Burton, Jonathon. *Race in Early Modern England* (New York: Palgrave McMillan, 2007).

Lubin, Alex. *Romance and Rights: The Politics of Interracial Intimacy,* 1945-1954 (Mississippi: The University Press of Mississippi, 2009).

Malcolmson, Scott. *One Drop of Blood: The American Misadventure of Race* (New York: Farrar, Strauss, Giroux, 2000).

Marx, Karl. *On Society and Social Change* (Chicago: University of Chicago Press, 1973).

McElya, Mickey. *Clinging to Mammy: The Faithful Slave in Twentieth-Century America* (Cambridge: Harvard University Press, 2007).

McGuire, Danielle. *At the Dark End of the Street: Black Women, Rape, and Resistance—a New History of the Civil Rights Movement from Rosa Parks to the Rise of Black Power* (New York: Vintage Books, 2010).

Mintz, Steven. *African American Voices: A Documentary Reader,* 1619-1877 (Oxford: Wiley-Blackwell, 2009).

Moore, Mignon. *Invisible Families: Gay Identities, Relationships, and Motherhood Among Black Women* (Berkeley: UC Press, 2011).

Moore, Rebecca and Pinn, Anthony, et al. *People's Temple and Black Religion in America* (Bloomington, IN: Indiana University Press, 2004).

Morrison, Toni. *Playing in the Dark: Whiteness and the Literary Imagination* (Cambridge: Harvard University Press, 1992).

-------------------. *The Bluest Eye* (New York: Plume Books, 1970).

Nelson, Jill. *Straight, No Chaser: How I Became a Grown-up Black Woman* (New York: Penguin Books, 1997).

--------------. *Volunteer Slavery: My Authentic Negro Experience* (Chicago: The Noble Press, 1993).

Newman, Louise Michele. *White Women's Rights: The Racial Origins of Feminism in the United States* (London: Oxford University Press, 1999).

Perry, Jeffrey. *Hubert Harrison: The Voice of Harlem Radicalism, 1883-1918* (New York: Columbia University Press, 2009).

Phelan, Peggy. *Unmarked: The Politics of Performance* (New York: Routledge, 1993).

Pinn, Anthony. *African American Religious Cultures* (Santa Barbara, CA: ABC-CLIO, 2009).

------------------. *African American Humanist Principles: Living and Thinking Like the Children of Nimrod* (New York: Palgrave MacMillan, 2004).

------------------. *By These Hands: A Documentary History of African American Humanism* (New York: New York University, 2001).

Roberts, Dorothy. *Killing the Black Body: Race, Reproduction, and the Meaning of Liberty* (New York: First Vintage Books, 1997).

Rodriguez, Havidad et al. *Latinas/os in the United States: Changing the Face of America* (New York: Springer Science, 2008).

Rosenblatt, Paul C. and Wallace, Beverly R. *African American Grief* (New York: Taylor and Francis, 2005).

Sharlet, Jeff. *The Family: The Secret Fundamentalism at the Heart of American Power* (New York: Harper Perennial, 2008).

Smith, Barbara. *Home Girls: A Black Feminist Anthology* (New Brunswick: Kitchen Table Press, 1983).

Stockett, Kathryn. *The Help* (New York: Penguin Books, 2009).

Sutton, Matthew Avery. *Aimee Semple Mcpherson and the Resurrection of Christian America* (Cambridge: Harvard University Press, 2007).

Takaki, Ronald. *A Different Mirror: A History of Multicultural America* (Boston: Little Brown Company, 1993).

Taylor, Cynthia. *A. Philip Randolph: The Religious Journey of an African American Leader* (New York: New York University Press, 2009).

Thompson, Gail. *Through Ebony Eyes: What Teachers Need to Know But Are Afraid to Ask About African American Students* (San Francisco, CA: Jossey Bass, 2004).

Walker, Alice. *In Search of Our Mother's Gardens* (New York: Harcourt Brace &Company, 1983).

Washington, Harriet. *Medical Apartheid: The Dark History of Medical Experimentation on Black Americans from Colonial Times to the Present* (New York: Anchor Books, 2006).

Washington-Williams, Essie Mae and Stadiem, William. *Dear Senator: A Memoir by the Daughter of Strom Thurmond* (New York: Harper Collins, 2005).

White, Deborah Gray. *Ar'n't I a Woman: Female Slaves in the Plantation South* (New York: Norton, 1999).

Wilson, Daniel H. and Long, Anna. *The Mad Scientist Hall of Fame* (New York: Citadel Press Books, 2008).

Wise, Tim. *Colorblind: The Rise of Post-Racial Politics and the Retreat From Racial Equity* (San Francisco: City Lights Books, 2010).

Woodson, Carter G. *The Miseducation of the Negro* (Radford, VA: Wilder Press, 2008).

Zafar, Rafia. *We Wear the Mask: African Americans Write American Literature, 1780-1860* (New York: Columbia University, 1997).

Zinn, Howard. *A People's History of the United States* (New York: Harper Collins, 2003).

Index

14th Amendment 67
15th Amendment 104
abolitionists 100
abortion 3, 54, 64, 81, 86, 90-91, 117-118, 123, 137, 148, 166, 177-178
Advanced Placement (AP) 44-45, 46-47, 148
African Americans/blacks
  academia/education and 35, 39, 46, 48, 96
  atheism and 119, 144, 147
  colonial law and 62
  Church/religion and 22, 61, 102, 112, 128, 127, 136, 139, 154, 157, 168
  colorism and 127-128
  communities and 6
  criminalization and 172
  death/homicide and 166, 170, 175
  depression and 40
  genetic heritage and 62, 164
  Great Migration and 58, 126
  grieving 173
  homelessness and 141
  homosexuality and 8, 19, 21
  immigrants and 32, 36
  lynching 56
  media representation and 173
  mass incarceration and 154
  race construction and 68
  racial politics and 36
  segregation and 80, 126, 131, 135, 155, 160
  science and 34, 45, 50, 88, 133-134
  secularism and 11
  socialism and 129
  stereotypes and 4, 5, 10, 29, 30, 33, 35, 42, 65, 67, 88
African Americans for Humanism 119
African American women/black women
  atheism/non-belief and 119-120
  beauty standards and 128-129, 161
  criminalization and 90-91
  depictions of 63-64, 66, 73-74, 120, 164
  feminism and 103
  hypersexuality and 16, 76-77, 111, 157
  medical experimentation and 161
  oppression and xiv
  public space and 78
  rape and 4, 56, 72, 163
  religion/religiosity and 102-103, 105, 125, 128-129, 138, 155-156
  scientists 44, 49
  slavery and 61, 92-93, 101-102, 177

stereotypes and 10, 50, 104,
work and 70
American Atheists 143-145
American Humanist Association 147
Anthony, Casey 76, 89
Anzaldua, Gloria 20
Apostle, The (film) 63, 66
Art-making 153, 158-159
Atheism 38, 116, 133, 146
Ardiente, Maggie 147
Arellano, Diane vii, 108, 118, 122, 148

Bacon's Rebellion 67-70
Benson, Ophelia 38
Bey, Jamila 119
Bible Belt 21, 31, 53, 59, 65, 69
Black Atheists of America 119
Black Canadians 38
Black Church 11, 21-22, 102, 109, 114, 119, 127, 137, 155-156
Black Non-Believers of Atlanta 119
Black Non-Believers of Chicago 119
Black Skeptics Los Angeles 22, 119, 147
bullying 16, 19, 20
Butler, Carrie 72-74, 87, 92, 97

Camping, Harold 54, 56, 66
capitalism x, xiv, 27, 30, 65, 84, 130, 141, 146
charter schools 197, 205
Chicano student walkouts xii
Children of Ham 29, 105
Christian fascism 54
Christianity 6, 26-27, 54, 60-61, 63, 71, 80, 127, 135, 138, 141, 155, 157, 159
Christian nation 5, 18, 26-27, 29, 63, 80, 97, 131, 179
Church of God in Christ (COGIC) 156
cisgendered 15
Cisneros, Sandra 106, 118, 179
college preparation xii, 45, 47-48
colorblind/colorblindness ix, xi, 13, 29, 34-35, 37, 51, 142, 153, 164
Communism/communist 18, 59, 81, 83, 146,
Communist Party 127
Covenant House 14-16
Crisostomo, Paula xii
Cromwell, Ian 38
cultural relevance xi

Dawkins, Richard 142
Day of Solidarity for Black Non-Believers 146
Death
children and 175, 180
pervasiveness of 168, 174
race and 165-167, 170, 172
religion/faith and 118, 141, 173, 178-179
youth of color and 171
Douglass, Frederick 5, 101
Downey, Margaret 114-116
Dreiser, Theodore 122
DuBois, W.E.B. 11, 174, 214
Duvall, Robert 63, 66

economic justice 145-146, 168, 176
Enlightenment 60-61, 101
Epicurus (on God) 180
evangelicals 26, 32, 41, 59, 112
evolution 115, 134, 166
Exceptionalism (American) ix, xi, xv, 2-3, 30, 33, 60, 62, 65, 84, 97, 104,

femininity 17, 57, 76-77, 84, 86, 107, 157, 159
feminism 55, 75, 100-103, 115, 118

Fox News 26, 29
freethinker/freethought xiv, 18, 100, 102, 104-105, 142-143, 148

Gaudette, Bridget 118
gay conversion therapy 3, 8
Gay/LGBT 3, 6-14, 16-18, 20-22, 26, 32, 147, 153, 166,
gender
- identity 15
- inequality xiii, 39, 45, 56, 86, 95, 102, 104, 115, 130
- race and 93, 100, 109-110
- religion and 113-114, 138, 142, 145, 155
- roles 2, 7-10, 16-17, 83, 89, 108, 137, 157
- secularism and 115, 118
- stereotypes 87

gender norms 10, 20, 106, 108
gender politics 100
gender queer 14
Giddings, Paula 102, 190, 192
Gingrich, Newt x, 2, 33, 59, 70, 131
God xiv, 1, 3-4, 6-12, 14, 18, 20, 22-23, 26, 28-29, 30, 40-41, 54, 60, 62-63, 72, 80-82, 84-85, 91-92, 97, 99, 101, 105, 107-108, 111, 113, 115, 117, 118, 123, 129, 131-132, 136-142, 149, 154-155, 165, 169-170, 174-175, 177-179
Goddard, Debbie 119
Graves, Joseph 34-35, 187
grieving 173, 175, 180
Grimke sisters 101

Harris, Sam 133
Harrison, Hubert Henry 53, 127
Hedges, Chris 54
Hensler, Rebecca 180
heterosexism x, 6, 13, 157
high stakes tests xi, 96
Hitchens, Christopher 142
HIV/AIDS 7, 154, 157
homelessness 13, 15, 17, 141
homophobia 13, 15, 17, 19, 22, 148,
hooks, bell 156, 198
Hoover, Herbert 27
Hudgens, Monica 73
Hughes, Langston 17-18
Humanism vii, x, xii, xiv, 133, 135, 142
Hurston, Zora Neale xiv, 58, 77, 100,
Hutchinson, Earl Ofari 56, 190
Hutchinson, Maria 72
Hutchinson, Yvonne Divans vii, 178

imperialism x, 35, 146
intimate partner violence 110
Islam/Islamic 6, 134

Jacoby, Susan 84, 100
Jefferson, Thomas 4, 60
Jezebel 2, 10, 16, 76, 87, 105-106, 137, 163
Jim Crow xi, 9, 30, 34, 37, 55, 61-62, 67, 77-78, 83, 85, 88, 96, 105, 112, 115, 154, 163, 166, 175-176
Jones, Jim 167-168
Jonestown massacre 167-168

Kelley, Stephen vii, 180
King, Martin Luther 139, 161, 176

Larsen, Nella 100, 139
Latinas xii, 106, 107, 113, 116-118, 133
Latinos ix, 21, 39, 42, 65, 131, 155, 173
- Immigration and 32, 62, 67, 69, 96
- racial identity 35, 126
- religion and 107, 111, 112, 116-117, 141

voting and 67
Lesbians 8, 16-17, 22
Ligon, Glen 152
Long, Eddie 136
Lorde, Audre 20
Los Angeles Unified School District (LAUSD) 12
lynching 55-57, 79, 81, 120, 157

Mammy, the 10, 37, 64, 92-93, 104
Manifest Destiny 28, 55, 59, 97
Mapplethorpe, Robert 153
Martin, Trayvon 33, 87, 94, 171
Marx, Karl 18, 168-169,
Masculinity 7-9, 15, 16, 19, 33, 35, 138
Mass incarceration 19, 13, 31, 59, 124-125, 130, 134, 145, 153, 154
McGuire, Danielle 76
McMahon, Derrick 7
McPherson, Aimee Semple 18
Megachurches 67, 155
Mendez vs. Westminster 67
mental health 16, 95, 125, 148
miscegenation 4, 62, 73
Miss Ann 103-104, 163,
morality 13, 29, 30-31, 56, 60, 64, 103, 114, 118, 162, 179
Morrison, Toni 30, 51, 58, 82, 103, 179
mortgage lending 28
Mott, Lucretia 101
Myers, PZ 39

Native Americans 62, 68
Navarro-Rivera, Juhem 117
Nelson, Jill 36, 121, 138
New Atheism 145-146

Obama, Barack x, 2-3, 21, 25-26, 31-32, 45, 52, 59, 64, 149, 155
One-Drop rule 36, 61-62, 74
Operation Rescue 177
Ozzie and Harriet 83, 135

Parks, Rosa 161
Parr, Russ (*The Undershepherd*) 137
patriarchy x, 2, 84, 93, 101, 120, 161, 178
Pentecostalism 32, 111-113, 133, 142
Perry, Rick 26, 65
Perry, Tyler 154
Post-racial/postracialism ix, 50, 58, 60, 124, 131
Prayer 6, 26, 63, 80, 99, 113, 122, 140-142, 154, 156, 173, 178, 179
Prosperity gospel 52, 136-140, 155

Race
class and 67-68, 147
construction of 35-37, 62, 146, 162
education and xi, 17, 95
feminism and 100-101, 108
interracial/mixed race 4, 61, 78, 83
religion and 61, 63
science and 43, 45, 133
Race, The Power of an Illusion (documentary) 34-35
racism xii, xiv, 6, 13, 19, 23, 28, 35-36, 38-39, 43, 45, 51-52, 54-55, 57-59, 66, 68, 74, 81-82, 100, 102, 105, 110, 112, 121, 131, 143-144, 146, 157, 174, 176, 178-179
Randolph, A. Philip 11, 127
Rape 3, 41, 56, 73, 76-79, 85, 87, 110-111, 120, 144, 157, 161

Religion
- cultural identity and 6, 149
- economics and 129, 145
- gender and 81, 100, 107, 108, 113
- hypocrisy of 178
- Marx and 168-169
- politics and xiii, 2, 13, 39, 61
- race and 26, 40, 71, 127-128, 145, 155, 162
- rejection of 6, 18, 117
- segregation and 156
- science and 4, 133
- unknown and 40
- War on 26

Religious Right x, 2, 12, 25-26, 29, 31-32
reproductive justice 148
Rhoades, Raina 144
Roberts, Dorothy 91-92
Romney, Mitt 32, 65
Rose, Ernestine 105
Rubio, Marco 33
Rustin, Bayard 20
Ryan, Paul 65

Shakespeare 179
same-sex marriage 10, 21
Santorum, Rick x, 26, 33, 85
Science
- bias 40, 44, 49, 51
- higher education 35, 48
- image/ideal of 41, 104, 133-134, 169
- people of color in 38, 42-43, 45-47, 50

scientism 66
segregation xiii, 11, 18, 28, 38, 51, 77-81, 92, 96-97, 100, 125, 129-131, 145-147, 155, 166, 175
sexism xiv, 19, 100, 102, 109-110, 117, 120-121, 178
sexual assault xiii, 15, 75, 110-111, 157, 161
Shermer, Michael 38, 142
slavery 3-4, 9-10, 51, 57-58, 61-62, 68, 79, 81, 90, 97, 100-103, 105, 139, 144, 173
social justice x, 11, 17, 19, 38, 113-114, 127, 130, 143-144, 147, 168, 179,
South Los Angeles xii, 19, 28, 43, 95, 100, 109-110, 123-127, 166, 171, 175
Stanton, Elizabeth Cady 100, 104
Stewart, Maria 101-103, 110, 120
storefront churches 123, 129, 135, 149, 155, 169
suspension/expulsion rates 48, 94-95

Taylor, Nicome 119
Tea Party 55, 59
Thomas, Mandisa 119-120
Thurmond, Strom 72, 77, 78
transgender youth 3, 15
Tripp, Andrew 148

undocumented immigrants 3, 31, 54, 67

Veal, Kimberly 119

wages of whiteness 59
Walker, Alice 57, 99, 158, 160,
Washington, Harriet 50, 161
Washington, Naima vii, 144
Washington Prep High School xii, 19, 28, 100, 123
Watson, Ayanna 119
wealth gap 124, 134

welfare queen 3, 23, 32, 64, 67, 121
Wells, Ida B. 55, 110, 120,
Wheatley, Phyllis 60
whiteness 10, 37, 39, 40, 57, 59, 68, 70, 92, 148, 162-163, 166
white people 28, 29, 32-33, 39, 51, 65, 69, 74, 78, 111, 128, 135, 147, 172
white privilege 37, 74-75, 122, 126, 143
white supremacy ix-x, xiv, 6, 13, 35, 37, 58-60, 63, 74, 77, 79-80, 100-102, 120, 144, 162
white men ix, xi, 4, 27, 56, 73, 78, 92-93, 104, 106, 121, 153, 159, 164, 179
white women 16, 22, 56, 75-77, 81-84, 88, 91-92, 100-106, 108, 116, 120, 154, 157, 161-162,
white working class 27, 68-69, 81-82, 103, 135
Williams, Essie Mae Washington 72-74, 77-78, 92
Wright, Donald 143, 146
Women's Leadership Project xiii, 19, 99, 109, 123, 148, 171

Zimmerman, George 33
Zion Hill Baptist Church 22, 135

① Christianity cannot liberate black people because it's ideology is so imbedded in white hetro male supremacy as is American Exceptionalism & Patriotism

② If Black Christians can never truly be Christians

Dr. Amos ~~Wilson~~ Wilson

Blueprint for Black Power

Black on Black Violence

(Dr. Kamau Kambon?)

Racketeering in Medicine: The Suppression of Alternatives by James P. Carter

Medisin by Scott Whitaker

The Medical Mafia by Ghislaine Lanctot

Survival into the 21st Century by Viktoras Kulvinskas

Ann Wigmore

19334179R00127

Made in the USA
Charleston, SC
18 May 2013